Like a Bullet of Light
The Films of Bob Dylan

Like a Bullet of Light
The Films of Bob Dylan

BY C.P. LEE

Helter
Skelter
publishing

This edition published in 2000 by
Helter Skelter Publishing
4 Denmark Street, London WC2H 8LL

Helter Skelter Publishing is part of
The Foundry Creative Media Company Ltd
Crabtree Hall, Crabtree Lane, Fulham, London SW6 6TY

Cover design by The Foundry
Typeset by The Foundry

Printed in Great Britain by Redwood Books, Trowbridge, Wilts.

ISBN 1-900924-06-4

A CIP record for this book is available from the British Library

Thanks to Derek Barker for the use of the images on front cover and on pages 16, 19, 22, 24, 26, 32, 35
& 37
Thanks to C.P. Lee for the use of the images on pages 39, 60, 66, 117, 125, 133, 140, 144, 160, 161, 165,
168, 172, 174, 177 & 204

REEL TO REAL

Francisco Sabate

(El Quico)

'caballeresco pero espiritual'

&

Pamela Lee

Mi corazon

Foreword
Into The Past

'The aim of every artist is to arrest motion, which is life, by artificial means and hold it fixed so that a hundred years later, when a stranger looks at it, it moves again since it is life...' William Faulkner, 1956.

Bob Dylan is inarguably one of the greatest artists of the twentieth century. Though his reputation is founded on his chosen medium of musical composition, recording and performance, he has made several attempts in his career to cross over to the world of film. However, while Dylan's achievements in contemporary music are undeniably great, there is less consensus on the success of his forays into visual media. This book sets out to assess the true merits of this work.

The material in this book falls under several categories: Dylan as participant in documentaries; Dylan as actor in filmed drama; Dylan as director; Dylan as special guest; Dylan and music video; and Dylan in TV specials. I've focused on particular items and mentioned many more in passing, though I have consciously made no attempt to catalogue all known footage. Anybody seeking an exhaustive listing of visual material is directed towards Glen Dundas' superb *Tangled Up In Tapes*.

For my generation, living before the days of video recorders, cable and satellite, there were only two ways to see Bob Dylan in action – in concert or at the cinema. My first opportunity to see him on the big screen came in 1968 at the Arts Lab in Drury Lane, London, when the cinema there screened a copy of DA Pennebaker's classic 'rockumentary', *Dont Look Back*. In the movie Dylan came across as the King of Cool: sharp, witty and pithy with a screen presence that filled the frame with charisma. The film was a revelation.

After the crushing blow of having the BBC reject the Dylan episode of the *Johnny Cash TV Show* on grounds of its alleged 'inferior' quality in 1969, it was 1972 before I got the chance to see new footage of Dylan – this time in *The Concert For Bangladesh*. Even if Dylan was only in it briefly as a guest it was better than nothing. At last, the big screen was filled with images of him singing four of his best-known songs. A year later I was at the Scala Cinema in Withington, Manchester to watch Bob Dylan's feature film debut in Sam Peckinpah's *Pat Garrett and Billy The Kid*. Even more magical than the previous film, Dylan gave of an aura that filled every inch of the frame. Sitting in a darkened cinema listening to Dylan intone those famous lines – *'Beans – Baked beans –-Curried beans ...'*, it seemed obvious that he had great promise on screen. Truncated though his part was, it seemed to promise greater things to come.

That opportunity arose for me in late 1978 at the Aaben Cinema in the run down inner city suburb of Hulme, Manchester. Sitting inside that cinema for over four hours watching *Renaldo and Clara* was a revelatory experience; I was so completely absorbed in Dylan's creation that I was completely unaware of the movie's four hour running time. Despite the film's unorthodox length and structure, Dylan was mesmerising and it was exhilarating to be witness to his cinematic vision.

After that, nothing for ten years until the ill-fated *Hearts of Fire*. There were infrequent TV appearances, some of them, like his 'performance' at Live Aid, spectacularly bizarre; others, like his appearance at the 1998 Grammy Awards, astoundingly good. But of course, by now we were in the video age and we could watch them over and over again if we so desired.

Bob Dylan's musical influences are well documented, but the shadow of the screen has always been beside him too. Still, it took him a while to act on any desire to involve himself in visual media, though it was not for want of opportunities. Offers of film work were being forwarded to his manager Albert Grossman's office throughout the 1960s. Amongst the many film roles he declined were Holden Caulfield in *Catcher In The Rye*; and the part of Marlon Brando's younger brother in the unmade *Fargo*. He was also considered the ideal choice by Warren Beattie to play outlaw Clyde Barrow in the seminal Sixties' movie *Bonnie and Clyde*, before Beattie decided to take the role himself.

In 1965/66, there was talk of a movie collaboration with Allen Ginsberg which was to be shot in a variety of international locations during Dylan's forthcoming world tour. However, the tour was cancelled after Dylan's motorcycle accident, and so it remains one of the great 'what ifs' of Dylan and film. Apart from the crash and his withdrawal into self-imposed exile in Woodstock, there is another reason why Dylan probably didn't make any feature films until the 1970s. Prior to 1966 his priorities were writing, recording and performing; it's highly unlikely that he could have found the weeks or months necessary to be involved in a movie shoot even if he'd wanted to.

From my earliest experiences of Dylan and film I knew that people's opinions are fiercely divided about his qualities, or lack of them, as an actor and filmmaker, but one thing remained the same throughout the debates and reviews – this was Bob Dylan, and as such, he was bound to be original.

C.P. Lee
2000

Reel One
Dont Look Back

One evening in 1956 the three members of a junior high school band called The Golden Chords came out of the Lybba Cinema in Hibbing, Minnesota. They'd just been to see a film called *Giant* for the fourth time. It was the last movie to star the ill-fated young screen actor James Dean. Thousands of young people across America were obsessed with the late star's short, frantic life and The Golden Chords were no exception. Along with rock 'n' roll and rhythm and blues, James Dean was one of their main topics of conversation. One member of the band, Robert Allen Zimmerman, was to become increasingly infatuated with the star's life, rushing to newspaper stands to buy the latest magazines cashing in on Dean's death. He bought posters and postcards, and assiduously clipped items about Dean from newspapers. He even developed a kind of ersatz Dean persona, wearing a leather jacket and letting a cigarette dangle from his lips, shrugging and pouting, gazing through half lidded-eyes. For a while, Robert Allen Zimmerman held back from the idea of becoming Little Richard and wanted to be James Dean.

With the determined obsessiveness that was to become the hallmark of his musical 'training' over the next few years, Robert Zimmerman studied everything he could about the late, great James Dean, from how he walked to how he talked and what he wore. He could tell you every minor detail of Dean's tragically short life. In later years he would remark to people how much he and Dean looked alike in photographs, begging people to look at them closely to see the similarities.

The young Zimmerman's obsession with Dean even began to cause dissension at home. One freezing cold winter's evening in 1957 he went on his own to the Lybba and sat through another screening of *Giant*. When he came back late that night to his parents' house at 2425 East Seventh Avenue, they were up waiting for him and according to Robert Shelton, a blazing row ensued.

First his mother tackled him in the parlour, asking him why he had to stay out late all the time, roaming the streets? He tried to explain but his father, Abraham Zimmerman, interrupted, telling him not to talk back. The teenager stalked out, heading for the basement where he had a kind of shrine to Dean with pictures and articles tacked on the walls. His father followed him, going on about his attitude –

'*Robert, you come back here! We've given you a good home. We buy you the best of everything. What more do you want? I never had it so soft when I was your age ...*'

In the basement den, father and son confronted one another. Again Robert tried to explain that he had to go and see James Dean. Didn't they understand? His father exploded and tore down one of the pictures of Dean and ripped it in two, flinging the pieces to the floor. Robert was crushed.

Shortly afterwards The Golden Chords went their separate ways and Robert Zimmerman, of course, became Bob Dylan, one of the most important musical figures of the twentieth century. When we look at Dylan's career in terms of songwriting, recording and concert performances we get an image of a prolific, sometimes mercurial artist, who has mastered one of the most important creative genres of his time. When it comes to watching images of this most talented of people, things tend to go a little out of focus.

When pressed, even people with little more than a passing knowledge of Dylan and his career might be able to recall his appearances in D.A. Pennebaker's ground-breaking rockography, *Dont Look Back* and possibly Sam Peckinpah's *Pat Garrett and Billy The Kid*. But there are more films and dozens of TV appearances that have been forgotten by all but the diehards. This Film and Television guide will tell the story of Dylan's relationship with moving images.

Take One – Framing The Shots

By the early 1960s, Popular Music was rapidly increasing its influence on American culture. After the initial burst of enthusiasm following Elvis Presley's arrival in the mid-1950s, the rock'n'roll scene had descended into a moribund state, watered down and confused, unsure of its direction. But the so-called 'British invasion', brought about by groups such as The Beatles and The Rolling Stones had revitalised the creative energy of American musicians. Added to this was the rapid growth in popularity of the 'Folk Revival', acting as a kind of antidote to the watered down pop-pap of Tin Pan Alley.

While popular music was on the rise, by 1963 it had so far eluded any serious analysis – either in book or film form. But all this was about to change. An independent filmmaker called D.A. Pennebaker had been nurturing plans to shoot a music documentary for some time, when out of the blue he was approached by Bob Dylan's manager, Albert Grossman, about working with the young singer.

'…Music was interesting,' Pennebaker later reflected. 'I had talked to someone who knew the Stones… and so I thought of [making a film about them] and went over [to England], but that didn't seem quite right… So I was thinking about it – had been for about a year and a half… And then Albert Grossman came in one day.'

According to Pennebaker he was out of the office at the time and so Grossman spoke to his partner, Richard Leacock. Pennebaker:

'…Albert came in and said, "I represent Bob Dylan. Is anybody here interested in making a film about him?" And Leacock said, "Who's Bob Dylan?" So Albert said, "Maybe I'd better come back again."'

Fortunately Grossman returned. Pennebaker recalls: 'Albert said, "My client's going to England; would you like to make a film about it?" I said, "Sure."'

Take Two – The Eye And The Mouth

Donn Pennebaker was born in Illinois in 1930. Before entering the world of documentary filmmaking he was an artist and an electrical engineer, designing, amongst other things, the world's first computerised airline reservation system. In the 1950s he began to turn towards the medium of film, which had always fascinated him. He was able to use his skills as an engineer to devise several technical modifications which transformed the way that documentary, and film in general, could be made. Pennebaker fitted a handle onto the front of his hand-held, 16 mm camera, added a shoulder pad and created a powering system that cut battery weight from forty pounds to twenty. This gave the camera operator a much greater freedom of movement and fluidity. Pennebaker even went so far as to design and grind his own lenses.

Operating out of New York, Pennebaker began the early 1950s making short documentary films about subjects like the YWCA and the Boy Scout movement. Later in the decade, he became actively involved with a group of young American filmmakers, working under the banner of 'Direct Cinema', which included the Maysles Brothers, Richard Leacock, and Robert Drew.

Direct Cinema was a documentary form inspired in some ways by the radical experiments of 1920s Soviet Bolshevik filmmakers such as Dziga Vertov, who had revolutionised the genre with his experimental epic, *Man With A Movie Camera* (1929). This new breed of Soviet documentary makers simply filmed life as it happened, with no intervention by the director. Their films are direct precursors of today's 'fly-on-the-wall' docu-dramas. The objective was to record a kind of 'truth', unmediated by the auteur or the camera. Importantly, there was no commentary and no direct questioning of the subjects being filmed. Pennebaker's new, lightweight camera was perfect for this unobtrusive style of documentary making.

In 1960 Pennebaker directed a film charting presidential hopeful John F. Kennedy's New England campaign called *Primary*. As a result of the success of this and other projects he and the other rising young Turks of Direct Cinema attracted the attention of Time-Life Inc. who were looking to expand TV journalism through the format of documentary. Pennebaker and Richard Leacock set up their own production and distribution company and in the early 1960s they began to receive a series of TV commissions from ABC and NBC. They subsequently set up a liaison office with Time-Life and recruited new personnel, including a young woman called Sara Lownes who happened to be Bob Dylan's girlfriend. It was Sara who suggested Albert Grossman should contact the company. Pennebaker:

'For a long time [Sara] worked up at the magazine for our unit – we were a kind of secret unit working on "Life". I had a studio downtown and she took charge of the uptown office; so she and I were really managing the whole operation in 1963.'

Grossman arranged for Dylan and Pennebaker to meet and then dealt with the thorny problem of financing the movie. According to Shelton, Grossman put up an initial $3,000 seed money and left Leacock Pennebaker Inc. to sort out the rest. However, in a 1986 interview with John Bauldie, Pennebaker remembered it differently:

'We put up all the money for the film. Albert didn't put up any money. He put up the tickets for Jones and Howard Alk to get over there, that's all, and they were friends of his so I didn't figure that was too administrative – and so in the end we put up all the money for the film.' (Jones and husband Howard Alk were friends of Grossman. Alk, who ran the Bear Club in Chicago where Dylan played early in his career, had an interest in filmmaking.)

With Grossman apparently not contributing, Pennebaker approached Dylan's record company Columbia for funds, but was astonished at how unwelcome his advances appeared to be. Finally, after being shunted from department to department and from executive to executive, the frustrated Pennebaker made an offer:

'I said, "Look, I'm not looking to make a lot of money out of this, but if I could get our expenses paid – just getting to England and back – we'll put up all the film and everything, as long as we can get that back ultimately. For $5,000 I'll give you half the film." They said, "No".'

Fortunately Pennebaker went to see an old friend, Ike Kleineman, one of the production team who was setting up CBS Television's prestige current affairs programme 60 Minutes. According to Pennebaker, Kleineman told him, 'Well I'll buy some footage from you – maybe $500-$600 worth of footage – if it's terrific footage".'

Pennebaker managed to scrape together just enough money to fund the rest of the filming costs. Over a Manhattan restaurant meal,

Dylan and Grossman came to a loose agreement with Leacock Pennebaker Inc. that they would be reimbursed for $100,000 when the movie had gone into profit. According to Pennebaker the contract was 'written on a piece of paper, the bottom of a menu somewhere, it was a handshake deal... Dylan and I just shook hands and that was it.'

Take Three – 'What Is Your Real Message?'

By the time Pennebaker and his crew began shooting in England, the filmmaker had obviously given a lot of thought as to how to present Dylan and his music on film. He spent a great deal of time listening to his records and familiarising himself with the lyrics.

'With a music film your first concern is the actual performance...' Pennebaker later explained. 'You must use a hand-held camera – that is fundamental. You cannot become part of the music unless you are free to move that camera in any direction at any time.'

Pennebaker had quickly developed an affinity for Dylan. During the concert shoots, he was particularly aware that something remarkable was taking place in front of his camera:

'The songs really hit me. From then on I knew that by total chance I'd fallen right into the place that I should be. That happens maybe ten percent of the time in filmmaking.'

Technically Pennebaker had to work within the confines of a restrictive budget, seldom shooting a song all the way through:

'I shot about twenty-five thousand feet, at about two and one half reels a day. I was really hoarding film. I'd shoot a line of a song here, another line there. When we got down to the editing ... I found that we'd wasted very little film.' One of the strengths of *Dont Look Back* is that the viewer is never aware of the financial constraints.

In spite of the many hurdles D.A. came up against, he managed to produce a unique portrait of a young artist. What is interesting is that Pennebaker claims that at first he never thought about the film in

"AN EXCEPTIONAL PORTRAIT OF THE YOUNG MAN WHO IS PROBABLY THE MOST POTENT SINGLE INFLUENCE ON YOUTH IN THE WORLD TODAY!"
—John L. Wasserman, San Francisco Chronicle

terms of a documentary. He envisaged it as an 'entertainment film'. But Pennebaker was too deeply immersed in the cult of Direct Cinema and its attendant cultural baggage for *Dont Look Back* to have been anything else. So how did he sell himself and his vision of truth to Dylan? Surely Sara and her experiences of working with Leacock Pennebaker Inc. must have had some bearing on it? It's hard to imagine Dylan allowing just anybody interfere with his own personal take on things. When asked by John Bauldie what he thought Dylan's motivation was in taking part in the film, Pennebaker replied:

'I don't know. And I'm not sure that it's meaningful to try and second guess. My sense is that ... I think that he thought that this was a way to learn about films and basically, Dylan always counts a nickel, it was gonna be cheap – it wasn't gonna cost him anything!'

Take Four – 'Oh Strewth!'

From its opening moment, *Dont Look Back* contravenes immediately the format of the documentary. Instead of the customary credit sequence, the viewer is plunged directly into what was, for its time, a ground-breaking celluloid presentation of a tune. The song, 'Subterranean Homesick Blues', acted as a kind of chorus throughout the movie: Dylan may have been touring England solo, acoustically, but his heart lay somewhere else. The electric muse that had been creeping slowly into his recorded output during the last few months was now being unleashed in the form of a 45 rpm single that was to reach anthemic proportions on Britain's pirate radio stations.

The clip that accompanied 'Subterranean Homesick Blues' is what was known at the time as a 'promo(tional) film'. Nowadays it would be called a 'rock video'. In the mid-Sixties it was common practice for all top ten artists to make promo films. Billy J. Kramer's 'Little Children', (February 1964), Nashville Teens' 'Tobacco Road', (July 1964), and The Stones' 'Little Red Rooster' (November 1964) were all fairly typical examples. Promos such as these were shown on television and as short features at cinemas. Promos were also often used on British TV by American artists who couldn't get over to the UK because of other commitments.

Pennebaker is convinced that this was part of Albert Grossman's reasoning in allowing *Dont Look Back* to get made. 'I'm sure that Albert explained to him,' Pennebaker recalled, 'that the deal was for them to pick up some footage they could use for commercials abroad. Everybody – The Beatles, The Stones – they did these TV promo things free. That was standard, that's what you did on English TV at that time to sell a record.'

According to Pennebaker, the concept for the shoot came from Dylan himself. Once again Dylan demonstrated how differently he perceived things. The standard manner of filming promos was fairly straightforward. The group or musician would stand somewhere and mime to their latest single. Sometimes it was done in a studio, occasionally at some sort of exotic location. Arguably for Dylan – so concerned with truth and authenticity – to mime his vocals would have seemed false. According to some contemporary sources he's still unhappy about miming for his promo videos. But, what he may have considered a problem he brilliantly subverted by the use of cards with key lyrics written on them. These signs were handmade the night before in the Mayfair Hotel by Dylan, Joan Baez and Donovan! Pennebaker:

'You know Donovan's a very good drawer? He turned out to be the artist, so everybody gave him the hard ones to do.'

Three different versions were shot, all using the locked-off camera single shot. One was done on a roof, one in an alleyway by the side of the Savoy Hotel and a third in a nearby park. This particular location filming was interrupted half way through by the arrival of the police who closed down the shoot just as Dylan was reaching the end of the cards.

The 'Subterranean Homesick Blues' footage was later shown on British TV as a stand-alone promo. Like so much that Dylan has done over the years, it has exerted an enormous influence on popular culture. Its highly original style has been adapted, borrowed and plain ripped off for the last three decades. Its influence has manifested itself in everything from other musicians' videos to advertisements for banks and batteries.

From a strict chronological sense 'Subterranean Homesick Blues' should appear at the end of a film that documents Dylan's last solo acoustic tour. The raucous, punk-like 'Subterranean' is ushering in a whole new era of sound, and yet Pennebaker has chosen to place it like a slap in the face at the top of the movie – Wham! – No introduction, no quarter asked, no quarter given. It ends on a quick fade to black.

Take Five – 'Keep A Good Head and Always Carry A Lightbulb'

Next is the title sequence – the point where we'd normally expect a film to begin. We join Dylan and several members of the entourage, Neuwirth, Grossman, etc, backstage in a provincial dressing room. Dylan is fretting about his missing cane, Grossman is doing his famous Buddha pose, inscrutable and calm, yet somehow cheerfully menacing all at the same time. Dylan takes the stage, lit by a single spotlight. The screen fades black as he sings the opening of 'All I Really Want To Do' over a black screen. The credits roll upwards finishing in a single title – *London 1965*.

It's as simple as that. We are transported back in time by the briefest of information and even when the film was released in 1967 it must have seemed like a document from a time long past. In those two years, Dylan's image had shifted from the directly confrontational to that of a mysterious rock hermit.

Then we're at Heathrow Airport in London and the camera disembarks along with Dylan and his crew. Pennebaker follows the giggling, nursery rhyme ('London Bridge Is Falling Down') singing group as they leave the tarmac and enter the terminal. Dylan cadges a light off a young journalist, or it could be just a fan. He doesn't appear to realise how

> "Youth will make this one of the most popular films ever produced. It will quickly rank with that small number of totally contemporary films that include The Beatles flicks, 'Morgan,' 'Blow Up' and a very few others.
>
> "Dylan expresses something very, very important about the New Youth. Our sons and daughters are beyond our command, and Dylan offers us clues as to why.
>
> "It is the most effective presentation of the reality of contemporary youth attitudes that I have ever seen. It is also one of the best, if not the very best, portrait of a performing artist to be shown publicly.
>
> "It ought to be seen dozens of times!"
>
> — Ralph J. Gleason, San Francisco Chronicle

popular he is and in a moment Pennebaker's camera catches a bit of fan frenzy as a crush of youngsters try to touch their idol. This is where hand-held cameras come into their own. The camera's proximity intensifies the excitement and adds to Dylan's (and our) surprise at his reception. There's something about the jerky *cinema verite* style of rolling and bucking that adds an extra edge to a scene like this that could quite easily have been shot from above, or some distance away but wouldn't have been half as effective.

The film then shifts to the first of a series of 'meeting the press' episodes that will pepper the movie. Before Dylan emerged as a radically different kind of performer, 'someone with a message', pop artists had generally been interviewed by showbiz columnists and their exploits carried little or no importance outside of glorified gossip sheets. Dylan, on the other hand, was perceived by the media machine as an oddity – a 'Protest singer', something beyond their ken.

This fascination with Dylan as some kind of prophet or poet had obviously been fuelled by the chart success of songs such as 'Blowin' In The Wind' and 'The Times They Are A-Changin' '. Music, or so it appeared, no longer had to preoccupy itself with the Tin Pan Alley banalities of Moon/Spoon and June. Here was a form of contemporary song, call it Folk if you will, which in terms of its subject matter and its sophistication went light years beyond the simple parameters of Pop. Small wonder then that the British (and American) press were fascinated by Dylan and his audience.

But what becomes painfully apparent throughout the movie and is later drawn to its hideous conclusion in *Eat The Document* is the media's total inability to cope with the uniqueness of Dylan's persona. Drawing strength from clichés and succour from banality they ask almost universally the most obvious questions. The interview, per-se, is always a battle of wits, and throughout *Dont Look Back* the subtext to Dylan's behaviour is how he deals with the question – *How can a performer give suitably animated replies day after day to the same old queries?* Especially questions such as 'What is your real message?' Dylan – who until now has apparently been trying to be helpful, his replies free from sarcasm or boredom – allows a look of whimsical playfulness to pass across his face.

'*Keep a good head and always carry a lightbulb.*'

Now bear in mind that he's actually carrying a large, oversized lightbulb and he's already answered another journalist's question – '*Why have you got that lightbulb?*' with the very reasonable reply – '*Oh it was just a gift. Somebody very close gave it to me*'. Meaning, I think we can reasonably assume, that it was given to him as a kind of gag/gift, either at Kennedy Airport or on the flight (he's carrying it off the plane at the beginning of the movie), but now the deal is, these people are making an issue out of it. They are uncool. They will be gently put down. He glances quickly around, sees the lightbulb and incorporates it into his Zen koan. The assembled journalists fall into the trap and very carefully write it all down.

Pennebaker's camera is active throughout, sometimes giving us Dylan's view of the press pack, other times their view of him. At one point he actually interrupts Dylan's press conference by focusing in on Bobby Neuwirth who is sitting with the journalists. From his privileged vantage point Pennebaker captures this bit of immortal dialogue.

Journalist – *Are you Folk?*

Neuwirth – (incredulously) *Am I Folk!? – Oh no, not me. I'm not Folk.*

Take Six – 'I'm Glad I'm Not Me!'

Essentially *Dont Look Back* consists of a series of scenarios or motifs that interweave and intersect with one another. These can be broadly broken down into –

1. Backstage
2. Onstage
3. Hotel Rooms
4. Interviews

To this we could add another element threading its way through the film and that is 'Travel'. There is constant motion: limousines, trains and planes. People come in and go out. The only point of stasis is the performances, where Dylan stands like a hub at the centre of a wheel.

Throughout the other scenarios, a cast of characters led by Dylan stroll and struggle their way through the greyness of mid-Sixties'

England. Marianne Faithfull, curled up on a sofa, listens attentively to Joan Baez and Dylan singing. Tito Burns and Albert Grossman play out their roles as Svengalis of Pop. High Sheriffs' Ladies queue with science students for audiences with the Folk troubador. Teenage girls squeal and howl as teenage boys run alongside limousines. John Mayall sits silently in the back as Alan Price sucks on vodka and orange squash. Donovan becomes jester to the high court and Horace Judson from *Time* magazine is ritually sacrificed on the altar of Hip (how that must have amused Pennebaker).

As described above, we see Dylan interacting with a variety of people in many different situations and, though some may argue that it is a cultivated mystique, Dylan's changing behaviour – hip one second, petulant the next – is an innate chameleon-like response to suit given situations. In *Dont Look Back* he is at times disengagingly charming, at others blisteringly acerbic in his handling of naïve hangers on.

Richard Goldstein in *The New York Times* summed up the problem of representing Dylan on film when he said 'Without a programme you can hardly tell the vaudeville from the verite...'

Whatever, Dylan's circus is in town and it's hard to tell the geeks from the freaks as he cuts a broad swathe through the sensibilities of the England of the time. All the while, Pennebaker's camera reveals Dylan as an exotic creature, an alien-like hybrid of Byronesque good looks and existentialist put-downs, but it also reveals a young man who is working very hard at everything he does – a young man who is succeeding brilliantly.

Take Seven – Backstage (interior)

The actual film proper opens with an apparently nervous Dylan stalking and pacing around a dressing room, guitar and harmonica round his neck and a cigarette clamped firmly between his lips. Dylan is revved up and ready to go. Different towns but always the same dressing room.

It's an hermetic atmosphere backstage, insular and usually private. All performers have rituals that they go through before and after performances. What makes *Dont Look Back* so uniquely unusual, certainly for its time, is the apparent freedom of access that Dylan allowed Pennebaker. His camera roams freely around the vignettes and cameos that are laid out for our pleasure like paintings in a gallery. For the first time in a rock film the viewer is allowed, apparently, to participate in, or, more properly, glimpse at the world of the artist in a way that would be emulated by all the rockumentaries that followed. How privileged we actually are I guess we'll never know, but much of it seems genuine enough. There is a certain candour about Dylan that shines through the masks.

'It's not so much 'about' Dylan,' Pennebaker later explained. 'Because Dylan is sort of acting throughout the film. And that's his right. He needs some protection in a sense against that process. But I think that what you do find out a little bit is the extraordinary pressure of having to go out and be absolutely perfect... He had to be extraordinary where most of us settle for just being adequate.' Still, I agree with Paul Williams that the great thing about

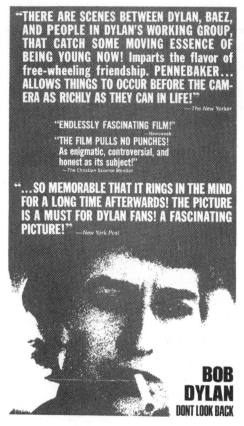

"THERE ARE SCENES BETWEEN DYLAN, BAEZ, AND PEOPLE IN DYLAN'S WORKING GROUP, THAT CATCH SOME MOVING ESSENCE OF BEING YOUNG NOW! Imparts the flavor of free-wheeling friendship. PENNEBAKER... ALLOWS THINGS TO OCCUR BEFORE THE CAMERA AS RICHLY AS THEY CAN IN LIFE!"
—*The New Yorker*

"ENDLESSLY FASCINATING FILM!"
—*Newsweek*
"THE FILM PULLS NO PUNCHES! As enigmatic, controversial, and honest as its subject!"
—*The Christian Science Monitor*

"...SO MEMORABLE THAT IT RINGS IN THE MIND FOR A LONG TIME AFTERWARDS! THE PICTURE IS A MUST FOR DYLAN FANS! A FASCINATING PICTURE!" —*New York Post*

BOB DYLAN
DONT LOOK BACK

Dont Look Back is that it 'humanises' Dylan.

Visually the scenes are in true Direct Cinema style, with Pennebaker's raw technique creating an easy flowing rhythm that places the viewer as the dispassionate observer. His hand-held camera hovers like the ubiquitous 'fly on the wall', for sustained takes with minimal editing. These became the hallmark of his distinctive style. Sometimes his camera lingers on the subject after they've finished talking – gauging reactions. At other times he focuses on a scene's principal players, occasionally at Dylan's expense: there is the wonderful meeting backstage in Newcastle, between Dylan and Alderman Mrs Jim Clark, the High Sheriff's Lady.

Opening on a wide shot that establishes the scene, a slightly incredulous looking Dylan is introduced to an archetypical female civic dignitary, circa 1965. With her fur stole and matinee gloves she's a working facsimile of a member of the Royal Family spending a night at the opera. You half expect Dylan to curtsy or bow. As Pennebaker moves into close up on Her Royal Highness, Dylan can barely contain the smile behind his hand.

The High Sheriff's Lady – *I'm the Sheriff's lady. And I'm happy to say on behalf of all of them I've come to say how very happy we are to have you here. And we hope you have a very successful night because everybody loves you.*

She proceeds to extol the virtues of her fair city. Soon, she enthuses, she is to become the Lady Mayoress. This information is verified by a gentleman whom Albert Grossman would no doubt term 'a flunky'. Dylan's grin grows and his hand becomes busier concealing it. Strangely, Grossman, who has previously hovered around the periphery of many of the film's scenes, is absent from this one. He's possibly just out of sight, behind the door from which Bobby Neuwirth is soon to enter, doubled up with helpless laughter. Without pausing for breath the High Sheriff's Lady charges relentlessly on. She tells, or possibly orders, Dylan –

High Sheriff's Lady – *I'll have you as my guest in the mansion house*. And then goes on –

High Sheriff's Lady – *I think the songs are very wonderful, and you write them yourself too, don't you?*

Before Dylan can reply she adds –

High Sheriff's Lady – *Sometimes?*

Bobby Neuwirth enters the room clutching gifts of harmonicas for Dylan's guest. After graciously accepting the gift she beams at all around her –

High Sheriff's Lady – *And I really mean this, I think you're a really good example for the youth.*

The 'youth' in question (well, there actually appear to be three of them) are all male, all clearly embarrassed and all standing about three feet behind the High Sheriff's Lady. She actually introduces them as her sons. She says that one is called Stephen and then introduces another one as Stephen too. It is true that her son Stephen is present, but both?...!

The High Sheriff's Lady then sweeps imperiously from the room with a final observation.

High Sheriff's Lady – *He's charming.*

He's also hardly managed to get a word in but that doesn't matter because clearly she's been totally won over by Dylan's disingenuous 'oh, shucks' manners. The winner of this bout is most certainly her good self. Dylan has merely been an innocent bystander in this particular section of the movie.

Take Eight – Onstage

There's a brevity in the musical numbers in *Dont Look Back*. We know from Pennebaker this was partially an economic imperative, but for the sake of argument let's assume it was also an aesthetic one.

There's a Jamaican phrase – 'short cut draw blood' – that is particularly apt in the movie. The cuts and thrusts of the short musical extracts are effective in reminding the viewer why Dylan is in England in the first place and where he was musically at the time. In a sense there is no need for full-length versions of the songs. By the time of the tour, Dylan was almost past performing a large chunk of them anyway. Particular songs from his repertoire such as 'The Times They Are A-Changin'' could be viewed as ancient history from Dylan's perspective. If anything he was performing them as a favour to his British fans who lagged somewhat behind their American counterparts in 'hipness'. For documentary purposes the film (and the filmmaker) is much more interested in the phenomenon of the paraphernalia of the tour, the comings and goings, the questions and answers. Pennebaker's all-seeing eye is the matrix of events, not Dylan the prophet's.

Quite often it's the music that's not played onstage that commands our attention. There are moments when we the viewers are left feeling in a privileged position, when we catch a glimpse of the creative artist at work, gently teasing out threads of structures, using the building blocks of chords to try out new ideas on the piano.

Still, the live stage numbers, no matter how truncated, do offer a snapshot of the artist at a time of near perfection in his performing capabilities. Some critics, citing Dylan himself it must be said, have claimed that there is a certain staleness about the shows, an almost palpable air of boredom to his playing. But I don't feel that they come across that negatively, though of course, cinematically, ways of shooting a solo performer in concert are fairly limited. Pennebaker is

> **As film, it is pure art; as a documentary of an artist it is pure poetry; and as a commentary on our world, well, that's the way it is. Ralph J. Gleason**

renowned for his unobtrusiveness, and the onstage sequences are simple as befits the mood of the shows. One shot, however, at the end of the movie when Dylan is playing his final concert at the Albert Hall is quite breathtaking. It's a simple one-cam shot that begins as a fairly tight close up of Dylan singing. It then pulls out slowly until we realise that it must have been taken from the balcony. Dylan, bathed in a single spotlight, grows smaller and smaller until he is just a tiny image in the bottom left hand corner of the frame. No other single shot has ever come quite so close to demonstrating the essential loneliness of performing, the distinct feeling of distance and separation. It is worth the price of admission alone.

Take Nine – Hotel Rooms

As you'd imagine in a documentary about 'life on the road' a lot of the action in *Dont Look Back* takes place in hotel rooms, in this case, principally The Savoy in London. One sequence in particular has since gone on to provide the name for a fanzine and has also, over the years, been the focus for much discussion: the (in)famous – 'Who threw the glass?' incident.

It opens with a shot of a poster for a Donovan concert that segues into a shot of Donovan himself, self-consciously smiling at the camera. Without warning we then cut to an extremely angry Dylan. This is a shock. We're not used to this. Normally we'd expect a cool Dylan or an aloof Dylan, sometimes occasionally a smiling Dylan, but this is a whole different creature. This is a hopping mad Bob. For years I'd thought Dylan was referring to a drinking glass that had been thrown out of the hotel window, but according to Anthea Joseph (a London Folk promoter who befriended Dylan in 1962) it was a glass shelf from the bathroom that had been thrown out by two English drunks who were partying with the entourage in Dylan's suite.

'There's this perfectly good party going on,' Joseph recalled. 'All sorts of people turned up. Allen [Ginsberg] was there. I mean everybody was there. And I was going round dishing out the drinks. And then this row broke out... These two bozos had locked themselves in the bathroom, where it had beautiful glass shelves.

These wonderful sort of thirties bathrooms! Vast marble bath. They were just chucking them out!'

Dylan is standing with his back to us in the hotel doorway –

Dylan – *I just want to know – who threw that fucking glass into the street?!*

Bobby Neuwirth stands protectively on one side of Dylan. Howard Alk stands on the other. Neuwirth stretches his arm out to prevent the camera from coming closer, but Pennebaker manages to get in tighter – Dylan shouts –

Dylan – *Who did it? Somebody better tell me who did it or you're all gonna have to get out of here and never come back!*

A drunken English Bohemian wobbles uncertainly in front of Dylan and tries to explain that he didn't do it and anyway, he's pissed.

Dylan (in a rage) – *Don't tell me you're pissed! Don't tell me you're pissed! You were there. Who threw the glass into the street???*

What we have here is a slight problem of English language vernacular. In the Queen's English to be pissed means to be drunk. In American usage it means to be angry. Dylan then gives the guy ten seconds to bring the culprit before him. The guy sways unsteadily and looks incapable of bringing anything near Dylan other than his previous night's dinner. All the time an acoustic 12-bar jam is going on in the background.

The shot changes to inside the hotel room and onto Donovan who is sitting next to a guitar-wielding John Mayall.

Dylan – *I'm gonna clean up the glass.*

Donovan leaps up, and grinning amiably says –

Donovan – *I'll help you man!*

Another cut and we see American Folk singer Derroll Adams trying to quieten things down a little while Anthea Joseph looks on. Dylan speaks again, this time presumably to the main perpetrator of the glass incident –

Dylan – *Either be groovy or leave man.*

After a brief scene in which Dylan apologises to a hotel representative we cut to Dylan shaking the drunk's hand and carefully explaining to him that he just didn't want anybody to get hurt by the glass. The recumbent drunk scowls upwards as Dylan asks Adams if there are any good poets in town. Adams replies that Dominic Behan is around but Dylan doesn't want to see him. The drunk rouses himself from his stupor and announces in an imperious tone –

Drunk 2 – *Dominic Behan is a friend of mine!'*

Dylan's response to this is again placatory. He's really trying to cool things down –

Dylan – *Hey, that's fine, man. I just don't wanta hear anybody like that though.*

The scene cuts and we go into a more conventional sequence in which Donovan and Dylan trade off songs. Dylan wins.

So there we have the 'Who threw the glass?' scene. It is tense and fraught. Our sympathies fly round from character to character, but essentially remain with Dylan. Have we been given a glimpse of his real persona? I think not. Pennabaker's avowed intention with Direct Cinema was to represent truth, but this is a conundrum that continues to tax all filmmakers. This is not to say that the event was staged for the cameras. Dylan's anger is certainly real, but ultimately if there was no camera present, would Dylan have been the one to do the questioning? Surely, any potential hassles or problems would have been dealt with by Grossman, conspicuously absent from this scene, or by Neuwirth. He was the tour manager – things like this were his responsibility. And, if the drunks do not appear to be aware of being filmed, the grinning Donovan and the dismissive Mayall certainly do. Perhaps the only absolutely true Direct Cinema is the footage we get these days from security videos but whatever, this scene makes for gripping viewing.

For anybody interested in the identity of the glass-thrower, there was a booklet published in the UK in the mid-1980s called *The Circus Is In Town* which claimed that it was either Folk singer Louis Killen or another Folk singer who shared the same name as an old Village friend of Dylan's, Fred Neil. Killen's accent is markedly different from that of the voice in the film and in the Winter 1999 edition of *The Bridge* fanzine Killen denied that he was the culprit.

Take Ten – Interviews

Dont Look Back has attained legendary status for a lot of reasons, not least the sequences where Dylan is confronting or being confronted by the press. From the mauling given to Terry Ellis – (who would later leave the heady atmosphere of academia and found Chrysalis Records), the young science student who said later, 'I remember he had a wicked glint in his eye – I couldn't tell you if it was chemically induced. In retrospect, I don't think he was actually being cruel to me, he was being quite pleasant – but in his own caustic way…' all the way through to his encounter with Horace Judson from *Time* magazine. From the way the scene is edited it looks as if Dylan is playing with Judson as a cat might play with a mouse –

Dylan – *Are you going to see the show tonight? Are you going to hear it?– It's gonna happen fast and you're not gonna get it all –*

– There's no great message

– You've got a lot of nerve asking me a question like that!

And on and on throughout the scene. Dylan's blistering attack on the establishment press is a *tour de force*… or so it seems –

Anthea Joseph recalled that, '[Judson] was quite abusive as well. He was extremely upset, he really was, and in a way I suppose, it wasn't really his fault, not properly briefed, treating Bob like some sort of curiosity, not as a serious artist.'

Before the film moves into its final section, the Albert Hall concert, Dylan leaves Judson with one of his more hilarious semantic observations –

I'm just as good a singer as Caruso… You have to listen carefully, but I hit all those notes. I can hold my breath three times as long if I want to…

Take Eleven – Cameos

'Well, you've got to understand a peculiar situation around royal entourages, palaces, courts in general, politics, and that is that you can be number four or five, but if you're used to being number one or two it's a big jolt.' D.A. Pennebaker

A variety of people flit around the periphery of *Dont Look Back*, some as fleeting cameos, others with a more extended role to play in

Pennebaker's absorbing psychodrama. Former Animal, Alan Price seems to occupy more screentime than his persona deserves; ever present with his bottles of vodka and orange. Pennebaker recalls one scene between Dylan and Price when he felt the presence of his camera may have been too intrusive:

'When he asks Alan if he's playing with The Animals anymore, and he says, "No, it happens," and Dylan starts to chord in those blues. And then he looked at me like he was kind of pissed that I was filming. But I didn't give a shit. It was one of those things where we were looking right in the eye. And he looked away. But you can see that mean look he sometimes gives.'

Joan Baez's participation in the movie is at times almost heartbreaking. Flying into Heathrow at the head of the entourage, she had just completed an American tour with Dylan. To certain sections of the media she and Bob were the uncrowned King and Queen of Folk (and to other sections, the crowned King and Queen). It's apparent from Joan's behaviour in *Dont Look Back* that she expected to be Dylan's special guest at his English concerts. It wasn't to be, as Baez herself explained:

'I never sang with him [on the English tour]. He wouldn't let me sing to put it bluntly. I should never have gone on that tour. It was sick… But you see, I thought he'd do what I had done with him, would introduce me, and it would be very nice because I'd never sung in England before… I was very, very hurt. I was miserable. I was a complete ass; I should have left, I mean, I should have left after that first concert. But there's something about situations like that – you hang around. I stayed for two weeks and then I walked out of that door in the film. I never came back after that.'

She actually did return after Dylan's concert tour programme was over and he had been taken ill while waiting to record two shows for the BBC. She rushed to his hotel room after hearing just how sick he'd been (Dylan had actually been admitted to St Mary's Hospital in Paddington and was back in the Savoy Hotel recuperating). When the door was opened by Sara Lownes, Joan Baez realised that it was finally over.

Pennebaker's camera shows us an unflinching, no-holds barred record of the end of the affair and it's very hard not to feel a great deal of sympathy for Ms Baez, as she shuffles aimlessly through the footage from one freeze out to another. Apparently, her saviour throughout the sorry mess was Bobby Neuwirth.

'One night I went into Neuwirth's room crying,' she recalled. 'He put his arms around me and mopped a pint of tears off my cheeks and chin, and begged me to pack up my bags and leave the tour. "But Bob asked me to come. He asked me," I protested...'

Said Pennebaker, '... well she loved him.'

Take Twelve – Pancho & Lefty

Dont Look Back offers us one of the most (unintentionally?) funny scenes in a rockumentary – Albert Grossman and English impresario Tito Burns taking great pleasure in screwing a number of British television producers, extracting the maximum amount of geld for their golden goose.

Burns was one of England's top promoters. He'd seen it all, from the dance bands of the Forties through to the rock'n'roll boom time of the Fifties, and now he was finding a lucrative market for 'Protest'. He claimed to have watched one of the first tour concerts in Sheffield.

'I have never seen Dylan work before and I went in for a few numbers,' Burns recalled. 'I stayed there two hours, because it got to me. I'm not an intellectual, and I only understood about half of it, but the magic still got to me...'

Burns was from the old school – and loving it. You can almost hear him counting heads and costing the take as he reminisced in 1965:

'In 1964, I don't think he took a lot of money at the Festival Hall. In 1965, he took the maximum. In his coming concert tour in spring

1966, when he could double the price of tickets, he's refusing to do that…'

You can almost hear Tito's jaw dropping. But if Albert said that, Tito would go along, because you can see the symbiosis between the two men bubbling. Besides, Dylan was attracting the right sort of people. The people who would give this East End son of Jewish immigrants a credibility that he appeared to crave. One that rock 'n' roll would never have in Tito's lifetime. It would be decades later before Royalty took to summoning Pop stars for galas and such-like. Tito Burns:

'The Beatles and The Stones were at the Albert Hall and we had to get them boxes way back… Everyone was there! Marianne Faithfull rang up for eight tickets. Her mother is a Baroness you know… Just about everybody was there… The names that were coming through… The Earl of Harewood… fantastic!'

In their scene together in *Dont Look Back*, the two Svengalis of the Pop world sit opposite each other in Tito's office on Denmark Street in London, then known as the English Tin Pan Alley. The street housed management offices, agencies and recording studios, nestling side by side with coffee bars and guitar shops. Tito Burns' office was at the top of a flight of rickety stairs.

Tito is on the phone to the BBC and Johnny Hamp at Granada. He and Albert are playing the two off against each other. Tito's gold cufflinks are flashing in the light coming in through the office window as Albert reclines in a chair. Tito puts the phone down on Stuart at the BBC. Albert leans forward mysteriously –

If you get him back, why don't you leave me to have a crack at him?

Together, they weave, duck and dive, wringing the best price out of the Brits that they can.

Well, you know Granada – They pay for the taxi as well…

Two grand, that's our final offer.

And so on as they bat the producers around like killer whales with a penguin.

Albert Grossman occasionally regretted allowing Pennebaker to film the scene. Pennebaker:

'Albert did say that after a while he got tired of little girls coming up to him in clubs, telling him how gross he looked in that scene. He almost wished he hadn't done it; but Tito, he wrote me a letter and he thinks he's a movie star! "I'll be with Albert in about ten minutes" – you couldn't get people to act funnier.'

Take Thirteen – The Final Cut

By the end of May 1965, Pennebaker was back in New York and trying to work out what to do with the footage that he'd shot. It wasn't until the winter of 1965/66 that he began to work on it properly.

One of the film's significant moments is a cut that occurs just after the journalist from the BBC's African service asks Dylan – *How did it all begin Bob?*' – and it goes to archive footage of Dylan singing 'Only A Pawn In The Game' from a Civil Rights march in Greenwood Mississippi, shot by Ed Emshwiller in 1964.

Pennebaker had stuck it over his editing desk, not having a clue what to do with it, principally because it had been shot on a wind-up 16 mm Bolex with a separate soundtrack. As he was watching the African service interview, Pennebaker began to get excited:

'And then I saw that thing sitting on the shelf, and I decided I might as well look at it. Now, when you use a viewer to edit, you have the viewer and you have a synchroniser sitting here with a reader on the synchroniser, and they're roughly 22 frames apart. So you never let anything go out,' cos once it gets out you have to thread up – and it's hard to do that. So I had these pieces of film from the last scene still sticking out – "How did it all begin Bob?" – And I just spliced the Greenwood film on, just to look at it, not as part of the film, 'cos that's the way you look at stuff. And when I looked at it, I thought, "Holy shit!" And I never took it out of the film.'

Dont Look Back was ready by the end of January, but it wouldn't be until early April 1966 that Dylan was able to see the finished cut. He was preparing for his world tour at the Columbia Rehearsal Rooms on Sunset Boulevard in Los Angeles. Pennebaker:

'When Bob first saw the film in North Hollywood, he was shocked and said we needed a lot of changes. The second time he saw it, with a writing pad in his hand, he came out saying, "no changes".'

After the second screening Pennebaker remembers only two changes that he and Dylan discussed:

'This particular thing where he is playing for a long time and it's kind of back-lit, it's a beautiful scene, he's all by himself with Tom Wilson (Dylan's record producer at the time), who I liked a lot. So anyway, he's sitting there and Bob is fiddling around with this song and singing these scat words to it, and I'd cut that scene a little bit, the original song goes on much longer. Dylan said, "Well, uh, that scene where I'm workin' on that song at the piano, I bet you never filmed anybody writing a song before?" I said, "Well no. I didn't actually." Dylan said, "Maybe you oughta put some of that back then." So I thought about it, and I thought he was right, and I did put it back.

'The second thing he said was, "An' all that stuff in the room with the glass, you don't need to have that, that's so noisy, I hate that." I thought about it and I said, "Well I understand, but my sense is that you really need that for the story to work. It's very essential and I don't know exactly why, and I'm not going to try and defend it psychologically or anything 'cause I don't care about that, but I think it matters to the story and I can't cut it out." And he said, "OK".'

Dylan's mercurial mood swings meant that Pennebaker now had the green light for showing the movie, though it would be a year later before it was finally premiered in San Francisco on May 17 1967 exactly one year after the legendary 'Judas' confrontation at Manchester Free Trade Hall. But it didn't premiere easily. Both Dylan and Albert Grossman were unhappy. Pennebaker:

'There were a lot of big hassles with Albert. I wanted to go to the quality art theatres. I felt the film, like Dylan, should be hard to see… anyway, I remember that Albert never really thought of my film as a real film, it seemed awfully home-movieish to him to have any kind of reality…'

In later years, Pennebaker explained the financial costs of the film to Robert Shelton. With editing and music rights, plus the cost of blowing up the print from 16 mm to 35 mm, the movie was coming in at around $40,000. One third of the box office gross ($1 million) went to the producers (Leacock, Pennebaker). After distribution and advertising and sundries, Dylan was splitting around $100,000 with the producers and Albert Grossman. No wonder then that his exchange took place in a 1969 interview –

Q – *Don't you like Dont Look Back?*

Dylan – *I'd like it a lot more if I got paid for it.*

Still, Dylan's fans flocked to see it. The main reason, of course, was that in the intervening period between the film being shot and its release, Dylan had seemingly assumed the mantle of a recluse after an apparently life threatening motorcycle accident in July 1966. In actual fact, we now know that he was extremely busy recording with The Band at Big Pink and recuperating from several years of excess.

Whilst his hordes of admirers must have felt that the film was like manna from heaven, the scribes from the 'overground' press were not all convinced -

Life Magazine's reviewer bemoaned, 'What we do not see, or feel, is what is going on inside Dylan...' while *The Kansas City Star*'s critic deemed it, 'The worst film I have ever seen, as organised as a small boy's room...'

The Atlanta Journal dismissed it as a 'Boring, off-color home movie of the neighborhood's biggest brat blowing his nose for 90 minutes...'

The Cleveland Plain Dealer was even more vehement in its criticism: 'SHOULD BE BURIED... This is a cheap, in part, dirty movie, if it is a movie at all. It is a chopped up "story" of Bob Dylan's stormy visit to England. It is certainly not for moviegoers who bathe and/or shave. It is "underground" and should be buried at once. Burn a rag, as was once said of filth. Phew!'

In spite of the adverse contemporary critical reactions *Dont Look Back* has been doing the rounds for over three decades now and was re-released in a brand new print in 1998 to almost universal

"GROOVINESS GROUND ZERO" -NY POST

BOB DYLAN
DONT LOOK BACK

approval. Frequently shown on TV, and readily available on video (at least in the USA) it has at last been recognised as the first serious study in documentary form of a performing artist.

One final point – How did the film get its name? Pennebaker:

'*Dont Look Back* was my idea for the title, and was a bit of wisdom from Satchel Page, an old-time baseball great who remarked, "Don't look back it may be gaining on you". I realise that there is a line in one of Bob's songs: "She's an artist, she don't look back," but it was coincidence, and the song wasn't in the film. The title came to me either when I was filming or editing. I don't remember which now.'

Reel Two
Eat The Document

In a 1978 interview, Dylan claimed that he had been shocked by *Dont Look Back,* however his complaints about Pennebaker and Grossman's business arrangements mentioned towards the end of Reel One wouldn't surface until after *Dont Look Back* premiered in 1967. In the meantime, Dylan requested Pennebaker's assistance on a proposed TV project that was under negotiation.

America's ABC TV television network had coughed up a $100,000 advance for a sixty-minute programme about Dylan to be aired as part of a series called *Stage 66*, promising –

'What you always hoped television would be. Great Theatre. Created by great writers, performers, artists... All in color, starting this October.'

Dylan presumably brought in Pennebaker because he felt comfortable with his techniques. Arrangements were made for him to assist shooting the European leg of the 1966 world tour.

'Dylan wanted to make a film of his tour with the band and he

wanted to direct it and he asked me if I would help him film it…' Pennebaker explained. 'It was to be a TV show, that's what I was told, and later on I did have some talks with ABC about it. I wasn't supposed to be the producer… and I wasn't supposed to be the editor necessarily, though it was unclear. We were going to do it as we went along.'

The documentary would be shot by the same crew as *Dont Look Back* – Pennebaker, known to the Dylan entourage as 'The Eye', sharing camera duties with Howard Alk while Alk's wife Jones recorded the soundtrack on a Nagra tape recorder. Dylan's stipulation that it was to be *his* movie – quickly dispensing with the original title of 'Dylan by Pennebaker' – was bound to make Pennebaker's task harder than the year before. Although it wouldn't lead to any discernable friction there was a certain element of artistic schizophrenia in the way in which certain scenes were shot. Pennebaker:

'…it was Bob's film, and he wasn't really interested in making a concert film. He was interested in making a film for television… he was interested primarily in directing material off the stage. Stage material did not interest him, and in fact I shot a lot of it kind of on my own…

'In the beginning I was only trying to respond to Dylan, what Dylan wanted. Dylan said, "I'm going to direct you. Get the camera and we'll decide what to do." He would direct people and say, "Can you film it this way?" "Did you get that?"…

'Making home movies – well, it's simply that it doesn't interest me very much, as a rule…

I felt very ambivalent as to what I should be doing: and I never did sort it out…'

Take One – 'Ever Heard Of Me?'

Eat The Document opens with a shot that would be considered quite outrageous today, let alone on American television in 1966. Although discreetly edited it's fairly obvious what's just taken place – Dylan is raising his head up from the top of a piano, his cupped hands around his nose. He is laughing, coughing and spluttering simultaneously. While a bemused waiter looks on, Richard Manuel snorts something up his nose then puts the lid back on a small snuff box. Maniacal laughter and rolling, dramatic piano music underpin the scene. They are both out of their heads.

This opening sequence sets the movie's tone – fast, frenetic, disjointed and, sometimes just plain strange. Beagle dogs cross roads as Scottish schoolgirls giggle. Enigmatically beautiful women flit in and out of scenes as buses, trains and cars dash madly across a mid-Sixties' landscape. Visits are made to suicide sites, police dog displays and balconies. The film is in colour, but one cannot escape the feeling that it should really be in monochrome; the footage has an old-fashioned European air – nearly every male character is in a suit and sporting a short haircut, while the women tend to be demure and proper. Dylan and his cohorts, on the other hand, appear to have descended on an unsuspecting Europe like exotic animals from an intergalactic zoo. They pick and preen their way around a variety of locations, Copenhagen, Glasgow, Paris and London. They observe the native fauna from the back of limousines, carriages of trains, dressing rooms, stages and hotel rooms.

Some of the cast are familiar from *Dont Look Back* – including Albert Grossman, Howard and Jones Alk, Neuwirth and Fred Perry, the English road manager. Most notable amongst the new faces are band members Robbie Robertson – nicknamed 'The Limpet' because of the way he attached himself to Dylan's side at every available opportunity – Garth Hudson, Rick Danko and Richard Manuel of The Hawks (soon to be The Band) and Mickey Jones brought into replace Hawks drummer Levon Helm who had jumped ship. Interspersed throughout the footage there are also cameo appearances from visiting celebrities like Johnny Cash, Cathy McGowan, The Spencer Davis Group and John Lennon.

However, beneath the fleeting comings and goings and the chaos and apparent madness, there is some structure and method. For instance, though it is not done obviously, each member of Dylan's band is introduced in a short vignette before a number in which they feature. After Manuel and Dylan meet a young Scandinavian couple, we cut to Manuel playing the keyboard lead into 'Baby Let Me Follow You Down'. After the strange back-stage scene where Dylan appears to be shouting at Robbie Robertson about whether he knows 'Tom Thumb's Blues', we cut to Robertson's solo in the same number. Similarly oblique entries are provided for the rest of the musicians.

For all this, the key to *Eat The Document*'s structure is its lack of structure. It is part travelogue, without ever telling you where you are; part rockumentary, with a quite limited performance content, though the music when it does appear is frighteningly good; part documentary (though far from fly-on-the-wall verite); there is almost a complete absence of grounding facts or explanatory features – the film's confusion is its very coherence. Quite simply – this is what life is like on the road.

Take Two – 'Are We Ready To Move On?'

Because of its fragmentary nature *Eat The Document* is difficult to pin down. Many commentators have criticised its apparent 'pseudo-intellectualism', and there are moments when Dylan's vision of life on the road is frustratingly confusing for the viewer. Clearly Dylan's aim was not to make an ordinary documentary but to create something new that goes beyond the natural realism, warts-and-all format of *Dont Look Back*. As we will see, it may have been something of a hit-and-miss experiment but it would provide the blueprint for Dylan's feature film, *Renaldo and Clara*, ten years later. Still, Pennebaker would defend the project:

'This time Dylan got more involved in the actual filmmaking. My new high-speed film really caught the psychedelic aura of drugs and rock onstage. Whatever Bob's reservations, I think it was a major jump forward from *Dont Look Back*.'

Eat The Document is very much a creature of its time. The dialogue that punctuates its fractured structure is enigmatic to say the least. Certainly a Fellini or Bergmanesque quality hovers over the first part of the movie. '...in some sense [Dylan] thought he was going to be Ingmar Bergman or something,' Pennebaker reflected, 'and make some new kind of film.'

What we have here is a collection of scenes recorded in conventional documentary format, but assembled by a low-budget, art-house movie director. Left to his own devices, Pennebaker would have come up with an aesthetically more pleasing version of this footage (and according to various sources – has). But he most certainly could never have come up with anything more challenging to the precepts of conventional narrative cinema. Dylan is a unique artist, and what he tried to do on the tour, and later, during the editing, was expand his oft-mentioned concept of 'mathematical music' – 'I'm more of a mathematical singer,' he insisted at a December 65 press conference. I use words like most people use numbers' – into the visual realm.

In *Eat The Document*, people look up and people look down. Scenes cut dynamically, faces flicker in and out of the main strip of celluloid, collide and then career off into the void. Snatches of overheard dialogue echo salvation, betrayal and perhaps damnation. The important thing is to remember that it is all relevant to the mind that put this thing together – like the heavens, *Eat The Document* has mathematics at the heart of its chaos theory.

Take Three – 'I'm Sorry For Everything I've Done'

'I saw my role there as helping him if I could, but it was really hard for me because Dylan was a very peculiar director. He didn't know what he wanted, and people wandered around, so you ended up filming things for no particular reason...' – D.A. Pennebaker

OK. So Bob Dylan says to you – 'Rick Danko and I are going to snort some methedrine. This is what it's like. This is life on the road. Film it, let truth be our judge,' or something similar. So, as a respected documentary maker, you do just that, knowing full-well that it'll never make it onto prime-time TV. Bob Dylan wants to recreate the last supper, so you all sit down in some hotel, but one of the guys figures it'll be funnier if you only have one plate of food, and if you passed it all the way around the table and everybody takes a little bit but you don't let them. Then the whole thing gets messed up because when it gets to Bob he doesn't want to play the game anymore and the whole scene fizzles out.

And then, in Paris, he wants to do a scene with a French actress named Zuzu who doesn't even speak English – but it's cool. Bob puts on a white matinee idol jacket and a fake villain's moustache, and before you know it, he's recreating scenes from *The Perils Of Pauline*. Grimacing at the camera and saying –

You're not the type to be hypnotised – You must be the type to do something else!

The Mod-looking French girl has enough about her to realise that a reaction is called for, and, raising up her arms to ward off the evil attentions of Dylan, Le Diabolique, she incants –

Que?! Que?! Que?!

Dylan, as the evil whatever, attempts to justify his actions –

I am very tired... I just have to be entertained before... Before lunchtime!

There are very few of these staged scenes in *Eat The Document*, considerably less than one might imagine from reading D.A. Pennebaker's accounts of the tour. However, who knows how many reels may actually lie in their cans, buried somewhere in a Manhattan vault?

We do know that the scenes drawn together in *Eat The Document*'s final cut seem to rely on the absurdity of spontaneous reality. The construction of the narrative owes more to Surrealist concepts of 'automatic writing' (words chosen quickly and randomly that somehow when interpreted give insight into the unconscious mind), than to the kind of formal template that Pennebaker would have used. Pennebaker:

'Maybe he's gotten himself into some kind of film competition with me which I didn't want at all, and I said, "Listen Bob, you can take this footage out and burn it if you want, but I think there's a film in there", because I'd gotten tired of just shooting anything that took place and I started making a film the only way I know. I mean, I started looking for certain things and doing certain things. Because you know, that's what I do. I don't know how not to make a film. So I was caught up in it a little bit and made a film over three or four days and then I kind of let it go.'

Take Four – After Death, The Judgement

After the opening 'snuff' shot, accompanied by the 'silent cinema' piano playing, the movie cuts to a train journey from Dublin to Belfast. Dylan wanders through the footage, smoking, observing, sitting and standing. The rest of the entourage, Grossman, Howard Alk, et al, stare out of the train's windows, the scenery rushing by. Enigmatic art-house dialogue wafts over the scenes.

Are we ready to move on?
Are you out for long here?
Well who would know?
Not too far…

As a scene setter for disorienting the viewer it works according to what we might call 'Dylan's Law', that is to attack the senses with a random sequence of images and sounds. And so it continues – gear being unloaded, musicians noodling around at a sound-check. We are never told where we are or what's happening – again it is possible to argue that this is what it was like for the people on the tour, simply being shunted around and deposited in various concert halls and hotels with no knowledge of your surroundings. Mickey Jones found it difficult to interest his fellow band members in sightseeing. They generally considered it 'uncool', or simply something that interfered with sleeping or partying.

An auditory transition takes place as Garth Hudson tries out the bagpipe sound on his organ. This is segued on the soundtrack to real bagpipes and it suddenly becomes clear we're in Scotland. In keeping with 'Dylan's Law' a series of shots taken there are juxtaposed as follows.

The camera lingers on a sandwich board man. On the board on his front are the words: *'IT IS APPOINTED UNTO MEN ONCE TO DIE'*.

When he turns round we can see a photograph of what looks like a disaster and the words: *'AFTER THE JUDGEMENT'*.

Dylan, Neuwirth and others of the crew are watching a police-dog display. Valiant Alsatian dogs leap at 'armed' criminals. The Glaswegian public politely ignore them, even though Dylan's crow's nest hair was unprecedented for either a man or a woman at that time.

A Highland pipe band marches backwards and forwards, pibrochts blaring, drums rattling. This is the only scene in the movie that we might label as a traditional piece of documentary making, albeit without any signposts denoting where in Scotland we might actually be. (For interest's sake, the location is George Square, Glasgow.)

Take Five – Thin, Wild, Mercury Music

One of the many frustrations Dylan has presented us with in *Eat The Document* is his apparent disregard for the musical content (or at least his refusal to conform to his audiences expectations of a tour documentary). In one respect, it is an extension of the way Pennebaker used the musical interludes in *Dont Look Back* – punctuating the narrative rather than being part of it. Dylan is saying, 'there's more to me than music', but his technique in *Eat The Document* is too fragmentary to be as effective as Pennebaker's. The concert footage is disappointingly scant, but it does begin to make a certain kind of sense. Dylan uses short sections of the ensemble numbers to present himself and The Hawks in as dynamic a light as possible, a kind of 'we are a band and we rock' statement.

The electric performances heard in the second half of Dylan's 1966 concerts reached a peak of intensity that had rarely been matched at the time. The interaction between Dylan and Robertson is exciting and dangerous. Hudson, Jones, Danko and Manuel have honed their performance down to bare electric bones, shorn of any superfluous notes. Dylan's howling impassioned vocals and harmonica are the bare ground on which The Hawks have built their new house of steel, and no amount of huffing and puffing from the Folk Traditionalists in the audience is going to blow it down.

When Dylan and Alk began editing *Eat The Document* the jury was still out on whether Dylan had betrayed the Folk movement by going electric. This TV special offered Dylan the chance to point out once and for all how wrong his detractors were. Obviously aware of the time constraints of a TV documentary, Dylan chooses to edit in the most dynamic ensemble moments from as many electric numbers as possible, rather than feature only a couple of them in their entirety.

That's why his inclusion of many of the lead breaks from the electric set makes a lot of sense. Some of his other ideas in relation to the presentation of the songs, however, don't.

The musical sections of *Eat The Document* open up with a blistering version of 'Tell Me Momma'. The extract consists of a verse, the lead break and then a slow fade down on the following verse. Visually the number is presented in a manner that we would nowadays normally associate with an MTV video. Indeed, Dylan and Alk have used 34 edits during the duration of the song. What we have to bear in mind is that there was only one person operating the one camera at any one time, so any cutaways, such as separate shots of other musicians or the audience, would have to be edited in during post-production. On 'Tell Me Momma' we have at least four different angles indicating at least four different venues. There are front of house shots, back shots, side-stage shots and in your face close-ups, probably a bit of every gig that was committed to film.

'I filmed two or three concerts very hard,' Pennebaker explained. 'And then I filmed in France and at the Albert Hall. I missed three concerts … I was shooting it the way you do stage performances with a long lens, because you can isolate it.

'About the second concert I really got totally bored looking through that lens at him 'cause I wanted to go out there on stage with him… So I just got out there and he didn't know what I was gonna do… I was standing there with my camera and Dylan came out, saw me and he just really broke up. He totally cracked up, it killed him because it was such a funny idea… I had a very wide angle lens and I could just stick it right in front of their faces, and it was so marvellous to get that close.'

In addition to 'Tell Me Momma,' a number of other songs are presented in truncated but reasonably lengthy extracts, including, 'Baby Let Me Follow You Down', and 'I Don't Believe You.' However, as explained above the norm was for much shorter clips and songs such as 'Like A Rolling Stone' and 'Ballad Of A Thin Man' are particularly frustrating.

In fact we only get one whole verse of 'Like A Rolling Stone' before cutting away to audience interviews, Garth Hudson serenading British teen-queen Cathy McGowan on organ, and sundry other odds and ends. Worse still, the one verse we do get is given a rather desultory treatment. Considering 'Like A Rolling Stone' was Dylan's most famous song to date, this was a powerful exercise in the deconstruction of his own myth. Perhaps he was concerned that in *Eat the Document*'s world of confusion, this hit single, with its particularly anthemic chorus, would provide the audience with to much of a grounding reference point. Then again, maybe he was just tired of the song by the time it came to editing.

There are however two stand-out musical numbers in the film. The first, 'Ballad Of A Thin Man' was shot in either Glasgow or Edinburgh and has since been shown in its entirety in two different TV series – *Heroes Of Rock And Roll* and *Dancing In The Streets*. In Dylan and Alk's edit it is cut into segments of three verses, each one broken by other scenes. Visually however, it remains stunning cinema with one particular shot of Dylan with a halo of light hovering around his head worth the price of admission alone.

'You know, that was a homemade lens,' Pennebaker explains. 'I made that lens. There was no lens like it then, it made marvellous distortions. I love it. The light would flare out... I loved doing that stuff... I mean, I had the feeling without knowing it, that it had to do with drugs... what I saw was the amazing effects of it, not how terrible.'

The final concert number featured in the film, 'Mr. Tambourine Man', is another interesting anomaly. It's the only song from the first acoustic half of the shows in 1966 that made it into the final cut. All the reports from the tour indicate that Dylan was more than bored with the acoustic numbers, and he could barely contain his excitement to get back on stage for the electric second sets. The inclusion of this performance suggests that Dylan realised it was in some way special.

Visually, it is nothing special – exterior shots of a Scandinavian crowd of schoolchildren gawping as Dylan is hustled into a limo followed by a series of cutaways of Dylan blowing into a harmonica, intercut with tight focused on-stage footage of him performing the song. While we barely hear more than a fragment of Dylan's vocals, the clip is essential as a virtuoso demonstration of harmonica playing that *blows* everything else you've ever heard, out of the water – it clearly leaves the audience (but not Dylan!) breathless. As the notes from Dylan's harmonica swoop and soar amidst repeated riffs and beautiful extempored phrases it is clear that he is taking the much maligned instrument beyond the musicianship of the likes of Little Walter or even Larry Adler. It is a very effective counterpoint to the frenzied combo work of Dylan and The Hawks.

So indeed are a short series of numbers filmed in a Glaswegian hotel bedroom on a rainy afternoon during the tour. Shot intimately by Pennebaker with just the occasional 'art' angle or reflection in a mirror, these moments give a wonderful insight into Dylan's style of songwriting. Earlier in the tour Australian actress, Rosemary Garrette had been witness to one of Dylan and Robertson's hotel sessions:

'I was able to listen to a composing session,' she explained. 'Countless cups of tea... Things happened, and six new songs were born. The poetry seemed already to have been written. Dylan says "Picture one of these cats with a horn, coming over the hill at daybreak. Very Elizabethan, you dig? Wearing garters." And out of the imagery, he and (Robbie) work on a tune and Dylan's leg beats time with the rhythm, continuously, even when the rhythm is in his own mind.'

Carefully and methodically Pennebaker charts the progression of one of these composing sessions. For a moment we are reminded of the scene in *Dont Look Back* when Dylan is playing the piano in Newcastle, watched by producer Tom Wilson. 'I bet you never filmed anybody writing a song before?' the singer had wagered Pennebaker earlier that year.

Now it really did appear that for all his elliptical answers to questions about his work processes, and for all his cultivated mystique, Dylan did want people to see something of what went into his art – though of course he has chosen to give this rare insight in the middle of a carefully planned exercise in disorientation.

Take Six – 'He Wants Shooting – He's A Traitor!'

If Dylan was using *Eat The Document* as a forum for demonstrating his creative processes, he also used it to show what he was up against in 1966 as he tried to extend his art through a new electric sound. Several short sections of the film are intercut with comments from concert-goers who are in turn annoyed, confused, upset and, occasionally, it must be pointed out, pleased, with this new musical direction.

The majority of these voxpop segments are interior shots taken by Howard Alk – simple 'headshots' of the respondents punctuated with a couple of wide lens pans, with interviews by Bobby Neuwirth – in the foyer of the Manchester Free Trade Hall after Dylan's confrontational appearance that evening – the appearance that had resulted in the legendary 'Judas!' shout from the recently identified Keith Butler.

Pop groups could produce better rubbish than that. It was a bloody disgrace, it was. He wants shooting. He's a traitor!

He shouldn't have had the group.

He may think it's gimmicky, but I think it was rubbish, and I'm not going to another one of his!

You know, he's always pretending he's for the person in the gutter. Well, if that's how he walks, in the gutter I'd rather walk with my head up in the gutter rather than like he is, crawling through the bloody gutter. Just making a pile out of it. Yeah, he's making a pile out of people he pretends he's for...

Then there are the few who speak up for Dylan –

I think Bob Dylan's the greatest, every time, everything. Yes!

The words are good. All the songs are good. He's better than Donovan... And he's better than Elvis too!

Several of the foyer interviewees thought the TV crew were from a US news network.

They said they were from American TV. They had a NBC sticker on the camera. They wanted to know if we were angry at what we'd seen.

The sticker could possibly have been left over from Leacock Pennebaker's time with TV documentary making. What seems apparent is that they were on the look out for disgruntled audience members as opposed to 'fans' – an approach much more likelier to have been taken by a news crew than Dylan's own team.

What's also surprising is how 'straight' the interviewees look nowadays. Contemporary accounts of the tour place a great deal of emphasis on the 'bohemian' appearance of the crowds. In reality most of the males wear suits and ties with hair barely touching their collars. The women are smartly dressed too – more mod than boho. Many, of course, were students and there is an abundance of college scarves. Still, the overwhelming atmosphere is one of a time that is not yet 'in time' – the beginning of the counter-culture that has yet to find its place and strength.

One proto-hippie however, has an enhanced cameo role. He's the only person to be interviewed outside London's Royal Albert Hall, and he's an American. Wearing sandals and Indian robes, he wears his hair in a plait and is festooned with beads. He and the interviewer are engaged in a kind of Zen battle of hipness. The hippie, demonstrating remarkable media savvy, directs all his answers straight to the camera.. The sequence starts with the hippie.

Hippie – *Your mind is only a tool.*

Film Crew – *Why?*

Hippie – *And it represents what's inside you.*

Film Crew – *Why?*

Hippie – *'Why?' is not a question.*

Film Crew – *What are you doing here?*

Hippie – *You've already asked me that one.*

Film Crew – *What are you doing here?*

Hippie – *You must be cleverer when you're interviewing*

And so on through an interesting extended repartee before the hippie gets bored and wanders off to do something much more interesting – watch Bob Dylan. It's a great introduction to the counter-cultural revolution that was looming on the horizon. In fact, this particular sequence is one of the few in the movie that is shown uninterrupted. Dylan may have felt that here at last was someone who was totally sympatico to where his head was at.

Hippies, earnest young students, giggling schoolgirls and bewildered concert-goers are all sieved through the filter of the camera, chopped up and regurgitated for the audience of *Eat The Document* to peruse. But one particular group of Dylan's traditional sparring partners are more or less ignored this time round – the press.

Perhaps because Pennebaker had handled that theme so well in *Dont Look Back*, Dylan felt there was no use in re-treading old ground. We do get snatches of press conferences, principally at The Savoy Hotel on 3rd May, and in Paris on the 23rd, but the verbal sparring that characterised his confrontations with Horace Judson, et al, in the previous year's movie is missing.

Take Seven – Fixtures, Forces And Friends

Like *Dont Look Back*, *Eat The Document* contains a number of cameo appearances from the famous and not so famous. The attractive blonde woman who features in a number of close-ups at the previously mentioned press conferences is Jones Alk, Howard's wife and Pennebaker's sound mixer. Amongst the celebrity guests this time are The Spencer Davis Group, Johnny Cash and John Lennon. Steve Winwood of the Spencer Davis Group got on so well with Dylan that they headed off on a trip together.

'Stevie Winwood came to see us [at the Birmingham show],' Dylan explained. '…[Shortly afterwards,] we went out to see a haunted house, where a man and his dog were supposed to have burned up in the 13th century. Boy, that place was spooky…'

What we have on film, however, is a bit more mundane: a standard rockumentary backstage scene where the Spencer Davis Group musicians discuss influences, while Dylan, very much holding court, and Robertson recline in chairs.

They discuss Leadbelly, Big Bill Broonzy and Stevie Winwood's Ray Charles-influenced vocal style before a quick edit to a silent girl who's been listening to the conversation.

Dylan – *Hey. Could you get me some more tea? Hey. If you're sitting near the tea, could you get me some more tea? Tea, and some water?*

Dylan's distinctly un-rock'n'roll passion for tea is mentioned a lot throughout the movie and makes a nice counterpoint – here and elsewhere – to the chaos, craziness and occasional po-faced seriousness of the disorienting world of the international rock tour.

Johnny Cash's cameo appearance – filmed in London when his and Dylan's tour itineraries coincided – is much shorter and even more frustrating than Winwood and co's – especially considering the long affinity between the two artists. When Columbia considered dropping Dylan after the disappointing sales of his first album, Cash sent a letter to the company's executives praising Dylan's talents. Cash also dashed off letters to Folk magazines like *Broadside* defending Dylan from the critics who were already gathering in 1964 to protest about his 'introverted' lyrics. At that year's Newport Folk Festival, Cash was there singing Dylan's praises *and his songs*.

Here, in *Eat The Document*, Cash attempts to duet with Dylan hammering away at the piano, on a version of his own, 'I Still Miss Someone'. Cash tries again and again to hit the same melody that Dylan is dragging out of the recesses of his mind. Interesting though it is, it doesn't quite gel and at the end of Dylan's peripatetic version, Cash diplomatically announces –

We'll just check the words through...

Dylan sits at the piano and listens attentively to Cash's pronouncements on the tune. Cash, leaning attentively with his arm on the piano, helps Dylan along –

The tune's completely different.

Dylan looks on up at him and enquires –

Is it different? How different is it, man?

Cash demonstrates by singing the first line in his rich, deep baritone voice –

At my door the leaves are falling –

And then, sadly, the scene ends.

The fact that Dylan kept this in the final cut is telling. He doesn't care. Whatever's going down, he still has a lot to learn from Cash in terms of the 'Tradition'. Cash was an heir to a direct line from a centuries old legacy of authentic American music and Dylan makes it obvious that he is ready, willing and eager to learn from the master – though the public would have to wait until 1969 to hear Dylan and Cash actually dueting together.

This short scene is a simple piece of interaction shot simply in keeping with Pennebaker's notion of Direct Cinema, that reveals something of Dylan's basic honesty about himself while at the same time containing a great deal of cultural significance.

Cash was a leading light of Country music – a style traditionally representative of the values of red-neck, right-wing, patriotic middle-America. Dylan, on the other hand, was regarded by many of his fellow Americans as a long-haired, left-wing, beatnik protester – all the things despised by Country music fans at the time. These two seemingly diametrically opposed figures symbolised an America on the verge of being torn apart. In choosing to include Cash in *Eat The Document*, Dylan sends out a very clear signal to both camps to accept and embrace harmony.

A more peculiar set-piece occurs about two-thirds of the way through the movie, though it was shot on the day that Pennebaker joined up with the tour in Denmark. Dylan and Robertson are trekking through an unidentified Danish village. The film then cuts to Dylan and Manuel carrying potted plants wrapped in cellophane ... Dylan speaks –

I wonder how long it'll take us to get back to LA from here?

We catch a glimpse of a young Scandinavian couple, before Dylan stands back and orders Manuel to barter for the girl. He offers his jacket which is refused. He offers to throw in his chap-stick, a can opener and finally his shirt. All the while, the girl looks on uncomprehendingly. Finally the boyfriend asks if they have any money. Manuel asks –

How much?

On being told two thousand crowns Manuel replies –

Will you take Australian money?

All the way through the rather strange exchange Dylan is pensive, allowing Manuel to do all the talking. Dylan generates these dramatic situations, when people are filmed goofing around, but as in other scenes in *Eat The Document* he appears incapable of following them through, relying again on his 'bit players' to carry the day. If anything, it demonstrates Dylan's unease with improvisational reality – a point which would later become more apparent during *Renaldo and Clara*, where long moments of Dylan silence would be punctuated with attempts by the actors to get some reaction from him.

A Danish journalist, Carsten Grolin, accompanied Dylan during his visit to Elsinore and commented in *Ekstrabladet*:

'Without the strain of having to be a "public figure", he became less reserved and strolled around asking plenty of questions ... he wanted to know everything about the history of Kronborg – if Shakespeare had ever been there, where it was that Hamlet had met his father's ghost. All the time the film crew were shooting the episode for the TV film, which will be called *The Twentieth Century Hamlet*.

Take Eight – 'Do You Suffer From Groovy Forehead?'

The most famous celebrity encounter in *Eat The Document*, is Dylan's legendary limousine ride with John Lennon through a dull London dawn in May 1966 – though we only get one minute or so of the two reels shot. Dylan and Lennon are ensconced in the back of a chauffeur-driven Austin Princess lent to Dylan by the Rolling Stones. After a couple of establishing shots of the drizzle-drenched streets we cut to a close-up of Dylan looking decidedly 'out of it'. Lennon speaks –

Lennon – *Do you suffer from sore eyes, groovy forehead, or curly hair? Take Zimdon!*

A bleary Dylan doesn't respond. Lennon pretends to berate him –

Lennon – *Come, come boy! It's only a film. Come, come. Pull yourself together. Another few dollars, eh? That'll get your head up. Come on, come on. Money, money!*

Another shot of a wasted Dylan and that's that.

Watching the twenty-minute footage from which this was taken is a gruelling experience. The party had started the night before in the Mayfair. According to one source who was there, Beaujolais and marijuana were the intoxicants of choice. By five in the morning it must have seemed like a good idea to rouse Pennebaker, and set off on a drive round the deserted streets of London to film whatever happened. Lennon's acting credentials had already been established in two successful Beatles' movies. Put he and Bob in front of a camera and something was bound to happen.

However, while Lennon tries to start a few improvised dialogues, any magic that might have been there at the hotel is sadly gone. Dylan gets progressively sicker and sicker, turning white and green before the camera's all-seeing eye. Lennon sits by his side looking and sounding remarkably together.

By reel two Dylan is reduced to repeating how sick he's feeling – in between asking how long it'll be before they get back to the hotel. After being told by chauffeur Tom Keylock that they should be back in about five minutes Dylan makes a very revealing comment –

Dylan – *Oh God, I don't wanna get sick here...*

He then lunges forward with his head in his hands, rubbing his eyes and groaning –

Dylan – *What if I vomit into the camera? I've done just about everything else into that camera, man. I might just vomit into it.*

History does not record if Dylan did just that, but it has recorded Lennon's comments on filming with Dylan –

John Lennon – *I've never seen it!* [Eat The Document] *I'm in it, you know! Frightened as Hell, you know! I was always so paranoid. He said, I want you to be in this film and I thought, Why? He's going to put me down! It's gonna be... You know, and I went through all these terrible things. So in the film I'm just blabbing off, just commenting all the time like you do when you're very high and stoned. But it was his scene, you know, that was the problem for me. It was his movie. I was on his territory. That's why I was nervous, you know. I was on his session.*

Take Nine – The First Cut Is The Deepest

By the end of May 1966, Pennebaker was back in New York and work began on creating something suitable for ABC.

'Well, we got it processed first,' Pennebaker remembered. 'Then we had to sync material up, so two or three people were put to work syncing it up... it took maybe a month to sync it up.'

Meanwhile, Dylan and his wife Sara went off to Spain before returning to Woodstock. When they got home, Dylan had to complete work on his novel *Tarantula*, and begin preparations for another world tour scheduled to kick off in only a few weeks' time. For the moment he seemed happy to let Pennebaker work on the movie.

'Dylan was in a really strange state of mind...' Pennebaker recalled. 'He was up in Bearsville and didn't want to get into it. We were supposed to deliver this thing to the ABC and the ABC kept calling me because they kept thinking that I was the director/producer... In a way I'd gotten my film, as Dylan said, "I've made your film, now you've got to help me make mine".'

Dylan drove to New York in late July and spent two or three days looking at the rushes.

According to Pennebaker, Dylan then told him, 'Well, I want you guys to go ahead and make some sort of rough edit to get an idea of what you did', because ABC were coming after it... So Neuwirth and I started to edit something together – We did a twenty to thirty-minute thing, just a rough idea. Then Dylan had his accident.'

'His accident' was Dylan's motorbike crash on July 29th. It was supposedly this crash that forced Dylan into semi-retirement for a number of years, though he was actually using the accident as a God-given excuse to withdraw from his punishing schedule and take stock of his life to date. It didn't stop the TV project though. Pennebaker went to visit Dylan shortly afterwards and found him walking around in a neck-brace. Pennebaker:

'Albert [Grossman] got pissed at me because he said I wasn't helping [Dylan] edit enough. And I explained to him that I was never supposed to be editing it. I had another film to make... [Dylan] didn't appear to be very knocked out by the accident so I never quite knew what happened, or talked to him about it... But he was very pissed at everybody and I don't know whether it was because they were putting pressure on him to get the film ready for TV and he didn't want to do it, or whether he felt he was in some kind of film competition with me, which I certainly never wanted to get into... So we just tucked away the film that Neuwirth and I had worked on. We just buried it, and they went on and made a film...'

Despite stating that he had no desire to work with Howard Alk on the movie, the mercurial Dylan soon changed his mind. In the fall of 1966 he and Alk presented a thirty-minute rough cut to ABC executives. It was obviously too late for the current fall schedules so they were viewing it for a possible screening slot in the cunningly titled *Stage 67* series. Reports at the time suggested that the executives were horrified by the film, considering it 'too freaky'. These reports were denied in 1971 by ABC executive producer Hubbell Robinson:

'We didn't know what we had because when we saw the film in the Fall of 1966 it wasn't yet edited. By that time we had to make other programming commitments for the spring of '67 and Dylan didn't know what the film would be and when it would be finished.'

Eventually Dylan had to pay ABC back their advance, which in turn gave him complete control over all the footage. Meanwhile, he and Alk carried on editing, though that is perhaps too gentle a word to describe the process.

What was actually going on in the sunless little editing room Dylan had built in his Woodstock home, as he and Alk hunched over their Moviola, was a form of deconstruction. Dylan, whilst rebuilding his strength after the years of intense performing, recording and writing, was taking apart the mythology that had been built up around him and was forging a new mystique. We know that he was concerned by how many of his audience regarded him as some sort of prophet. What he was doing now was creating an anti-documentary that he hoped would contribute to a new anti-mythology. In effect, he was displaying his refusal to be pinned down. In an act of psychic survival he was preparing to give the public another version of the way he saw things – a way that he hoped would be as radical as his music. And it was towards music that he looked for a way of editing the now re-named *Eat The Document* – 'It's like "*Eat shit*",' Pennebaker said, explaining the baffling title.

Dylan and Alk assembled all the different elements and themes captured in the footage – 'trains', 'fans', 'cameos', etc, and placed them in piles. They assigned a number to each pile and then thought long and hard about how they could structure them to establish a rhythm, an inner structure that would appear to emerge under its own steam. They viewed the spools as one would notes in a musical composition. If they were put together in the right sequence the editor could create cinematic chords out of the harmonic juxtaposition of visual notes – an idea very much in keeping with Dylan's conception of his music as 'mathematical'.

Another way for Dylan to debunk the mythology surrounding him was physically to destroy the film footage as he edited it. According to Pennebaker, Dylan and Alk were working from the original reels he supplied:

'They cut the original... so, at this point, no original even exists to make that film. That film is irrevocably lost to the process... They cut a final release print of *Eat The Document*, and to do so they took the original. I said someday somebody's going to want to look at that... I said you don't have to cut the original; go in optically and make an optical dupe... But they chose not to. They actually cut.'

And cut the original they did. With scissors. And they threw the unused footage in a garbage bin. In a 1968 interview with Happy Traum, Dylan went some way towards justifying his actions:

'What we had to work with was not what you would conceive of if you were going to shoot a film. What we were trying to do was make a logical story out of this newsreel footage... to make a story which consisted of stars and starlets who were taking the roles of other people, just like a normal movie would be...What we did was construct a stage, and an environment, taking it out and putting it together like a puzzle.'

What they were actually doing was physically cutting up the myth and then dumping the pieces into garbage cans. This is exorcism under *heavy* manners.

Take Ten – 'Free Bob Dylan!'

Alk and Dylan finished editing *Eat The Document* sometime in early 1967. It then remained unseen – though much speculated on – until its premiere at the Academy of Music in New York in February 1971. The occasion was a benefit for the Pike County Citizens' Group

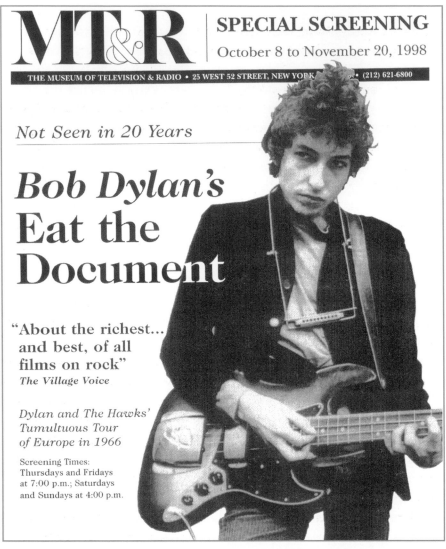

MT&R

SPECIAL SCREENING

October 8 to November 20, 1998

THE MUSEUM OF TELEVISION & RADIO • 25 WEST 52 STREET, NEW YORK • (212) 621-6800

Not Seen in 20 Years

Bob Dylan's Eat the Document

"About the richest... and best, of all films on rock"
The Village Voice

Dylan and The Hawks' Tumultuous Tour of Europe in 1966

Screening Times:
Thursdays and Fridays
at 7:00 p.m.; Saturdays
and Sundays at 4:00 p.m.

campaign to stop strip-mining, organised by The Band's manager, Jon Taplin. Jonathan Cott wrote an amusing review of the night's events in the 4th March 1971 issue of *Rolling Stone*. Reports were printed in the English music press that members of the so-called Bob Dylan Liberation Front led by A.J. Weberman mounted an attack on the screen and that Dylan had decided to withdraw the movie from distribution.

Sometime during the mid-1970s Howard Alk gave a one-off screening of his own personal copy at the Toronto Film Festival. And then suddenly out of the blue, *Eat The Document* appeared where it was supposed to have been seen in the first place, on TV – shown on New York's educational Channel 13 in a joint venture with WNFT (a National Educational Channel) and Channel 13 PBS TV (a Public Service Channel) in September 1979.

It then immediately disappeared from view once more and wasn't seen again in public for nineteen years. In 1998 Dylan's office allowed *Eat The Document* to be screened at a variety of venues across the United States. In Los Angeles it was accompanied by panel discussions featuring D.A. Pennebaker, Mickey Jones and Greil Marcus. These events were well attended, with audiences ecstatic at finally seeing a proper print, interspersed with commercial breaks from the period. Efforts to have the film screened in the UK continue, most recently by BBC Radio 1 DJ Andy Kershaw.

Take Eleven – The Other *Eat The Documents*

In a manner of speaking there are two other versions of *Eat The Document* in existence. One of them is supposed to be named *Something Is Happening, But You Don't Know What It Is*. Allegedly this is Pennebaker's personal compilation of material culled from the out-takes of the European tour and represents what he himself would have put together if asked by Dylan or Grossman. Popular legend has it that it runs for two hours and, because of copyright reasons, is usually kept firmly under wraps, though reports have emerged that it has been seen privately, under controlled conditions, three or four times over the last thirty years.

How true this is has yet to be verified. Pennebaker certainly has sound tapes from the 1966 tour, and it wouldn't be unreasonable to assume that he has ciné footage too. He also has a lot of out-takes from the *Dont Look Back* tour carefully preserved in a private vault.

The second *Eat The Document* does actually exist. It's a forty five-minute or so home movie of the 1966 tour shot by Mickey Jones who took along his Standard 8 movie camera and in 1997 finally edited all his footage together.

A lot of it is typical 'young American' abroad vacation stuff. Mickey, after all, was the band member who was most interested in taking a look round the places they were playing in, so there are quite a few plain tourist shots of famous buildings, etc. But one or two sections are of particular interest.

Mickey himself shot several sequences of Dylan's solo acoustic set; then, when he wanted footage of Dylan and The Hawks he would pass the camera over to a roadie who would shoot either from the side of the stage or from out front. On one of these occasions they appear to be on a kind of TV set. Mickey maintains that it was shot in Australia. The viewer can clearly see TV cameras around the stage. Confirmation has recently emerged that this was the first night of the Melbourne concerts.

The second piece of footage of significant interest is a section shot by Dylan himself that can only be described as a view of the world through Dylan's eyes. Taken on board the airliner carrying the Electric Messiah and his unholy crew from Australia to Europe the sequence is, at first viewing, fragmentary. On repeated viewings however, it begins to make a kind of sense. It shares a lot of similarities with ideas of time, motion and space that Dylan was trying to get across in the editing of *Eat The Document*. It even possesses many of the attributes of Cubist painting or sculpture in that what he's trying to do is give a three-dimensional representation of the journey within the restrictions of a flat screen. Conventional film making will usually begin with what is called 'an establishing shot', that is, generally speaking, a wide, open shot that displays the physical space where the action is about to take place. Then the director will cut to a tighter shot that focuses in on a character or object that will propel the narrative. Dylan reverses the procedure so that he finishes his sequence with what we would usually get at the beginning, a long shot of the interior of an airliner. In the thirty or so seconds leading up to this shot he tracks the camera in medium close-up across the faces of fellow travellers, editing with the camera itself – some shots are held as he pans and swoops, then he'll stop the camera and move further down the plane's fuselage to his next vantage point. Dylan not only does left to right sequences, he also does up and down, trying to take in the entire enclosed space. What this achieves for the viewer is to give them a graphic simulation of the claustrophobic conditions on the flight. By only holding the shot for a second on each portrait, Dylan is suggesting the unreality of air travel where people are forced into intimate proximity within an enclosed space, where we may get to see them but never to know them. Straights and freaks alike are segmented in the same frenetic manner as the camera, ever so briefly, pauses for a second to observe before dashing off to the next parcel of the human cargo. After the closing shot, a full length view of the interior from the tail towards the cabin the screen fades to black before resuming with a view of their stopover in Beirut. It's a fascinating glimpse of the world tour and hopefully maybe one day Mickey can be persuaded to release it.

Take Twelve – Postscript

Since the end of his working relationship with Dylan (they still remain friends), the great Direct Cinema director D.A. Pennebaker has worked on some of the most influential rockumentary movies of our age. Immediately after *Dont Look Back* premiered, Pennebaker made the seminal 1960s' festival film *Monterey Pop*. This was followed in the 70s and 80s by a whole stream of musicographies, biographies and hagiographies of some of the leading and not so leading artists and groups of the times, including David Bowie, Nick Cave and Depeche Mode. Essentially though, Pennebaker will be remembered neither for these, nor for his pioneering political documentaries (though he did win an Oscar for *The War Room* in 1996), but for his encounters with a tousle-haired young proto-poet in the mid 1960s.

Reel Three
Pat Garrett and Billy The Kid

This is how Billy The Kid met his fate,
The bad moon was shining,
And the hour was late.
Shot down by Pat Garrett,
Silver City's best friend,
The poor outlaw's life
Finally reached its sad end.
Traditional American ballad (19th century)

Take One – A Man Called Alias

From the dawn of his career, there had been speculation and even, on occasion, mooted plans for Dylan to star in a 'real' movie. He did play a young American folksinger in a 1963 BBC television play, *Madhouse on Castle Street*, but after difficulties in rehearsal, Dylan asked for his role to be made a singing-only part.

Though Dylan's record producer, John Hammond, introduced he and Grossman to the head of the Music Corporation of America's talent agency, with a view to finding him a movie role as early as 1962, nothing came of it. Likewise the intriguing talk of him playing Holden Caulfield in a film adaptation of J.D. Salinger's novel *Catcher In The Rye* came to naught. It would have been quite normal for the era, if his manager had pushed him into cash-in movie territory, however this exploitative approach did not sit well with Grossman's hands-off approach or his belief that, 'If the bird ain't happy, the bird don't sing'. When quizzed about making movies on Les Crane's chat show in February 1965, Dylan made light of the subject –

Dylan – *Well, I'm going to try and make a movie this summer which Allen Ginsberg is writing – I'm rewriting...*

Les Crane – *What's this movie about?*

Dylan – *Oh, it's a sort of Horror Western – Takes place on the New York Thruway.*

Les Crane – *Are you going to star in it?*

Dylan – *I'm the hero – I play my mother.*

Predictably, nothing came of this bizarre plan. In spite of his youthful James Dean obsession, Dylan spent the rest of the 1960s concentrating on music, without apparently evincing much interest in movie acting. It would be 1973 before he made his feature film acting debut.

Take Two – 'Who Is That Kid? Sign Him Up!'

In October 1972, young novelist and screenwriter Rudy Wurlitzer sent Dylan a screenplay entitled *Pat Garrett and Billy The Kid*. The movie was already in pre-production with Sam Peckinpah as director. Wurlitzer's first feature film, *Two Lane Backtop*, a kind of hippie road movie starring James Taylor and Dennis Wilson, had been well received by the critics and he hoped that Dylan could be persuaded to write a tune or two for his next project. As *Two Lane Backtop* had become something of an 'underground' hit as well as a commercial success, Wurlitzer possibly felt that Dylan might regard him more 'sympathetically' than other film-makers. Everyone knew that Dylan's track record on film soundtracks was disappointing. He wrote 'Lay Lady Lay' for *Midnight Cowboy* but delivered it too late for inclusion. He demanded his name be taken off the credits of *Easy Rider*, although he had co-written the theme song with Roger McGuinn of The Byrds. This time however things ran more smoothly.

'Rudy needed a song for the script,' Dylan explained matter-of-factly. 'I wasn't doing anything. Rudy sent the script, and I read it and liked it and we got together and he needed a title song... So I wrote that song "Billy" real quick.'

Dylan had already demonstrated on his album *John Wesley Harding* his knowledge of the Western ballad form – a narrative style dealing with mythological concepts of good and evil, damnation and redemption, treachery and friendship. All these elements were reflected in the story of the outlaw Billy The Kid and his downfall at the hands of his former friend and accomplice in crime, the now reformed Sheriff Pat Garratt. The more Dylan read the script the more he became intrigued with the idea of becoming involved in the project – and not just on musical terms. Perhaps one of the parts would be suitable for him to play?

In fact, Wurlitzer felt there was a character in the script tailor-made for Dylan. Wurlitzer decided that one of Billy's gang known as Alias, a figure based on historical fact, would be an ideal role. In Garrett's ghost-written memoir, *The Authentic Life Of Billy The Kid*, published within a year of Billy's death, he wrote that 'Billy's partner doubtless had a name which was his legal property, but he was so

given to changing it that it is impossible to fix on the right one. Billy always called him "Alias".'

Peculiarly, after the film's release, Dylan appeared to have totally forgotten this fact, commenting in 1974, 'I don't know who I played. I tried to play whoever it was in the story, but I guess it's a known fact that there was nobody in that story that was the character that I played.' Eleven years later Dylan was even more dismissive: 'Rudy Wurlitzer was writing this thing, inventing a part for me, but there wasn't any dimension to it and I was very uncomfortable in this non-role.'

In the original script Alias is Billy's right-hand man. He has a stutter and figures in many of the set-piece scenes. How this changed will become clear as the story of the making of *Pat Garrett and Billy The Kid* unfurls.

In early November, Dylan flew to Durango to meet Sam Peckinpah, the film's director. Despite Dylan's legendary status, Peckinpah had never heard of him. James Coburn, who was to play Pat Garrett, took him over to the director's hacienda for dinner. James Coburn:

'... So the night we were over at Sam's house and we were all drinking tequila and carrying on and halfway 'tween dinner, Sam says, "Okay kid, let's see what you got. You bring your guitar with you?" They went into this little alcove. Sam had a rocking chair. Bobby sat down on a stool in front of this rocking chair. There were just the two of them in there... And Bobby played three or four tunes. And Sam came out with this handkerchief in his eye, "Goddam kid! Who the Hell is he? Who is that kid? Sign him up!" He was very moved.'

Peckinpah was so moved, in fact, that he immediately had the songs transferred onto tape so that he could play them anytime that he wanted.

For Dylan the offer of a film part, especially in a location as remote as Mexico, was most welcome. He'd been three years now in New York City and was feeling stifled – socially and creatively. He made arrangements for himself and his family to join the production as soon as possible.

Take Three – 'Everybody Hates Sam!
Everybody Loves Sam!'

Sam Peckinpah was many things to many people. But whether people loved or loathed him, they acknowledged that he was intense about his craft. When holding a master-class on Western film at the University of Southern California, he was asked by a student, 'What is the most important thing in the world to you,' he stared back for a long while and answered:

'Making films... That's everything. Nothing else matters.'

David Samuel Peckinpah was born in Fresno, California on 21st February 1925. Although his father was a lawyer, his grandparents had been cattle ranchers. The young Peckinpah spent a fairly idyllic childhood growing up in the territories north of San Francisco on the family ranch. It was there that his grandfather taught he and his brother 'how to cowboy'. During the school vacations the two youngsters would ride the range, break horses, hunt and fish.

In 1943 Peckinpah enlisted in the Marine Corps and in 1945 he was sent to China where he saw some action, before receiving an honourable discharge from the services. There was a portent of things to come on his arrival back at Los Angeles Airport. He was still in uniform.

'I was standing there [at the airport bar],' Peckinpah recalled, 'when I heard this voice behind me say, "Shove over," So I turned around, and as I did I cocked my leg back and I cocked both my arms, ready for a fight, when this somewhat stocky guy who was standing there said, "Hey, you don't have to do that. I just wanted to buy a serviceman a drink!" And that was Orson Welles – the only time I ever met him. And at that time I had no thought of entering the theatre or movies or anything like that. He just bought me a drink and I bought him one – and we went our separate ways.'

After leaving the Marines, Peckinpah enrolled at college, studying mathematics and engineering. In 1948 he married Marie Stelland who was majoring in drama, and through her developed an interest in theatre that eventually made him realise he wanted to be a director.

Peckinpah's first job in theatre was as a summer stock director. By

1952 he had managed to talk his way into KLAC TV in Los Angeles, where he got a post as a stagehand before making the slow climb up the ladder to editor and finally director. In the meantime, Peckinpah networked actively within the film industry and began to get work in a variety of production roles. To make extra money he wrote scripts for the proliferation of Westerns that dominated TV airtime – *Gunsmoke*, *The Westerner*, *The Rifleman*, and *Klondike*, among others.

In 1961, on legendary Western director John Ford's recommendation, Peckinpah was given his first feature film to direct – *The Deadly Companions*. It was the beginning of an extraordinary film career.

Peckinpah went on to establish his unique vision in a remarkable series of films that would include *Ride The High Country*, *Major Dundee*, *The Ballad Of Cable Hogue*, *Straw Dogs*, and perhaps most importantly, *The Wild Bunch*. It can be argued that the key shared characteristic of these films is a fascination with the myths and the values of 'manhood' and independence. Peckinpah was viciously anti-establishment. He was also notorious for his particularly powerful way of presenting violence.

It was Peckinpah in *The Wild Bunch* who developed the now common cinematic stylistic device known as 'the ballet of death', taking to its most extreme the idea introduced by Arthur Penn in *Bonnie and Clyde* (1967) which climaxed with the drawn out slow motion death of the two central protagonists as they are literally shot to pieces in a hail of bullets. Peckinpah's 'ballet of death' involves the violent end of a character filmed from a variety of perspectives, usually in slow motion, and edited as one complete montage. Film critic Robin Woods has gone so far as to claim that Peckinpah's 'films implicitly accept violence as a metaphysical act, a condition of existence, and go on from there at times equivocally to celebrate it.'

For all its much-criticised violence, Peckinpah's work is founded on a complex interweaving of mythological content, much of it similar to the traditional aspects of the Western ballad form. Maybe this is what attracted Peckinpah to Dylan's songs that evening in Durango. The visual storyteller could sense a link with Dylan the oral storyteller –

both artists blended a centuries old tradition with something new. The other key defining characteristic of Peckinpah's career was his fiercely guarded independence over the actual film making process. It would not be overstating things to say that the history of Peckinpah's work is one of struggle, betrayal and anger. Arguments with the studios occupied a major portion of his time in post-production and *Pat Garrett and Billy The Kid* would continue this pattern. Peckinpah felt the studios were insensitive barbarians; they felt he was a megalomaniac and a spendthrift – though in actual fact, Peckinpah generally produced his films on time and on budget. *Pat Garrett and Billy The Kid* was an exception to this rule, but for circumstances entirely beyond Peckinpah's control – the production was marred by faulty equipment, unfit locations and illness. Dylan's opening foray into movie acting was not to run smoothly.

Take Four – Picture Postcards Of Billy The Kid

The myth of the real Billy The Kid was in place before he died in 1881. Commonly known as William Bonney, he was probably born Henry McCarty, or McCarthy, in New York in 1859. In the words of the nineteenth-century Billy ballad, he headed out west with a gun in his hand. He ended up in New Mexico where a battle of sorts was being waged between rival ranchers – the infamous Lincoln County Wars of 1878. Bonney became a hired gun, his reputation based on the probably inflated figure of how many men he was supposed to have shot (which legend tallied as twenty-one). His first kill allegedly took place when he was only twelve. Pat Garrett was one of Bonney's compatriots in English rancher John Tunstall's desperado army, and together they fought the hired guns of rival rancher L.G. Murphy.

Reports about the New Mexico Range War in Tombstone and El Paso newspapers soon reached the east coast. Alarmed by the violence, the US government ordered Governor Lew Wallace (who later wrote *Ben Hur*) to step in and bring the fighting to an end. In the middle of all of this, Garrett acquired a sheriff's badge while Billy became a fully fledged outlaw. It was inevitable that the two men's paths would cross again and finally Garrett tracked Billy down and shot him dead as he lay in bed.

Almost before Billy The Kid was buried, Dime Novels (cheaply-printed paperbacks) started appearing telling fanciful accounts of his life. The romanticisation of recent history was in full swing and the public's thirst for such Wild West tales was unquenchable. As mentioned earlier, even Garrett obliged with a ghosted novella entitled *The Authentic Life Of Billy The Kid* (1882). Billy The Kid went on to enter the American consciousness as the archetype of the lone outlaw – one of the last 'true' characters of the frontier, too wild to be hemmed in.

If the tale was fine fodder for trash novels, it made even better cinema. The first Bonney movie, titled simply *Billy The Kid*, appeared in 1911. By the time Peckinpah accepted an offer from Metro-Goldwyn-Mayer to direct Wurlitzer's script, there had been over thirty feature films based around the Kid's exploits.

Take Five - No Romance In Durango

Before tackling a make-over of the script, Peckinpah began casting the movie. He had no problem with MGM over his choice for Pat Garrett - James Coburn - but ran into trouble with his first choice of actor for Billy. MGM wanted an established star like Jon Voight, but Peckinpah was adamant that he wanted someone fresh:

'I was looking at a lot of film over at MGM trying to cast Billy. And they were turning down my people and I was turning down theirs. Then I saw Kris Kristofferson in *Cisco Pike*, and I said: "I know I can work with that guy".'

Kristofferson was born in 1935. In the late 1950s he won a Rhodes scholarship to study at Oxford University, England. From there he joined the army and left with the rank of Captain in 1965, fancying his chances as a singer-songwriter. He got a job as a cleaner in CBS's Nashville studios where he first came across Dylan in 1966. Kristofferson recalls emptying ashtrays while Dylan recorded *Blonde On Blonde*. In 1968 he wrote his smash-hit song 'Me And Bobby McGee' and shortly afterwards he made a move into acting with *Cisco Pike*. The part of Billy The Kid would be his second major role.

MGM and Peckinpah agreed that shooting the film in Durango, Mexico would be a logical move. The Mexican crew would be cheaper while the sets were already there.

'...*Pat Garrett* should have been a walk in the park,' associate producer Gordon Dawson recalled, '...stationed in Durango, shooting in a hub around it, never making a major move, all Western, totally controlled sets because you're not shooting in practical locations where you have to worry about crowd control. Instead, it turned into a disaster.'

By the time Dylan travelled south to meet Peckinpah, the director was heavily into rewrites with Wurlitzer. Wurlitzer was not happy. He viewed the story as an 'existentialist' narrative, Billy and Garrett as two irreconcilable forces locked together by destiny, heading for a showdown, where the only way to avoid death was to change, whatever the cost.

'Rudy wrote a beautiful script,' James Coburn maintained. 'I thought it was one of the best scripts I've ever read. And Sam destroyed it. But the script has to crumble and die in order to be reborn in the form of a film... Creation involves destruction.'

In Wurlitzer's original script Garrett and the Kid never meet until the final scene. Garrett's death in 1908 is a postscript at the end of the movie. Peckinpah put it at the beginning thus making the film more cyclical. It enhanced Garrett and the Kid's relationship from the outset. In fact, it heavily resembled Peckinpah's own attempt at telling the legend in a script called *The Authentic Death Of Hendry (sic) Jones*, which ended up as Marlon Brando's *One Eyed Jacks*.

'I like Rudy,' Peckinpah insisted. 'He's got different ideas than I do, but he's a poet – a really fine writer. If I'd shot his screenplay, I would have had five hours of screen time. It was an epic confrontation with a great lyric quality to it...'

'The beginning was changed completely,' Wurlitzer explained. 'Extraordinary lines about male camaraderie made a soggy entrance into the script. The writer suspected that the script (not to mention himself) had been reduced to its most simplistic components... (The writer) drifted into being a witness to the actual filming...'

Peckinpah's changes allowed the epic confrontation to take place after two great circular motions – the individual protagonists each going their half of the full circle. By doing this the director was sign posting the movie's mythological thrust – examining the defining characteristics of masculine friendship as the friends in question hurtle towards destruction or salvation. Garrett and the kid are actually different embodiments of the same man: yin and yang; good and bad; light and dark; damned and saved. I feel it's fair to say that these elements are missing in Wurlitzer's original script.

With Peckinpah now happy with the revised script, it was time to start shooting. But just as the crew started work, Fate dealt another mean hand to the production – Influenza. In Durango thousands would die before the epidemic wore itself out, including Bud Hulburd, Peckinpah's chief special effects man. Peckinpah himself was ill throughout the production. Adding to this misery were the incessant clouds of dust swirling in the valleys around Durango. These consisted of dried topsoil and cattle manure, the spores of which gave many on the set, including Peckinpah, respiratory infections. There is a curious resonance between this and Dylan's 1997 heart condition, histoplasmosis, ostensibly caused by inhalation of dried chicken dung.

There were technical problems too, most crucially with a faulty Panavision lens that went unnoticed until the production was several weeks in.

'Somebody dropped the main camera,' Coburn explained, 'and for a while we had focusing problems – the left and the right of the screen were fine, but the bottom wasn't in focus. We needed to re-shoot when we finally got the camera fixed but the studio said, "No".'

When the first rushes were brought to Durango for screening and Peckinpah saw the damage caused by the dropped camera, he registered his displeasure by climbing on a chair and urinating a large 'S' on to the screen. It remained there for the rest of their stay, forcing everybody to view not just the rushes but Peckinpah's stained handiwork. Apparently Dylan was rendered speechless when the incident took place, Coburn allegedly saying 'Now you know what you've gotten yourself into'.

Peckinpah soon began to sniff a conspiracy to sink the movie. The film set was split into two camps, those who were on his side and those whom he perceived were working against him. Spies made regular reports back to the studio criticising his handling of the film. In turn, Peckinpah became increasingly furious at those he saw as saboteurs. Relationships grew so bad, and the misery so deep, that at one point MGM's unit manager allegedly threatened to take out a contract on Peckinpah's life. Gordon Dawson:

'Sam would tell me to set up a scene. Carroll [MGM's unit manager] would veto it because it wasn't authorised. Then there'd be a race to see if I could get a wrap before they could rip it out.'

And yet, somehow, they did manage to turn in a movie.

Take Six – Ready When You Are Mister Dylan!

According to Clinton Heylin, the first scene shot for the movie was the turkey chase which involved Dylan and Kris Kristofferson riding madly around on horseback. It was not a smooth take, as Kristofferson explained:

'This one scene, Sam wanted him to come riding up to me, and as usual, it wasn't in the script. So they put Bobby on a horse and told him what they wanted. Now, it's hard for Bobby to hit marks in a scene with his own feet 'cause he doesn't think like that. But he's supposed to come through these sheep to where I'm standin', and old Sam says, "Okay Bobby, you just come straight by the camera here." Well, Bobby went into a gallop, man, scaring sheep, horses, cameramen and everybody. And I was laughing so hard I was in tears. So was Sam. And old Sam says, "No, Bobby, I really didn't mean that." The strange thing is, though, I don't know yet whether Bobby did that on purpose or not.'

This was one of the scenes from Wurlitzer's original script that was supposed to indicate the importance of Alias' relationship to Billy. Unfortunately, Dylan's confidence as an actor was wilting, and he must have been conscious of his novice status working with the likes of Peckinpah and Coburn. The part of Alias began to be whittled down. First to go was the character's stutter. Although extant scenes survive in the vaults, none of them made it into the finished version of the film. Peckinpah thrived on improvisation and it's possible that the two of them decided that Alias should speak properly, particularly if that came easier to Dylan in rehearsals. But, truth be told, Peckinpah had more worrying things on his mind than Dylan's ability to carry off his role. Dylan, too, had problems of his own, though his were of the domestic nature. What he had hoped would be a fresh atmosphere after New York was beginning to turn into something else altogether.

'My wife got fed up almost immediately,' he recalled. 'She'd say to me, "What the hell are we doing here?"'

Much later, in February, Sara's worries bore fruition as one or more of the children fell foul of an unspecified illness and the family had to relocate to Los Angeles where they could receive proper medical treatment. In the meantime, back at the shoot, there were tensions of a different kind.

'The really interesting thing [is] what's going on between Peckinpah and Dylan,' Wurlitzer commented at the time. 'Sam is really Western, like an outlaw, looking to wide open spaces, and he didn't know about Dylan before. Dylan... brings a different point of view, especially to a Western. The part is small, but it's important in a funny sort of way. Do the two of them have any common ground to meet on?'

At Christmas, to provide a break for Sara and the children, Dylan flew them over to England where they spent the holidays with George and Patti Harrison, shopping in Chelsea and generally having a good time. Then it was back to Durango and the nightmare that the film had become continued with Dylan becoming increasingly withdrawn.

Peckinpah meanwhile was being continually harassed by MGM over production costs and he, being an irascible man at the best of times, grew more unstable, retreating into bouts of heavy drinking that made his ability to communicate with Dylan even more difficult.

'Unfortunately, Sam was going through so much shit with MGM that he was never able to sit down and figure out what Dylan *was* in the movie,' Kristofferson recalled '... Bob kept saying to me, "Well, at least you're in the script".'

Dylan was beginning to get hip to the ways of survival on a movie set. By his return in early January the character of Alias has lost his stutter and more significant scenes could therefore be worked on. Dylan also still found time to have some fun with his fellow actors. According to Kristofferson one bit of fun cost Peckinpah and the production budget about $25,000. The scene was almost the final one in the movie. Garrett has killed the Kid and is riding off into the sun. As is usual in the film industry, the scene was being shot at sunset, the so-called 'golden time', the time when the sun is just right.

'Well, Bobby wasn't in the shot,' Kristofferson explained, '... and he and Harry Dean Stanton decided they were going on a health campaign and [would] run five miles. Only the first part of the five miles was through the shot. I came out on the set, and it was like a tomb. I asked what had happened and I hear, "The Dylan boys just ran through the shot." And everybody is just sitting around not sayin' a word as Harry Dean comes walkin' in. It was about as quiet as a church, and old Harry Dean is sayin' "Hi Sam!" And everybody is sayin' to themselves, "Oh, shit," and Sam growls, "You just cost me $25,000." And Harry Dean says, "Sam, I knew it was wrong and I was running after him to tell him to 'Stop'."

Peckinpah spent his spare time doing three things: drinking; fucking and knife throwing. And he was pretty good at all of them. He chose to demonstrate his knife throwing prowess directly at Harry Dean Stanton. As a blade thudded into a door just behind him, inches from his head, Harry Dean Stanton shouted *'I promise Sam! It'll never happen again!'*

When told by Stanton about Peckinpah's reaction to their get-fit campaign, Dylan shrugged it off and suggested that they do a benefit concert for the director.

'Bobby Dylan is the most unusual dude I have ever known,' Kristofferson would reflect. 'I think he is a genius or somethin'. You can't really ever understand him completely. He is so much like a kid in a way... But he stuck it out, the whole movie without ever really knowin' what he was supposed to be doin'.'

Take Seven – Ready When You Are Again Mister Dylan!

Notwithstanding all the problems surrounding the location shooting, influenza, broken cameras, minimalist direction, etc, Dylan turned in a dedicated, workman-like performance, despite his demeanour. He never let it show on screen, but he was suffering and several cast members said that he didn't talk at all for days at a time.

'...but I never know where his head's at,' Kristofferson puzzled. 'There are times when it can be really upsetting when somebody doesn't talk. Hell, he doesn't even talk to his old lady sometimes for weeks... according to her.'

So how does Dylan come across? Well, not badly, considering all the restrictions placed on him, either by Peckinpah's lack of direction or his own insecurity. There are times when he appears to be shuffling his feet just a little too much, but on the other hand there are moments when he's a delight to watch. Several contemporary critics commented on the charisma of Dylan's performance. For a non-actor he glows and stands out in a way quite unlike most movie debuts.

'I couldn't believe it,' Kristofferson commented, 'he's got a presence on him like Charlie Chaplin... You see him on screen and all eyes are on him. There's something about him that's magnetic. He doesn't even have to move. He's a natural...'

But what is actually left of Dylan in the film after all the cuts and how did he create such an impression on people?

The first time that we see Dylan on screen is during Billy's escape from Lincoln County Jail. One can almost imagine the anticipation that this scene was greeted with in 1973. Peckinpah chose to highlight Dylan's first on-screen appearance with a series of close-ups that punctuate Billy's dramatic break-out.

Billy has just effected his escape from jail, blasted two deputies and made his way down the stairs from the jailhouse. Dylan is first shown, looking on as an innocent bystander. From the work clothes he is dressed in and the sign behind him – which reads 'Lincoln Bulletin' (the local paper that would help spread Billy's myth far and wide) – we can deduce that he is a compositor or printer's devil. As the scene progresses and we watch Dylan coming more and more under the influence of the Kid, it is possible to surmise that Peckinpah is making a play out of the fact that the Dylan character is a man of words. That is to say, a man who makes his living out of words (true?), whereas Billy, is a man who makes his living out of deeds. This is the first dichotomy.

Dylan's next scene is with James Coburn as Pat Garrett when he asks him, '*Who are you?*' and Dylan replies, '*That's a good question.*' Perhaps Dylan himself doesn't know, considering his feelings about his role. As the scene ends, and Alias decides to follow the Kid, he deliberately hands the tools of his trade to a young boy who's standing next to him and then throws his printer's apron to the ground.

In Dylan's next significant scene, he has arrived at Old Fort Sumner, Billy's hideaway from Garrett, along with three other outlaws. The Kid is testing them to see which ones are bounty hunters and which real fugitives. Once again the question, '*What's your name?*' is asked. Dylan again enigmatically replies, '*Anything you please.*'

His commitment to the outlaw band and dexterity with a knife are then displayed to Billy, who decides to take him into the group.

Now, this knife throwing business takes place in the middle of a gun battle. Dylan is patently not armed with a firearm. As Kristofferson and Harry Dean Stanton spin round fast firing at their targets, Dylan coolly throws his bowie knife through the neck of a man who's just about to shoot Billy. Obviously the fact that Dylan doesn't 'pack a rod' places him at a distance from the rest of the protagonists in the film. In the later cantina scene, his being 'unarmed' might well contribute to Garrett's sparing his life. It may have come from Dylan himself, possibly an acknowledgement of Peckinpah's prowess with throwing knives, or it may have come from Wurlitzer wanting the 'real' Bob Dylan to stand out from the other outlaws. According to several sources, Dylan practised his knife throwing so that these scenes would look genuinely authentic.

All Dylan's scenes that follow are secondary to the main narrative, but all of them confirm his charisma. He has several set-pieces with Kristofferson where he comes across quite professionally, if a little underused. In traditional terms he acts almost like the chorus in Greek tragedy. When alone in scenes with Billy, Alias is usually gently urging him to escape to Mexico, or anywhere –

Alias – *You could leave. You could live in Mexico!*

Billy – *Could you?*

Alias – *Yeah! – I could live anywhere – I could leave anywhere too! Mexico won't be had for a few months.*

Billy – *I guess that depends who you are.*

Probably the most famous scene involving Dylan takes place in an unnamed cantina when he and several other outlaws stumble into the presence of Pat Garrett. Garrett eliminates the outlaws, one by one, but allows Dylan to survive – keeping him away from the fighting by having him recite the writing on the labels of cans stacked on the shelves. With the benefit of hindsight, is it possible to speculate that this is how Peckinpah eventually came to see Dylan? As a speaker of dead words? Charming, yet hopeless?

Garrett addresses Dylan with a dismissive – 'Boy!' – And then proceeds to order him to perform a number of tasks: knocking out one of the bandits with the stock of a shotgun; 'blinding' Lemuel by pulling his hat over his eyes. He's ordered over to the other side of the cantina to read the can labels, and so begins his litany of banality –

Alias – *Beans – Beans – Beans and spinach – Beef Stew – Salmon – Tinned spinach –*

Dylan's voice becomes the background chorus to impending death –

Alias – *Fava beans – Quality, er, Quality salmon –*

Bang!!

Garrett's gun roars out and another one bites the dust. Dylan looks round, coughs nervously and carries on -

Alias – *Plums – Beans –*

Lemual, still blinded, sat across from Garrett –

Lemual – *You just made me have a bowel movement, Garrett! I'll never forgive you for this! -*

Dylan adds the coda –

Alias – *Succotash!*

The scene is bizarre, slow, arguably tedious and tinged with sadism.

Dylan's role as reader of labels appears on paper to be almost irredeemable, yet he pulls it off. Putting on his wire-frame glasses and at his most disarmingly charming, his reading actually dominates the scene, when, of course, it should be muted and in the background.

Garrett's dismissive use of '*Boy*', lends our sympathy to Alias when the action is supposed to be centred on the lawman. His stumbling delivery suggests an illiterate when we know that he worked in Lincoln for the local newspaper. It makes his character all the more intriguing.

After the cantina sequence, Dylan hovers around on the periphery of the action, even after the point where the Kid is killed. He's there the morning after Billy's death, in the shot that he screwed up with Harry Dean Stanton, charming as usual and, well, Dylanesque. But isn't that all that the audience had ever wanted anyway? So great was his mystique that he could probably have read from a telephone directory and people still would have gone to see it. As it was, he read from baked bean cans and it was great.

'He's like a wild card that none of 'em knew they had,' Kristofferson reflected. 'I think they just hired him for the name and all of a sudden you see him on screen and all eyes are on him. There's something about him that's magnetic. He doesn't even have to move. He's a natural.'

Take Seven – Knockin' On Heaven's Door

It was during the shoot that Dylan began to work his magic on the soundtrack for the movie. Shining in his natural environment, this was Dylan's opportunity to show Peckinpah where *he* was boss. Wurlitzer noted in his work diary that there was, by this time, a genuine struggle going on:

'Sam knows he's losing to Dylan. He's giving a screening of *The Getaway* in town tonight, but everybody wants to go to Mexico City with Dylan. [Sam] also just called a 6.30 rehearsal for Monday morning because he knows we won't be back till after eight. But I don't care man. I got to get away.'

In the CBS studio in Mexico City, one night in January 1973, Dylan led the charge. Kris Kristofferson had brought his backing band along to help Dylan. It appeared that Dylan was 'wary' of them. Kristofferson:

'I flew my band down figuring they would love to pick with Bob Dylan... So I went over to talk with them and he said something real curt like, "You can do this on your own song!" That really pissed me off, so I left him alone.'

Kristofferson though, was aware of Dylan's *modus operandi* in the studio. The ideas came so thick and so fast that no sooner has he shown the musicians how he envisaged a tune than he would spin off on another idea and expect them to follow instantly.

'And they were trying to be so perfect for Dylan!' Kristofferson explained, 'but he wanted their first impressions. He's like a certain kind of painter...'

The all-night session in Mexico City was Dylan's equivalent of an artist laying out all his colours on a palette and then beginning to mix them together to create the right hues. By four in the morning the happy-go-lucky partygoers from the film set were exhausted and went off to sleep. Dylan and a by now enthused producer, Gordon Carroll, carried on until seven in the morning when the studio technicians called it a day.

Unfortunately, only a few fragments of this session would be used in the movie – 'Billy', which appears on the soundtrack album as 'Billy 4', and thirty seconds of 'Billy Surrenders'. It was decided that Dylan would go into Columbia's studio in Burbank to finish the soundtrack. Carroll, who'd had such a good time in the studio in Mexico City, was still enthusiastic about Dylan scoring the film, but somewhere along the line Peckinpah began to get cold feet and MGM brought in Hollywood soundtrack arranger, Jerry Fielding. Fielding was from the old school of musical practitioners and had no empathy with Dylan. His memories of the Burbank sessions are revealing:

'Just because you play a guitar and sing doesn't qualify you for scoring a picture,' Fielding maintained. 'Everybody knew it, and everybody kept giving Dylan advice... And then, of course, he looked at me, and all he could see was "establishment". So he wouldn't listen to me at all. And I resent that kind of superficial shit. I paid my dues...

'I give Bobby Dylan credit for writing seven great pieces of music and a lot of nonsense which is strictly for teenyboppers. I also give him credit for having a way with words that is often very effective but just as meaningless. He plays a simple blues pattern and a number of repetitious chords that I honestly must say offend me as a musician.'

Dylan had gathered together a formidable array of talent for the sessions – Bruce Langhorne, who had last played with him on *Bringing It All Back Home*, drummer Jim Keltner, Terry Paul, Roger McGuinn, Carol Hunter, Brenda Patterson, Donna Weiss and many others. Even then, Fielding found it hard to stomach working with Dylan. He appears to have spent a long time trying to persuade Dylan to put his main theme 'Billy' into what he, Fielding, perceived as a 'natural order'. One that would fit a logical cinematic narrative. As Kristofferson observed, Dylan doesn't think like that, 'You think, "That son-of-a-bitch is doin' numbers on everybody." But I think really his mind doesn't go A-B-C-D-E, it goes A-F-W-Q...'

The movie score veteran obviously felt that Dylan was 'doing a number' on him. Fielding:

'It was my idea that having to sing a relevant verse as it fits the story at roughly nine separate points throughout the picture, it might be coherent. Dylan never understood what I wanted.'

On a surviving taped out-take, Dylan's feelings toward Fielding come across very clearly. Just as he and the band are about to go into a take Dylan says 'This guy Jerry Fielding's going to go nuts, man, when he hears this!'

But Fielding's disgust at working with Dylan was to explode when he heard 'Knockin' On Heaven's Door'–

'...he finally brought to the dubbing session another piece of music,' Fielding recalled. '"Knock-knock-knockin' on Heaven's Door". Everybody loved it. It was shit. That was the end for me... And it was infantile. It was sophomoric. It was stuff you learn not to do the second year you score a piece of film. And for me to go back and try to do that shit and tell them why I can't be a part of that - why it's wrong that he's singing "Knock-knock-knockin' on Heaven's Door" with a rock drummer in a scene where a guy is dying and the emotion speaks for itself. If I've got to explain that to a producer, then I've got to get out.

It's fair to say that the vocal version in the original release of the film is intrusive and too obviously mapping the drama and emotion of the scene, and in that way Fielding is correct, but the instrumental version works perfectly. That 'Knockin' On Heaven's Door' has gone on to become one of the best known Dylan tunes of all time speaks volumes about Jerry Fielding's capacity for musical judgement.

Stephen Scobie in Dylan fanzine, *On The Tracks*, has pointed out how Dylan's experiences with the soundtrack were matched by Peckinpah's experiences with the way *Pat Garrett and Billy The Kid* was handled after shooting was completed.

Take Eight – Bring Me The Head Of James Aubrey

Peckinpah was faced with the impossible task of editing the movie in time for the Fourth of July release, i.e. approximately two months. Peckinpah's contract allowed for two cuts to be made and he hurried back to Hollywood to begin work on them. Trouble started when he was refused permission to use his usual editors, Englishmen Garth Craven and Roger Spottiswoode. On the final credits five editors are listed.

Peckinpah, who had scented a conspiracy against him almost from the word go, found that MGM weren't interested in his cuts. His personal assistant, Katy Haber has her own theories about the studio's reasoning:

'So basically what MGM did was to hire Sam for who he was and then use his name to publicise the picture, even though it was no longer his cut. The sneaker ads in the *Los Angeles Times* were a four-by-four box with the name Sam Peckinpah in it and nothing else. I thought it was an obituary when I opened it up. I thought it was a joke.'

When Garth Craven saw what had happened to the picture he was horrified:

'It was a big picture. It was this sort of epic film, and that was not apparently what MGM wanted. I have not seen the film at the cinema. But people who were in the film have come along and said,

"Whatever happened to such and such?" And all I can say is that it was there when I last saw the film. Whole scenes and people were eliminated. It was more than a little bit heart-breaking.'

Practically all the people who'd worked on the film were bitterly disappointed, including Dylan who, as well as feeling an overall sense of shock at the way the film had been so brutally hacked to pieces in Peckinpah's absence, was particularly frustrated by what had been done with his musical contributions.

'The music seemed to be scattered and used in every other place but the scenes in which we did it for,' he later bemoaned. '… I can't say as though I recognised anything I'd done [as]… being in the place I'd done it.'

James Aubrey had ordered the heart to be torn out of Peckinpah's *Pat Garrett and Billy The Kid*. Peckinpah simmered with fury. When the film was released in the summer of 1973 the critics and public were equally confused and bewildered. *Variety* had this to say about Dylan:

'Bob Dylan makes his film debut in a part so peripheral as to make his appearance a trivial cameo. His acting is limited to an embarrassing assortment of tics, smirks, winks, shrugs, winks and smiles.'

The (London) *Times*' critic, David Robinson, however, considered Dylan 'a captivating little figure'.

Still, audiences stayed away in their droves and Peckinpah issued instructions to his lawyer to sue MGM for $2 million in damages. While Peckinpah's lawsuit soon ground to a halt, he achieved a victory of sorts when six months later MGM shareholders forced Aubrey to resign after a whole series of MGM movies failed at the box-office.

Although the movie became a cult hit of sorts on the art-house circuit it was a tragedy that at the time it failed to reach a wider audience in its original intended form, because it is arguably Peckinpah's greatest Western; even the scope and breadth of the original cut surpass the usual range of simplistic codes that go into the genre. Although in narrative terms, it's a simple tale of the fortunes of two men who were once close, Wurlitzer's script and Peckinpah's ensemble cast of actors take it far beyond the confines of such a simple plot. The director's camera work, as usual, is meticulous, and visually he manages to breathe new life into a cliched story in a cliched genre.

As early as November 1974, moves were afoot to release a director's cut. Vice-President in charge of production at MGM after Aubrey's departure was the more sympathetic Daniel Melnick.

'Sam has reedited *Pat Garrett*,' Melnick explained at the time. 'I have spent some time with him working on it, consulting with him on it… My own feeling is that it is really an extraordinarily good film, and that it may be flawed in various ways, but it remains an important film. I would like to see it released, but it will come down to economics and people's judgement as to how much it's going to cost to do that.'

It would be a long time before the definitive version was released. Sadly Peckinpah would not live to see it. He died in 1985.

Finally in 1988 American cable TV audiences were given the opportunity to view an edit completed by Spottiswoode that was as close to Peckinpah's original conception as was possible. At 122 minutes the cut was 16 minutes longer than MGM's 1973 version. Amongst other things, it reinstated Peckinpah's original beginning in which the murder of Garrett in 1908 is intercut with Billy and the gang shooting the heads off chickens in Old Fort Sumner in 1878. This opening and closing device provides the film with its circular structure and makes a hell of a lot more sense than the first version.

One change of significance to Dylan fans is the removal of the vocal on 'Knockin' On Heaven's Door', during the scene in which Slim Pickens lays down to die by the riverbank, and its replacement with a simple instrumental version. This change does work, not because the vocal version was too obtrusive, but now one's concentration can be centred on the scene visually. Perhaps the ghost of Jerry Fielding was stalking the re-edit?

In 1989 the newly restored/re-edited version of *Pat Garrett and Billy The Kid* was released in the UK at selected cinemas. The following year it was premiered on BBC 2 television. The critical reaction this time round was unanimously positive. At the time of writing, it still receives regular screenings in both Europe and America and is firmly ensconced in the canon of 'great westerns'.

Take Nine – Things To Look Out For

Dedicated movie buffs and Dylan fans alike may care to watch out for the following bits of trivia.

In the opening scene in Old Fort Sumner when Pat Garrett and Billy are chatting they speak the following lines –

Billy – *How does it feel?*

Pat – *It feels time's have changed.*

This is a nodding reference to two of Dylan's most famous songs, 'Like A Rolling Stone' and 'The Times They Are A'Changin'" possibly inserted by Wurlitzer when Dylan was taken on board.

Billy The Kid's Mexican girlfriend, Maria, is played by Kris Kristofferson's actual long-time partner, Rita Coolidge.

Screenwriter Rudy Wurlitzer was roped into the film, playing the part of one of Billy's gang called Tom O'Folliard. He's the tall, bearded outlaw being gunned down when Billy gets captured near the beginning of the movie. Dressed in full late-nineteenth-century costume, he actually bears a striking resemblance to Garth Hudson on The Band's early publicity photographs from Big Pink. One can easily detect a hint of irony in a remark made by his character just as the three of them are about to be assaulted by a deadly hail of bullets –

O'Folliard – *I ain't in this for my health...*

Peckinpah got into the act too, playing the part of a coffin maker who talks to Garrett just before his fateful, final confrontation with Billy. James Coburn found it very amusing:

'I think they cut most of what Sam said when it was released,' Coburn mused '...[it was re-instated in the director's cut], but his line to me was: "I'm going to take everything I've got and stick it in this box (casket) and bury it in the ground. Then I'm going to get out of this goddam territory." Then I offer him a drink from this flask I'm carryin' and he refuses it, which was hilarious because I think that's the only drink Sam's ever turned down and we got it on film.'

Peckinpah was notorious for his drinking both off and on set. His favourite quote when questioned about it was to say, 'I'm only an occasional drinker – I drink whenever the occasion arises.'

During production it's alleged by a former worker at the studio that MGM, wanting Peckinpah 'tamed', had spread rumours about his excessive on-set drinking. Peckinpah turned the tables on the gossipmongers by paying for a full page advertisement in *Variety*. The ad showed Peckinpah with as many of the cast and crew that remained loyal to him raising full glasses in a toast and the text that accompanied it read –

> *Dear Sirs,*
>
> *With reference to the rumours that seem to be spreading around Hollywood that on numerous occasions Sam Peckinpah has been carried off the set taken with drink. This is to inform you that those rumours are totally unfounded. However, there have been mornings....*

Finally, thanks to Stephen Scobie for reminding us of Jacqueline Bitz' observation that the Colt pistol, left in the outhouse for Billy's escape, was wrapped in newspapers. And who was working for the *Lincoln Gazette* while Billy was in jail there?

Take Nine – Postscript

Despite all the setbacks, illness, problems and madness, *Pat Garrett and Billy The Kid* was a learning curve for Dylan. His interest in making movies had been kindled by his involvement in *Dont Look Back* and *Eat The Document*. Now he'd seen at first hand the machinations of the industry, the backbiting, the feuds and the squabbles. More importantly, he'd seen how an artist's integrity could be compromised, and destroyed.

'Sam himself just didn't have final control and that was the problem,' Dylan later reflected. 'I saw it in a movie house one cut away from his and I could tell that it had been chopped to pieces ... Someone other than Sam had taken a knife to some valuable scenes that were in it.'

Dylan was determined not to let the same thing happen to him.

'I learned by working in *Pat Garrett* that there is no way you can make a really creative movie in Hollywood...' he commented. 'You have to have your own crew and your own people to make a movie your own way.'

And this is what Dylan set out to do several years later with *Renaldo And Clara.*

Reel Four
Renaldo and Clara

It is undeniable that Bob Dylan is one of the greatest songwriters of the twentieth century. However, when his dramatic directorial debut, *Renaldo and Clara*, appeared in 1978, many people questioned whether his genius extended towards filmmaking.

The answer does not come easy because nothing Dylan does comes easy. As with many of his most intriguing works, there is no easy way to pin down *Renaldo and Clara*. The film is part chronicle of a tour, part improvised drama, part mythological analysis. It is a logical progression from the experiments that Dylan and Howard Alk initiated with their work on *Eat The Document* back in 1966 and 1967. Back in 1968, while discussing *Eat the Document*, Dylan had already speculated on how he would go about making a movie in accordance with his own cinematic vision:

'What we tried to do was construct a stage and an environment, taking it out and putting it together like a puzzle... Now if we had the opportunity to re-shoot the camera under this procedure we could really make a wonderful film.' (See Reel Two.)

In 1975, Dylan would finally get a chance to 're-shoot' under his own procedures.

Take One – The Rolling Thunder Revue
In one of those simple twists of fate, Dylan's musical plans for 1975 nearly failed to materialise due to the offer of another film role. Producer Harold Leventhal and director, Alan Arkin, had several meetings with Dylan to discuss his taking the role of Woody Guthrie in a film biopic based on Guthrie's autobiography, *Bound For Glory*, which they had recently optioned. The part seemed tailor-made for

him. As things turned out the role eventually went to David Carradine, the director's chair went to Hal Ashby and the movie, which was released in 1976, was nominated for an Oscar. We can only speculate as to how Dylan would have made out playing his hero and mentor Guthrie. It remains one of the great 'what ifs' of film.

In France earlier in the year, Dylan had experienced an epiphany of sorts.

'I was just sitting in a field overlooking some vineyards,' he explained, 'the sky was pink, the sun was going down, and the moon was sapphire, and I recall getting a ride into town with a man on a donkey cart and I was sitting on this donkey cart, bouncing around the road there, and that's when it flashed on me that I was gonna go back to America and get serious and do what it is that I do, because by that time people didn't know what it was that I did... Only the people that see our show know what it is that I do, the rest of the people have to imagine it...'

Returning to New York, Dylan began hitting the streets of Greenwich Village with an energy and enthusiasm that surprised the people around him. He turned up at a Patti Smith gig at the Other End. He jammed along with Muddy Waters and Victoria Spivey at the Bottom Line. He spotted violinist Scarlet Rivera walking down Second Avenue with a violin case and invited her to come and play with him. He got on stage and played along with old friend Ramblin' Jack Elliott. He began writing with librettist Jacques Levy, resulting in several great songs including, 'Isis', 'Joey' and 'Hurricane' that would end up on his forthcoming *Desire* album.

Slowly a nucleus of musicians began to coalesce around Dylan.

'He started hanging out more,' Patti Smith recalled, '...People just started turning up in the Village. It happened very fast... Then one night Bob started going up on stage, jamming with these people. I saw him start getting attracted to certain people – Rob Stoner, Bobby

Neuwirth... And he was working out this Rolling Thunder thing –
He was thinking about improvisation, about extending himself
language-wise...'

Jack Elliott remembered Dylan asking him one night if he'd like to
go out on the road with him and 'play for the people'. Back in 1972
Dylan told Maria Muldaur about a dream he had of hiring a train
and just going off around the country with a bunch of musicians –
stopping off and playing wherever they felt like it. Bobby Neuwirth
remembered the excitement in the sultry heat of those Village nights
as the plans began to come together:

'It's gonna be a new living-room every night. This is the first
existential tour... it's a movie... a closed set... it's rock 'n' roll heaven
and it's historical... It's been Ramblin' Jack's dream for a long time..
He's the one who taught us all, and the dream's coming true...'

Take Two – Backtrack

Whether the idea for a 'rolling' tour was Dylan's or Elliott's is
extremely difficult to pin down so long after the event. The concept,
however, was hardly a new one. Groups of travelling players existed
as far back as the Middle Ages and Dylan himself was certainly
aware of the early tradition –

'Ever see those Italian troupes that go round in Italy?' he would
ask, 'Those Italian street theatres? *Commedia dell'arte*. Well, this is
just an extension of that only musically.'

A more modern example, one that interestingly *did* use trains,
were the Agitprop (Agitation and Propaganda) performers of the
early Soviet Union. The Bolshevik artists would decorate the trains to
resemble, for instance, buildings and battleships, fill them up with
film projectors, actors and props, then set off all over the newly
formed Soviet Union. Upon arrival at a village or hamlet, the train
would stop, the sides of the wagons would be rolled down to make
impromptu stages and cinemas and the artists would spread their
message of comradeship and revolution to the assembled peasants.

Arguably a more direct precursor of *Rolling Thunder* was the
Medicine Ball Caravan. Inspired by the success of the movie
Woodstock, Warner Brothers funded a trip across Europe and

America by proto-commune/hippy musical family Stoneground, led by ex-Beau Brummel, Sal Valentino. The 'family' travelled in an old school bus (shades of The Merry Pranksters) and performed in a circus tent (shades of the Rolling Stones' *Rock & Roll Circus*) at various venues en route. Among the entourage was Wavy Gravy, a.k.a. Hugh Romney, a former Village Folk habitué (who would be name-checked in *Renaldo and Clara*), BB King, Alice Cooper, Doug Kershaw and Delaney and Bonnie. The associate producer and editor for the resulting 1971 movie was none other than the director of *The Last Waltz*, The Band's farewell concert film, Martin Scorsese. (See Reel Five.)

Take Three – Is It Rolling Thunder Bob?

After talking to Jack Elliott in the Other End, Dylan paid a quick visit to Minnesota to visit his family, then to Chicago where he taped a TV tribute to John Hammond Senior, the record producer who originally signed him to Columbia, and then rushed back to New York brimful of ideas for the tour. First off, it was going to be called the 'Rolling Thunder Revue', because Dylan had simply been looking up at the sky, when he 'heard a boom. Then, boom, boom, boom, rolling from east to west. I figured that should be the name.'

He was later delighted to be told that in Native American it means 'speaking the truth'. When, later during the tour, the Revue was joined by a Cherokee medicine man called Rolling Thunder, the circle seemed complete.

Next, Dylan took the decision to have the tour filmed, and so a crew run by Mel Howard was duly hired. Whether it would be a rockumentary or a documentary or a what, nobody, least of all Dylan, had any idea. Gigs were going to be hit and run. Contrary to popular practice the tour would be 'secret' – word of mouth; the only publicity would be handbills. To book the venues and arrange accommodation and such like Dylan called in an old boyhood friend from Duluth, Lou Kemp, the 'Alaskan Salmon King'. The back-up band would include Rob Stoner, Scarlet Rivera, T-Bone Burnette, Howie Wyeth, Mick Ronson and David Mansfield. Other artists booked to join the entourage included film-star/singer Ronee

Blakeley, Bobby Neuwirth, Roger McGuinn, Ramblin' Jack Elliott and Joan Baez. Jacques Levy was drafted in to give the stage show some kind of structure. The eventual cast of musicians and road crew would run to over a hundred.

Dylan then decided he'd like a writer to collaborate on the screenplay and called Sam Shepard – a friend of Patti Smith's who had just returned to America after living in London. At one point Shepard had been drummer in The Holy Modal Rounders. By the mid 1970s he had a reputation as an up and coming young playwright. At the time of Dylan's call he was in California about to move onto a horse ranch.

Shepard tried to return Dylan's call, but kept getting put through to a confusing succession of secretaries, managers and lawyers, none of whom appeared to know what was going on. At one point Dylan's people confused him with a Doctor Shepard who was currently contesting a prison sentence for allegedly having murdered his wife (shades of 'Hurricane' – of which more later), and whose real-life story provided the inspiration for the long running TV series, *The Fugitive*. Shepard told them he was in actual fact, Shepard the astronaut!

After much to-and-froing, somebody in the office was finally able to tell him that Dylan was doing a movie and needed a writer.

'Ahaa! Writer! That's me. Writer.' Shepherd thought, replying, 'Okay, what's the scoop?' (In my best Chicago-reporter style.) Then comes a long vagueness about a projected film with me somehow providing dialogue on the spot for all the heavies,' he recalled.

Having vaguely expressed an interest Shepard was asked to get to New York as soon as possible to meet Dylan. And 'as soon as possible' was true. The tour would be leaving New York at the end of the week. Shepard, a non-flyer, got on the train at once.

Take Four – Plymouth Rock

By the time Shepard arrived in New York, the Revue company had grown even larger and preparations were in full swing. Allen Ginsberg came on board with his lover, fellow poet Peter Orlovsky, who was designated baggage handler. Howard Alk flew in from the coast to assist filming, and later, editing. It's possible that he began filming with Dylan that week. An interview with singer-songwriter, David Blue, that was supposed to act as a kind of chorus throughout the scheduled movie, was shot at about this time. Blue played pinball by the side of a swimming pool all the way through his scenes, whilst reminiscing about his and Dylan's early days in the Village.

Mel Howard also shot an early incarnation of a *Rolling Thunder* gig at Mike Porco's sixty-first birthday at Folk City. Amongst the musicians present that night were Dylan, Bette Midler, Phil Ochs, Joan Baez and Patti Smith. They sang, 'Happy Birthday' and 'One Too Many Mornings'. Many other songs followed. Porco was in ecstasy.

Mel Howard, though, found himself in much the same position as D.A. Pennebaker had a decade earlier when asked to help out with the shooting of *Eat The Document*.

'A lot of the stuff that we were shooting in New York and at the beginning was stuff that was conversational and worse than that...,' Howard remembers. 'To take the opportunity [to film Dylan] and just parade him around as though he were some kind of lame dick and everybody's gonna freak out over him and we can take funny movies of girls giggling, that to me was lame and a drag... I thought the stuff was home movies, and I really disliked it.'

Howard was pleased when Shepard arrived. Hopefully the presence of a recognised scriptwriter might help Dylan out of the mess he appeared to be getting into. However, the first meeting between Dylan and Shepard was not auspicious.

At the rehearsal rooms one of the crew asked Shepard if he'd like to meet Dylan, and led the playwright through a maze of corridors and into a small room. According to Shepard, Dylan appeared to be levitating, lying back on a metal chair with his feet propped up on a desk.

'He's blue,' Shepard recalled in his tour diary, *The Rolling Thunder Logbook*. 'That's the first thing that strikes me. He's all blue from the eyes clear down through his clothes. First thing he says to me, "We don't have to make any connections." At first I'm not sure if he's talking about us personally or the movie. "None of this has to connect. In fact, it's better if it doesn't connect." I start nodding in agreement as if I'm too cool not to understand, sliding something in half-baked about "surrealism". I stare at him. He stares back... '

Dylan then asked Shepard if he'd seen Marcel Carne's *Les Enfants Du Paradis*, or Francois Truffaut's *Tirez Sur Le Pianiste*? After admitting that he had, but it was a long time ago, the room fell into silence. Both men sat quietly until Dylan announced that he couldn't wait to get out of the city and onto the road. Then, they could get more into the movie, when things were happening.

The next day the Revue set out for the Seacrest Motel, Falmouth, Massachusetts.

'A-Unit Camera Crew (don't ask me how they came to decide who was "A" and who was "B") is the first to arrive in Falmouth with Dylan hot on its heels,' Shepard recounted. 'Dylan careens into the parking lot and approaches the camera crew. "Did you get any rivers? We're gonna need lots of rivers. And trains. Did you get any trains?"'

For the next few days the Revue went into rehearsals at The Seacrest. On the evening of the 29th October, Dylan's entourage decided to stage an impromptu concert in the lounge. The audience? Several hundred elderly Jewish ladies who had gathered there for a kind of World Championship Mah Jong play-off.

The women were heavily into their tournament and were surprised that evening when the hotel manager came out onto the little cabaret stage in the lounge and announced that one of America's leading poets was present and was going to read for them.

Ginsberg took the stage to a rousing chorus of 'Everything's Coming Up Roses' played by a cheesy house-band and immediately began reciting his poem to his dead mother, 'Kaddish' – a harrowing scream of frustration at her madness and fatal cancer and his inability to cope with it. Dylan ordered the crew to get it all on film.

'The cameras are weaving in and out of the aisles,' Shepard recalled, 'creeping up to tables, peering into their matronly faces. Dave Myers, the lead cameraman, is getting a little queasy and turned off by the atmosphere. It's not his style to have the emotional content of a scene so obviously contrived. The women wince as the 'cancer' stanzas of the epic grind their way towards the finale. Then it ends and there's a surprising burst of applause.'

Fragments of 'Kaddish' are interspersed throughout the film. Sadly Dylan didn't include his or Joan Baez's numbers that evening. Shepard described an ecstatic performance in his book, marvelling at how Dylan began stabbing at the keyboard of the hotel piano, pounding out a version of 'Simple Twist Of Fate'.

'Here is where it's at,' Shephard continued. 'The Master Arsonist. The place is smoking within five minutes. The ladies are jumping and twitching deep within their corsets. The whole piano is shaking and seems on the verge of jumping right off the wooden platforms... This is Dylan's true magic.'

The following day the first official *Rolling Thunder Revue* concert took place in Plymouth. It's impossible to know if Plymouth was chosen for its significance as the site where the Pilgrim Fathers (and, presumably the Pilgrim Mothers) landed, but if we take into account the encroaching American Bi-Centenial celebrations that were planned to take place there in 1976, it seems an apt starting point – Plymouth, site of the first proper American settlement. By 1975 the place had taken on the air of a heritage theme park. The good citizens of Plymouth were wont to dress in period costume. Tableaux and waxworks were everywhere. A replica of *The Mayflower* was docked in the harbour. Ramblin' Jack Elliott had helped rig her back in the 1950s and he was more than somewhat annoyed when he climbed barefoot to the top of the mainmast to discover that the camera crew had wandered off. Ginsberg stood by Plymouth Rock and proclaimed, 'We have, once again, embarked upon a voyage to reclaim America!'

Take Five – When I Paint My Masterpiece

The second night's concert was filmed and the opening credit sequence of *Renaldo and Clara* is taken from that footage.

Although basically simple – a camera shot with some zooms – the sequence is perturbing and disturbing. Here is a film by Bob Dylan and the first image we get of him is disguised by a plastic Richard

1. (Above) From left, Bobby Newirth, Dylan, D.A. Pennebaker and Howard Alk, Dylan's co-conspirator on *Eat the Document*, in Glasgow, May 1966.

2. (Right) *Tonight*, BBC TV, 1964. Dylan sings 'With God On Our Side' in front of a somewhat inauthentic farmhouse backdrop.

3. (Below) *Dont Look Back*, Dylan with Alan Price, 'ever present with his bottles of vodka and orange'. *Pictorial Press*

4. (Above) *A Concert for Bangladesh*: Dylan with organiser George Harrison and Leon Russell. *Ronald Grant Archive*

5. (Below) *Pat Garrett and Billy the Kid*: 'Dylan is first shown, looking on as an innocent bystander. From the work clothes and the sign behind him ... we can deduce that he is a compositor or printer's devil – a man who makes his living out of words, whereas Billy is a man who makes his living out of deeds.' *Pictorial Press*

7. (Above) *Renaldo and Clara*: Dylan and Baez during one of their less confrontational moments. *Ronald Grant Archive*

8. (Below) *Renaldo and Clara*: 'At the opening of the movie [Renaldo is] in a mask you can see through – it's translucent,' Dylan explained. 'At the end he's seen putting on face paint. Renaldo is a figure of Duality... He has no name...'

9. (Below left) 'The Woman in White, the Joan Baez persona,' Dylan commented, 'exists only in Renaldo's imagination in this movie'.

10. (Below) *Renaldo and Clara*: Dylan with Alan Ginsberg. *Ronald Grant Archive*

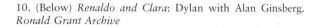

11. (Above) *The Last Waltz*: 'He looked amazing in the film, Bobby Dylan. Almost like a Christ figure. A Christ in a white hat. I mean, what *more* could you ask for?' – Robbie Robertson *Pictorial Press*

12. (Left) *The Last Waltz*: Van Morrison and Robbie Robertson share Dylan's microphone for grand finale, 'I Shall Be Released'.

13. (Top) After a short and rather bizarre set flanked by Keith Richard and Ronnie Wood, Dylan joined most of the other performers from the Philadelphia leg of Live Aid to perform 'We Are The World.' *Richie Aaron, Redferns*

14. (Above) *Getting To Dylan*, BBC TV, 1986: Interviewed in his caravan during the filming of *Hearts of Fire*, Dylan sketches his interrogator.

15. (Right) Filming promo video for 'When The Night Comes Falling From The Sky' with Dave Stewart in 1985.

16. (Above) *Hearts of Fire*: Dylan as retired rock star Billy Parker, with Rupert Everett as James Colt and Fiona Flanagan as Molly Maguire, at Colt's country mansion. Parker shoots pool while Colt and Molly watch a video of Parker in his prime – footage of Dylan from *A Concert for Bangladesh*. *Pictorial Press*

17. (Left) The promotional poster for the ill-fated *Hearts of Fire*.

18. (Above) *Hearts of Fire*: Dylan poses for the cameras with Flanagan and a distinctly uncomfortable-looking Everett. *Pictorial Press*

19. (Right) *Flashback* (aka *Catchfire*): Dylan sports industrial headgear for a 20-second cameo as a chainsaw artist, in obscure Dennis Hopper flick.

20. (Above) Dylan posing for the world's media at the *Hearts of Fire* London press conference. *Bleddyn Butcher*

21. (Below left) *Chabad Telethon*, 1989: Dylan plays with impromptu three piece, Chopped Liver.

22. (Below right) *Late Night With David Letterman*, March 1984: Dylan on tremendous form.

Nixon mask. For the entire duration of the song 'When I Paint My Masterpiece' the face of the man we all came to see is obscured by a synthetically rendered visage of a man we all came to hate. As the song progresses and the credits roll we get no closer to a proper view of Dylan. It's almost as if his first appearance is signposting all his subsequent ones in the film. Whatever preconceptions we had before sitting down to watch it had better be thrown out of the window straight away. We must also bear in mind that it was Halloween. As usual with Dylan, it appears that the unfolding journey will not be a straightforward one.

Take Six – 'Tell All The Truth, But Tell It Slant, Success In Circuit Lies'*

Several of Sam Shepard's constructed sequences would appear to have been shot, but most, if not all, of them 'ended up on the cutting room floor'. A discarded scene that is of particular interest is one filmed in a Falmouth diner with Dylan as an Alchemist and Ginsberg as the Emperor of a bankrupt empire.

Emperor – *What does he do?*

Alchemist – *Well, I've seen him touch fire to ice one time. That was interesting. The whole place melted.*

In *The Rolling Thunder Logbook*, Shepard outlined a whole series of potential scenes for the film:

'Boxing Match (Imhoff vs. Kemp)

William Burroughs – Magazine cutup (with Dylan in Boston)

'Alabama Song' – entire tour singing

Speaking in Tongues Sequence (Ginsberg, Dylan, Neuwirth)

Fishing...

And so on.'

It soon became apparent that Shepard, with the best will in the world, wouldn't be able to come up with workable scripts. It wasn't that he couldn't write them, it was more to do with the conditions

---

Emily Dickinson (written above Dylan's movie editing desk)

under which the film was being made. In fact, Shepard later claimed that this was the point where the filmmaking experience began to get interesting. He and Dylan had jettisoned the idea of having anything resembling a finished script, realising that it was hard to get actors involved in learning lines when they had so much else to do besides – partying, jamming or sleeping. A decision was made to attempt to improvise around loose themes and basically just see what happened.

Dylan didn't quite remember it that way though.

'*Renaldo and Clara* was originally intended as a more structured film,' he maintained. 'I hired playwright Sam Shepard to provide dialogue but we didn't use much of his stuff because of a conflict in ideas.'

Despite Shepard's set-back, filming carried on throughout the tour, taking place in a variety of locations including a bar in Quebec where Dylan, as the Renaldo character, is told how difficult love is by Maurice (Andre Bernard Tremblay). This, despite background noise problems, is an intriguing and well played out scene. Other locations included the Clinton Correctional Institute for Women in New York, Niagara Falls Hilton Hotel, 'Mamma's Dreamaway Lounge' (more of which in a moment) and Jack Kerouac's grave in Lowell, Massachusetts.

Dylan, Shepard and a couple of others drove to a bar called 'Nick's Lounge' that was owned by Kerouac's brother-in-law, Nick Sampas. Shepard remarked that it looked like the kind of place that would make even a redneck paranoid.

After a few drinks Sampas drove the party out to Kerouac's grave in his station wagon. After a little while Sampas pulled out a cassette tape. The ghostly voice of Kerouac played through the speakers as the driver explained that no one outside the family had ever heard the recording before. It set the scene perfectly for their arrival at the cemetery.

This scene appears about two-thirds of the way through the movie. It is intensely intimate and personal. Dylan and Ginsberg stood by Kerouac's grave with its simple marker, discussing graves and poets and the inevitability of death for us all. They sang in tribute to 'Ti Jean', aware of mortality. A touching interlude in a tapestry of sound and vision that can bewilder with its obtuseness, here is a moment that reaches out to the viewer and reminds us, not only of the transient fragility of 'stardom' but also of the fleetingness of being.

Dylan's concert 'white face' make-up, Mexican death rituals, Ginsberg's 'Kaddish', the visit to Lowell, all seem to point to an evocation of death in *Renaldo and Clara*.

'The idea of death in the movie is really the idea of life,' Dylan noted, 'like in a photographic negative.'

In many cultures sleep is linked to death. Western civilisation has long euphemistically referred to the dead as merely 'gently sleeping'. And in sleep, of course there are dreams, perchance. Finally, the Surrealist movement whose ideas so clearly influenced Dylan's lyrics in the mid-Sixties considered dreams to be absolutely paramount in revealing the workings of the subconscious mind, which they deemed the key to creativity.

Indeed, as scholar Franklin Rosemont explained, 'Surrealism aims to reduce, and ultimately to resolve, the contradictions between sleeping and waking, dream and action ... the conscious and the unconscious.'

Such ideas lie behind what little narrative the film features.

'At the opening of the movie [Renaldo is] in a mask you can see through – it's translucent,' Dylan explained. 'At the end he's seen putting on face paint. Renaldo is a figure of Duality... He has no name... The man on the floor at the end is the Dreamer. That's neither Renaldo nor the Chorus nor the man on the stage – the stage is part of the Dream. A man who's walking around seeming to be alive has dreamt nothing. But the man on the floor, who's obviously dreaming, no one asks him anything – but the whole movie was his dream...'

Howard Alk also tellingly described *Renaldo and Clara* as – 'The movie you haven't dreamt yet.'

In conversation with Allen Ginsberg, Dylan continued to elaborate on this dream theme.

When Ginsberg asked him what the significance was of the scene where the College Kid says he had no dream last night, Dylan replied:

'This whole movie is the dream the College Kid did not have. This whole movie has gone down and they haven't dreamt any of it. The movie that you never dreamt that you wish you'd a dreamt...'

Ginsberg followed by asking if Renaldo had a soul or if was simply in a succession of disparate illusory connected images.

'At the beginning he's locked in,' Dylan explained. 'He's wearing a mask you can see through, he's not dreaming. Most likely he'll become what he's dreaming about. Renaldo's dream almost killed him.'

'It's at the end of the movie,' Ginsberg offered, 'when he's putting make-up on – "What you can dream about can happen".'

'Exactly! You got it!' Dylan agreed. 'Renaldo has faith in himself and his ability to dream, but the dream is sometimes so powerful it has the ability to wipe him out. Renaldo has no ordinary mind – he might not even have a soul. He may in actuality be Time itself, in his wildest moments.'

Dylan had already spoken to several people about the 'magic' of cinema. That is, its ability to suspend time, particularly in relation to his concept of movie making.

'The movie creates and holds time,' he explained. 'That's what it should do – it should hold that time, breathe in that time and stop time in doing that. It's like if you look at a painting by Cezanne, you get lost in the painting for that period of time. And you breathe – yet time is going by and you wouldn't know it. You're spellbound.'

Take Seven – Women And The Key To The Mysteries

Dylan plays the part of Renaldo, a character 'with no soul', who is 'having a dream'. The part of Clara is played by his then wife, Sara, who also plays a kind of secret agent, and sometimes Sam Shepard's wife. Then there is Joan Baez, who plays a mixture of characters, the mysterious Woman in White (who, confusingly, is also sometimes played by Sara!), a Mexican whore and even occasionally herself. Ronee Blakely plays Sara as well as the wife of the Steve Soles character, Ramon. Ruth Tyrangiel is 'The Girlfriend'. To make things even more confusing, veteran rocker, Ronnie Hawkins, plays Bob Dylan! Though, it might be simpler to say that all the men in the movie play Bob Dylan and all the women play Sara?

Over four decades Dylan's representation of women in his lyrics have veered from the surreal majesty of 'motor-cycle black madonna, two-wheel gypsy queen' to classical Blues phrasing of 'riding in a buggy with Miss Jane', and his imagery from snarling cynicism or overwhelming love, to languid distancing. It has been argued by some critics that Dylan has used his songs to express his feelings towards women (principally Sara) because he may find it impossible to communicate with them in other ways. Taking all this on board makes his style of representation of women in *Renaldo and Clara* all the more mysterious. The female characters, are one-dimensional and curiously archetypical. There is little depth for Baez, Sara or any of the others to build on, though Dylan in his comments about their roles is unequivocal about their function: they are the symbol of freedom.

Perhaps the enigmatic roles played by the women can offer us a clue as to Dylan's intentions behind the film. In his conversations with Allen Ginsberg, Dylan claimed that the movie dealt with the transfiguration of the rose, and a red rose does appear frequently throughout the film, carried by one or other of the women. It first appears at a truck stop scene when the rose is picked up by (the real) Sara.

'In the symbol of the rose we see the vagina traveling around,' Dylan told Ginsberg. '...Go to the movie and pick up all the signs where the rose goes ... It was nobody's rose... We can also refer to the rose as "the dark opening". Scarlet constantly represents the vagina, the rose, the sweetness of it – always at the elusive Renaldo's right hand, that close. The man in the white face, the reasonable Renaldo, can always reach out to grab it.'

Mel Howard began to observe emerging from the improvisations certain themes – at the core of which lay Dylan's confused relationship with women.

'So we had a whole subplot,' says Howard. 'all of the women in the film, black magic and white magic, and the different powers of women and men and the focus of all this was Dylan himself ... but the thing that started to evolve as a general theme was Dylan, Sara and Joan. And Sara and Joan as opposing forces, in different mythological guises, Joan as a certain kind of energy, Sara as a different kind of energy, and Dylan in between, attracted to both ...'

This is exactly what had been happening in real life approximately ten years before, as outlined in Reel One.

For somebody who so consistently denies that his work is autobiographical there can hardly exist a more autobiographical scenario. Joan Baez seems to have taken a certain delight in using the situation to her acting advantage.

Several central scenes in the movie were shot at a small bar/diner called Mama's Dreamaway Lounge – a former brothel decorated with mountains of amazing religious kitsch and bric-a-brac, run by an 80-year-old gypsy. When Joan Baez arrived Mama immediately took her upstairs and fitted her into her own, ancient white wedding dress.

'Joan emerges from the closet in glistening white,' Shepard noted, 'The dress fits her like a snake. Mama starts crying at this vision and showers Joan with jewelry. The cameramen are freaking from lack of film. Gaffers are running up and down the stairs trying to reload the magazines at atomic speeds.'

(Mama would feature in a number of scenes with Baez and Ginsberg that made it to the final cut.)

Meanwhile, downstairs in the bar, Dylan was running through a scene with Ronee Blakely, but it wasn't quite panning out. Suddenly Baez appeared in her wedding dress. The cameras were rolling as she faced Dylan. If he wanted improvisational acting, he was about to get exactly that. Sam Shepard documented the ensuing confrontation:

'Why did you always lie?' [says Baez]

'I never lied. That was the other guy.'

'You're lying now.'

The cameras are crackling. Everyone's tiptoeing heavily, doing pantomime slaps on his knees at the outrageousness of this moment. Joan presses on.

'You were always calling me up and lying to me.'

'Aw, come off it. You think everything's bullshit. Now I'll admit there's some things that are definite bullshit but not everything.'

'Stop lying Bobby. You want them to turn the cameras off,

don't you?'

'Whatever happened to that boyfriend of yours?'

'Don't change the subject.'

'I'm making conversation.'

Baez beams at him, white teeth flashing over the top of Mama's blue necklace.

'What would've happened if we'd got married, Bob?'

'I married the woman I love.'

'And I married the man I thought I loved.'

The atmosphere in the bar grew edgy and nervous. To Shepard it resembled a prize-fight with Baez hurling her one-liners like kidney punches at the reeling Dylan as he tried to duck and dive. The film-crew tip-toed nervously around them as musicians giggled in the background.

Readers can draw their own conclusions as to why this scene didn't find its way into the final cut of the movie.

At this point, it is worth mentioning that Baez' beefs with Dylan were not just personal. As she noted in her autobiography *And A Voice To Sing With*, Baez was by now beginning to find Dylan's haphazard approach to the project embarrassing:

'One day I was trudging around in the snow on a farm in Canada with Dylan doing a "scene" … Naturally I was playing a Mexican whore – the *Rolling Thunder* women all played whores. The scene opened with Bob shoving me through the snow towards a shack. In fact there was neither plot nor a script so the characters "developed" as we went along… It was a cold day, and I wondered what I was doing in this monumentally silly project, and if Dylan was taking it seriously…'

Sara Dylan also echoed Baez's comment about the allocation of roles to women in the film. 'After all that talk about goddess,' she commented, 'we wound up being whores.'

The 'whores' were featured principally in a bordello that Dylan claimed was 'Diamond Hell' – presumably influenced by Ginsberg's association with Tibetan Buddhism. Diamond Hell is 'Vajra Hell', an inescapable level of imprisonment, a place of perpetual torment. For all his talk of the 'freedom of the rose' it is Dylan's women who are trapped in a Vajra Hell – or is it Dylan's perception of women that's trapped?

Eventually, the enigmatic figure of 'The Woman in White', played by Baez, arrives at Renaldo and Clara's love nest and confronts them. When asked by Ginsberg what Clara personified, Dylan's answered, 'Clara is the symbol of Freedom in this movie. She's what attracts Renaldo at the present.'

As for The Woman in White, Dylan explained:

'It's the ghost of Death – Death's ghost. Renaldo rids himself of death when she leaves, and he goes on, alive, with his greasepaint... The Woman in White, the Joan Baez persona, exists only in Renaldo's imagination in this movie.'

Yet, if this is so, why does he bring the two principal women in his life together towards the end of the movie? The confrontation that takes place is primarily to Dylan's detriment. He shuffles between them, embarrassed, awkward, like a small boy who's been caught eating candy. Sara and Baez appear to develop an affinity for one another and take turns in denigrating him. It's a remarkably strange scene, one fraught with emotion. The viewer definitely feels like a voyeur intruding on something deeply personal. It is intriguing that any glimpses we gain of the private world of Dylan and 'women' have percolated through the veneer of a supposedly dramatic narrative, not, through the lens of a cinema verite documentary maker like Pennebaker.

Take Eight – The Hurricane

Renaldo and Clara features a curious kind of addendum concerning Dylan's involvement with the campaign to free imprisoned Afro-American boxer Rubin 'Hurricane' Carter. This is the most documentary element of the film, and seems in some ways to have been created completely separately from the body of the movie. In fact it was shot at the same time and is an integral part of it.

Rubin Carter was jailed in 1967 for a triple murder he steadfastly denied having committed. Dylan became intrigued by the case when he read Carter's autobiography after his return from France in 1975.

'When I wrote the book *The Sixteenth Round*,' Carter recalled, 'I sent a copy to Bob Dylan because of his prior commitment to the [civil rights] struggle. I sent him a copy hoping that somehow I could influence him to come and see me. So I could talk to him... So, when he got the book and read it he came. And we sat and talked for many, many hours. And I recognised the fact that here was a brother.'

Dylan felt moved and inspired by Carter's plight and, in collaboration with Jacques Levy, put forward the case for the defence passionately and eloquently in a new song, 'Hurricane' – a stirring anthem that was arguably his first convincing 'protest' song for a decade. He recorded it for his forthcoming *Desire* album and plans were made to release it as a single as soon as possible. Indeed, *Renaldo and Clara* features a scene – shot very early in the filming schedule – where Dylan demands that Columbia executive Walter Yetnikoff allocates 'Hurricane' with an urgent release date.

Unfortunately, the lawyers at Columbia got cold feet over some of the lyrics and Dylan had to interrupt the *Rolling Thunder* rehearsals to return to the studio to record a 'cleaned up' version, accompanied on vocals by fellow *Renaldo and Clara* traveller, Ronee Blakely.

The second major 'Hurricane' segment is the concert performed by the Revue at the Clinton Correctional Institute, which is followed by a press conference given by Carter. In the film this sequence is followed by vox-pops filmed in Harlem outside The Apollo Theatre. Members of the public are asked if they have heard of the case and what their opinions are as regards Carter's guilt or innocence.

The single did have an impact in rousing public interest in the case. *The San Francisco Chronicle* hailed it as, 'One of the most convincing artistic statements of the year... [it] will stand with Dylan's greatest work.'

Throughout the Revue tour, Dylan plugged away at the case as an appeal was due to be heard any day. The Revue itself culminated in a huge final concert at New York's Madison Square Garden, called 'Night of The Hurricane 1'. Muhammad Ali and a number of other celebrities appeared on stage alongside Dylan to pledge their support for Carter's cause. Unfortunately, when the appeal was heard in

February 1976, it was thrown out and Carter was returned to jail. *(See foonote.)*

These 'Hurricane' sequences reflect another dichotomy in *Renaldo and Clara*. At a point when Dylan's song writing was strongly rooted in narrative structure, the visual elements of the film seem to be harking back to his mid-Sixties' surrealist imagery that peaked with *Highway 61 Revisited* and *Blonde on Blonde*. His work in collaboration with Jacques Levy is, as discussed later, cinematic in its style, sweep and scope and yet the random scattergun approach of Dylan's filmic vision flies in complete opposition to the structured order of reality he is now imposing on his song writing. Perhaps Dylan failed to appreciate the differences between song-writing and recording and filmmaking. The former is much lower scale, relying on a lone individual or a small unit of fellow artists. Filmmaking, on the other hand, is essentially bound to a different set of conventions and infrastructures. The lessons that he had learnt over long years in the studio, fast improvisational changes, completing lyrics on the spot, etc, couldn't be applied in front of cash-devouring cameras.

Take Nine – Rock 'n' Roll Heaven

Whatever confusion in people's minds has been created by *Renaldo and Clara*'s obtuse imagery, of one thing we can all be certain: the musical content of the film is above excellent. Dylan's fusion of stylistic forms represented an artist at a peak of perfection.

Dylan's plans for presenting his repertoire in revue form began almost as soon as he had finished recording his *Blood On The Tracks* album, which would be rapturously received on its release in January 1975. He began to gather round him a new group of musicians that he felt might best help him interpret the new numbers he had going round in his head. Many were called, from Eric Clapton and Emmylou Harris to Dave Mason and, more bizarrely, English Pub-Rock band Kokomo.

He would not be released until 1985. A film called The Hurricane, *directed by Milos Forman, based on Carter's struggle for freedom was released at the end of 1999. Dylan's ballad is featured in the movie.*

'He was trying to find a situation, you see, where he could make music with new people,' Clapton recalled. 'He was just driving round picking musicians up and bringing them back to the sessions. It ended up with like twenty-four musicians in the studio all playing these incredibly incongruous instruments, accordions, violin – and it didn't really work.'

Eventually Dylan narrowed the outfit down to the core unit that he would use in the Revue, and Jacques Levy was given the task of 'directing' the stage show.

'Bob said, "Can you figure out a way of doing it – a presentation? What would it be like?"... So I wrote up a thing...' Levy explained. 'And I left open spots so there could be guests and shifts. It wasn't really a rigid thing at all, the key point (was) how exactly we'd get to the point where Bob came on, and when to play the new material. We rehearsed the show in New York for almost two weeks. Again we had this enormous pile of material and it had to be arranged and worked out and staged. And the idea was that it should not look staged. We didn't want it to be a flash show, because that didn't fit anybody's style. The thing was to make it appear like it was a spontaneous evening... like a travelling vaudeville show or a traveling circus... There was almost a hootenanny feel... There was to be no tuning up between songs, there were no pauses. Big chunks of the show were the same every night.'

From the evidence we can glean from contemporary reviews and the concert footage included in *Renaldo and Clara*, all the pre-tour rehearsals and planning paid off. These were remarkable performances – carefully structured and skilfully played but emitting a phenomenal high-octane energy.

Conversely, Dylan has instructed the camera crew to shoot the musical numbers in a simple format and, as a result, the cinematic effects of the performances are visually unremarkable. There is no fast editing or gimmicky camera tricks. Generally they consist of one or two camera set ups, any pre-figuring of individual players is usually confined to zoom and our focus of attention, as directed by the camera's positioning, is Dylan. Editing is kept to a minimum, and there is very little intercutting.

In some of the non-musical sections of the film Dylan exploits the techniques of parallel editing, where two different scenes are edited together to appear as one, which he had been introduced to by Howard Alk ten years before. He even repeats a sequence familiar to us from *Eat The Document*, using footage from two different telephone calls edited together to appear as if they are being made to the people we see on screen. In *Renaldo and Clara*, Sara leaves Sam Shepard to make a phone call. We then cut to Columbia's Walter Yetnikoff answering the phone in his office and having a conversation, presumably with Sara. Dylan's use of sound-track music in the non-concert sequences also adheres to the principles of parallel editing. The music underpins, cross-cuts and punctuates the visual images. Sometimes it can be used to foreground a symbolic interaction or image. On other occasions the soundtrack too becomes multi-layered, threading its way through the sequence like a piece of yarn in a tapestry, invisible until you stand back and view the whole image. Here are several examples:

– Sara/Clara, this time wearing a voluptuous Sophia Loren type wig, is seen in long shot walking through a cityscape. She is carrying a coil of rope over one shoulder. We see her striding purposefully through the damp streets while the soundtrack has Allen Ginsberg reciting a poem which seems to be entitled 'Your Eyes'. Slowly, underneath the main voice-over, which has its own rhythmic cadence, we can hear a barrel-house piano, rumbling and striding through a twelve-bar. Suddenly, Dylan's voice becomes recognisable singing 'She Belongs To Me', a hymn to his muse. The subject matter of the lyrics is now given a visual frame of reference. The word has been made flesh.

– Throughout the background of the scene where Dylan trades Joan Baez for a horse, a particularly plaintive version of 'If You See Her Say Hello' is used to underscore the action.

– Sam Shepard and Sara are discussing what's gone wrong with their relationship. Music meanders in and out as the dialogue between the two becomes more jaded and pointless. As Shepard gets increasingly dismissive and unkind, we recognise the music as 'One Too Many Mornings', Dylan's paean to the inevitability of disaster in a relationship. As Shepard becomes more verbally aggressive the lyrics of the song become more and more sensitive. Dylan employs this technique adeptly on several other occasions in the movie, countering male negativity with a 'sensitive' song.

– Conversely, one rather amateurish example of flagging lyrical symbiosis with visual imagery takes place during an onstage version of 'It Takes A Lot To Laugh, It Takes A Train To Cry', on the line, '*if your train gets lost*', the film cuts to footage of Scarlet Rivera, backstage, lost, looking for the entrance to the stage. Then, in keeping with the links between sound and vision, the action cuts from the concert stage to a railway yard.

In the full-length version of the film there are over forty songs on the soundtrack.

Take Ten – Inside The Coliseum

The second phase of *Rolling Thunder* was over in May and, after a short break, Dylan and Howard Alk settled down to edit the footage in late summer 1976. They had over 240,000 feet of film in the can. The two men had to edit 100 hours down to a manageable size. The editing process was interrupted in early 1977 when Dylan and Sara's fragile marriage finally disintegrated – what had appeared as reconciliation during the filming, had now deteriorated into a bitter legal battle.

While Dylan has always been a mercurial figure, the *Renaldo and Clara* editing sessions proved to be one time in his life where he dedicated himself totally to the project in hand. With grim determination he remained more or less in one place until completion at the end of 1977. In the recording studio Dylan was renowned for constantly changing numbers, playing them in completely different time signatures and keys to the ones rehearsed and then often abandoning whole projects, seemingly out of sheer perversity. Now for *Renaldo and Clara*, he was like a man possessed as he single-mindedly stuck to one single vision.

It is perfectly normal for directors to over-shoot massively and rely on the editing process to mould the finished product, and Dylan had to learn how to create a film of marketable length.

'I knew it wasn't going to be a short hour movie because we couldn't tell the story in an hour,' Dylan explained. 'Originally I couldn't see how we couldn't do it in under seven or eight hours. But we just subtracted songs and dialogue until we couldn't subtract anymore.'

Cynics may argue that this is because the reels and reels of sprawling film were shot with no unifying concept in mind, but I think the point here is that Dylan does stick to his ideas, even if they appear confused on screen.

In a later interview he expressed surprise at how people reacted to the length of *Renaldo and Clara*, by pointing out that Indian films sometimes went on for as long as eight hours and in India nobody complained. One might comment that Dylan is conveniently forgetting the cultural differences between East and West, though he could have pointed to Wagner's *Ring Cycle* – performed over a period of several days and completely acceptable to opera buffs.

One of the reasons that Dylan devoted so much time, effort and money to the film was his distrust of the studio system, developed while working on *Pat Garrett and Billy The Kid*. He wasn't going to let the studios push him around the way he'd seen them do to Sam Peckinpah.

'My lawyer used to tell me there was a future in movies,' Dylan recalled. 'So I said, "What kind of future?" He said, "Well, if you can come up with a script, an outline and get money from a big distributor." But I knew I couldn't work that way. I can't betray my vision on a little piece of paper in hopes of getting some money from somebody. In the final analysis, it turned out that I had to make the movie all by myself, with people who would work with me, who trusted me.'

This is in keeping with Dylan's mode of operating within the recording industry. From quite early on in his career he has had total artistic control contractually, not only of his output but over other factors such as cover design and promotion.

In terms of *Renaldo and Clara*'s *avant garde* nature, it is worth remembering that Dylan's musical experimentation has been most evident in his lyrics rather than in song structure. There is no equivalent in Dylan's canon of Lennon's 'Revolution #9' or Lou Reed's *Metal Machine Music*. Dylan relies on instinct in music making and this is probably what he intended to do during the filming of *Renaldo and Clara*. In strictly commercial terms his instincts in this case let him down, possibly because the rituals of cinema going and concert attending are radically different. At a live concert both artist and audience are participating in a shared experience, in the cinema the director is removed from the process and can't fine-tune the 'performance' to suit the expectations of a particular audience. So, Dylan had shot the movie in his musical style and now with editing he attempted to apply a similar process.

'It's built in a very interesting way,' Ginsberg enthused. '...He shot about 110 hours of film, or more, and he looked at all the scenes. Then he put all the scenes on index cards, according to some preconceptions he had about them when he was directing the shooting. Namely, themes: God, rock & roll, art, poetry, marriage, women, sex, Bob Dylan, poets, death – maybe eighteen or twenty thematic preoccupations. Then he also put on index cards the dominant colour – blue or red... and certain other images that go through the movie, like the rose and the hat, and Indians – American Indians – so that he finally had a cross file of all that. And then he went through it all again and began composing it, thematically, weaving these specific compositional references in and out. So it's compositional, and the idea was not to have a plot, but to have a composition of those themes. So you notice the movie begins with a rose and a hat – masculine and feminine. The rose is like a "travelling vagina" – those are his words. The hat is masculine – crowns. The rose... travels from hand to hand... it's a painter's film and was composed like that.'

Clinton Heylin has observed, '[Dylan] perceived his primary influences not as Ford, Houston or Hitchcock, but Cezanne, Modigliani and Dali.'

This is an interesting point. Dylan's songwriting experiments with form and content had led him to an appraisal of Modern Artists and the philosophy of his art teacher, Norman Raeben, had taken him further into the concept of the 'conscious artist', yet much of *Renaldo and Clara* leant heavily on Surrealist ideas of the 'unconscious'. In terms of his painting and drawing, Dylan is a first-rate draftsman who often chooses not to demonstrate this. His style can vary from Realism to Surrealism, his life sketches are remarkably accurate, his large-scale canvasses vary in style from Figurative to Naïve–Primitive. There is a boldness and certainty about line and form and a strength in the use of colour. Clearly, to those who have been lucky enough to have seen more than just, say, *Writings and Drawings*, Dylan is an accomplished visual artist.

So what, we may ask, went wrong with *Renaldo and Clara*? Why, in spite of many fascinating qualities, was it received with such anger and confusion? Watching any movie involves an act of deliberate suspension of belief on the part of the viewer – Superman cannot fly, people can't just park their cars wherever they want, time is linear not sequential. We take such things on board quite easily when we go to the cinema because we go armed with a whole set of codes and conventions by which we understand the film and construct its meaning. The dominant cinematic form in our culture is narrative: films tell a story, usually one with a beginning, middle and end. This doesn't work with *Renaldo and Clara* and it is natural for the viewer to be disarmed. The key to enjoying the film is to watch it thoughtlessly and non-analytically. It is a series of impressions and emotions presented in an awkward but not inhibiting manner and the best way to view it is as a river flowing by. It's constantly in motion and possessed of its own rhythm.

It is true to say, as Paul Williams does, that Dylan is essentially a 'performing artist'. Maybe we should view the film in the same way as we would a concert – the artist appears, sings songs, the artist leaves – and so we have a beginning, middle and an end – the ultimate minimalist narrative. In a concert we don't question that the bit in the middle consists of many diverse mini-narratives.

But if we view the movie as an extension of his songs, watching it is a pleasure and its length no longer seems remarkable. It is unsurprising and almost inevitable that the man who had brought the eleven-and-a-half-minute song into Popular Music was going to bring the four-hour-long movie into our local theatre.

'Sad Eyed Lady of the Lowlands' is Dylan's 1966 magnum opus to his new bride Sara Dylan. It combines some of his most far out surrealist imagery with a haunting, repetitive chorus that pleads and begs for acceptance. In 1976, half way through the *Rolling Thunder Revue* tour and shortly after filming was completed, Dylan released the album *Desire*, featuring the song 'Sara'. Although Dylan claims in his *Biograph* notes that none of his songs are autobiographical, it's impossible to believe him in the case of *Sara*. It was recorded in front of her in the studio during a period of reconciliation in their failing marriage. Robert Shelton calls it 'an unabashed confessional to his wife. A plea for forgiveness and understanding.' We now have to ask the question: should *Renaldo and Clara* really be called *Robert and Sara*? Did the muse who inspired the sixteen-minute love song also inspire the four-hour movie? And can the viewer find the cinematic interpretation as enjoyable as the recorded?

Here is perhaps the key to the movie's problems – because Dylan has something interesting to say in 'Sara' he doesn't dispense with all the usual conventions of chord, melody and song structure. To produce cinematic work on a par with his greatest songs, he would have to combine an utter mastery of all aspects of filmmaking and script-writing with his own peculiar genius. This is as tall an order as expecting Martin Scorsese to produce an album on a par with *Blood on the Tracks*. This does not negate Dylan's mesmerising achievements with *Renaldo and Clara*, but it is worth remembering that Dylan, an artist legendary for refusing to explain the meaning of his work, went out of his way to try and explain what he was trying to say in the movie – even before its release, he gave numerous interviews where he tried to explain the nuances of the film's symbolism. Whereas the difficulty in interpreting the Surrealistic imagery of some of Dylan's best known mid-Sixties' songs is well documented, the impenetrable symbolism was overshadowed by the power of the melody, the strength of the playing and the ferocity of Dylan's delivery. In *Renaldo and Clara*, there was little else for the audience to focus on other than the imagery.

Take Eleven – 'It's Like Watching
The Defeat Of The Spanish Armada'*

On an early December evening in 1977 Dylan dropped into a restaurant near the Goldwyn Studios in Hollywood and invited surprised members of the public to a preview screening of *Renaldo and Clara*. Audience reaction was mixed – many of the invitees were perplexed. Undaunted, Dylan decided to press on with a January 1978 release.

The *Village Voice* assigned no less than four reviewers to assess Dylan's movie. All four duly tore the film to shreds. They accused Dylan of blatant narcissism and claimed he was comparing himself to Jesus. *The New Yorker*'s legendary critic Pauline Kael went even further:

'The Bob Dylan [his fans] responded to [in the Sixties] was a put-on artist,' Kael insisted. 'He was derisive, and even sneering, but in the sixties that was felt to be a way of freaking out those who weren't worthy of being talked to straight... In *Renaldo and Clara* his mocking spirit is just bad news... [He has] more tight close-ups than any actor can have had in the whole history of the movies. He's overpoweringly present, yet he's never in direct contact with us... we are invited to stare... to perceive the mystery of his elusiveness – his distance.'

Dylan had expected the film to get some criticism – as can be seen by his attempts to explain his vision in advance – but he could never have been prepared for the venom that was poured on *Renaldo and Clara*. It opened simultaneously in Los Angeles and New York to hysterically savage reviews. The critics seemed not only uncomprehending of the film's values, but seemed to have used it to attack Dylan personally.

'Reading the reviews of the movie, I sensed a feeling of them wanting to crush things. Those reviews weren't about the movie. They were just an excuse to get at me for one reason or another ...' commented Dylan in 1978.

---

*Village Voice *film critic*

It was only shown in a few other American cities, before Dylan withdrew it from US circulation – an act probably due as much to Dylan's fragile state of mind at the time, owing to pressures on both his personal and professional life, as to the critical reviews. The acrimonious divorce had left him emotionally drained, he was preparing a new band for a tour to promote the *Street Legal* album. For some inexplicable reason Dylan's star, so high in 1975, was waning and he appears to have become the victim of one of those strange fads of contemporary criticism when you knock somebody just because they've been successful.

Dylan never lost confidence in himself, his integrity or the film's worth and the movie's reception in Europe endorsed his validity as an auteur. The film was shown in May 1978 at the Cannes Film Festival and was well received. When *Renaldo and Clara* opened in London it ran for three months at one London cinema. On its opening, critic Nigel Andrews of the *Financial Times* wrote:

'… The mysteries exert an authentic fascination … I shall go out on a nervous limb and say that *Renaldo and Clara* is probably the most important film of the year … [it seeks] to define a new morality, a new religion; a new sense of direction for an age which has lost faith in doctrinal Christianity.'

The film continued to be a favourite on the late-night cult circuit for several years. Companies in England, Germany and Sweden also bought the TV franchise.

Back in America, though, a consortium of businessmen offered Dylan a deal he couldn't refuse. They wanted him to release a two-hour version, stripped down of the improvised scenes and consisting mainly of the film's on-stage footage. Dylan accepted their offer of $2 million, money he could use to recoup the losses incurred by the film's commercial failure, and the re-edited film was released in its new two-hour format to American cinemas.

We can presume that to be offered money to bowdlerise his finished work was adding insult to injury and, if so, he got his revenge by turning it into a parody of itself. Scenes were hacked to shreds arbitrarily and it became a concert film interspersed with barely-comprehensible vignettes. Like its full-length version it soon disappeared from the box office.

Dylan wouldn't return to film making for another eight years and then only as an actor. His forays into celluloid to date had been tremendously time-consuming and with little reward, either financial or artistic. This was not Roger Daltrey looking for an alternative career to frontlining the ailing Who. This was an artist looking for another way to express himself and he had been there, seen it and done it.

Before we see him in his next film in 1986, Dylan's energies were consumed by his conversion to Christianity, his subsequent re-emersion into an hedonistic rock'n'roll lifestyle of touring, recording and carousing. Towards the mid-1980s, though, he indicated to his agent that he would like to try another film role.

Reel Five
Hearts of Fire

There was a palpable air of excitement at the National Film Theatre on London's South Bank one Sunday morning in August 1986. Bob Dylan had arrived to hold a press conference about a movie called *Hearts of Fire* that he had agreed to make in England.

In the mid-1980s the fact that Dylan was holding a press conference in London was considered a major news-event. Extracts were shown on the BBC TV evening news bulletin. Monday morning's quality and tabloid newspapers featured the media-circus prominently in their pages.

FIONA **RUPERT EVERETT** AND **BOB DYLAN**

Hearts of Fire ⑮

If you want to feel the heat you have to play with fire.

LORIMAR MOTION PICTURES PRESENTS
A PHOENIX ENTERTAINMENT GROUP PRODUCTION A RICHARD MARQUAND FILM
FIONA RUPERT EVERETT AND BOB DYLAN HEARTS OF FIRE
ORIGINAL SCORE BY JOHN BARRY MUSIC BY BEAU HILL WRITTEN BY SCOTT RICHARDSON AND JOE ESZTERHAS
EXECUTIVE PRODUCER GERALD ABRAMS AND DOUG MORRIS CO-PRODUCER IAIN SMITH
PRODUCED BY RICHARD MARQUAND AND JENNIFER MILLER AND JENNIFER ALWARD
DIRECTED BY RICHARD MARQUAND
Soundtrack album available on CBS Records and Cassettes

DOLBY STEREO
IN SELECTED THEATRES

Released by Twentieth Century Fox through U.K. Film Distributors Ltd. Read the New English Library paperback
COPYRIGHT © 1987 LORIMAR TELEPICTURES DISTRIBUTION, INC. ALL RIGHTS RESERVED

LORIMAR
MOTION PICTURES
A LORIMAR TELEPICTURES COMPANY

'The NFT was the very last place I expected to see Bob Dylan,' journalist Patrick Humphries later recalled, 'The hacks had assembled for the press conference of *Hearts of Fire*... As the sun filtered in, I reckoned that none of us would be here without that first exposure to those scratchy mono LPs, a distant lifetime ago, and just for one moment, subs from *The Caernarvon Bugle*, national Sunday columnists, staid magazine editors, were briefly united. Instead of viewing the frizzle haired singer through binoculars here was the chance to get up close. Behind the façade of cool, we had all regressed to teenage fans.'

A few moments later Dylan, flanked by his co-stars and the film's director, Richard

Marquand, seated themselves on the stage and faced the number of photographers and journalists. If anybody was expecting a repeat of Dylan's acerbically witty 1960s' press conferences they were to be sadly disappointed. Whilst actors Rupert Everett and Fiona Flanagan mugged away happily for the cameras and Richard Marquand gamely answered questions, Dylan replied monosyllabically and with studied disinterest. So, how on earth had he gotten here?

Take One – In A Galaxy Far Far Away

Director Richard Marquand started out making documentaries for the BBC, before moving into feature film production in 1979 with a movie about the early years of The Fab Four, *Birth of The Beatles*.

That same year he directed an occult thriller, *The Legacy*, in former Who singer Roger Daltrey co-starred with American husband and wife duo, Katherine Ross and Sam Elliott.

Marquand's reputation was established with a film adaptation of Ken Follett's Nazi-spy-in-hiding thriller, *Eye of the Needle*, which ensured him a welcome in Hollywood and in 1983 he directed the third film in the Star Wars trilogy, *Return of the Jedi*.

In 1985 Marquand began a working relationship with screenwriter, Joe Eszterhas, which resulted in the high-class legal thriller, *Jagged Edge*, starring Glenn Close and Jeff Bridges.

Take Two – Telling Lies in America

Joe Eszterhas was born in Hungary and moved to America with his parents when he was six years old. He very rapidly assimilated American teen culture, watching movies, listening to Rock music and, as the 1960s progressed, becoming increasingly aware of the cultural upheaval that was taking place. He found his niche as a staff writer for *Rolling Stone*, where he blended hip musical taste with radical chic. His piece on the first anniversary of the Kent State shootings, 'Ohio Honors Its Dead,' was a particularly hard-hitting example of what became known as New Journalism.

Eszterhas' move to screenwriting came about in the late 1970s. While Hollywood obviously required he compromise his more radical concerns, Eszterhas did, initially at least, try and write about some of the serious issues that concerned him. Though the movie was inevitably a star vehicle, Eszterhas' screenplay for the 1978 Sylvester Stallone movie *F.I.S.T.*, centred on a Depression-era, blue-collar worker's struggle to establish a labour union and bore more than a passing relationship to the real life and times of Teamsters leader, Jimmy Hoffa.

Eszterhas' script for 1983's *Flashdance*, may have been a fairly conventional Cinderella meets Mills and Boon love story, but elements of the simple tale about an honest working girl supplementing her welder's salary by Go-Go dancing in a bar, while dreaming of ballet school, still harked back to the writer's earlier fascination with blue-collar aspirations. This time round Eszterhas' lean narrative was coupled to a driving Rock soundtrack scored by Giorgio Moroder. The critics remained resolutely unimpressed.

Cinema's grand dame Pauline Kael dismissed *Flashdance* as 'A lulling, narcotizing musical. It sells the kind of romantic story,' she added, 'that would have been laughed off the screen 30 years ago...', while Roger Ebert, another highly respected critic, singled Ezsterhas out for particular criticism:

'This poor kid is so busy performing the pieces of business supplied to her by the manic scriptwriters that she never has a chance to develop her character...'

Still, *Flashdance* was a big hit with audiences, pulled in an Oscar for best music and spawned a host of imitators.

Better still, Eszterhas' 1985 collaboration with Marquand, *Jagged Edge*, was both a commercial and critical success. Eszterhas and Marquand were riding extremely high when they were approached about a music film project that had originated with screenwriter Gerry Abrams.

Take Three – The Line Producer

'*Hearts of Fire* ... was in existence in one form or another for quite a few years...' recalled Iain Smith, one of the film's co-producers, who had previously worked on acclaimed projects such as *Local Hero* (1983), *The Killing Fields* (1984) and *The Mission* (1986). 'Richard [Marquand] saw in the script that he had the potential for a very interesting and exciting musical film – not a musical, but a film about music and musicians. It was what he wanted to get into at that point…'

Iain Smith developed the project in conjunction with executive producer Gerry Abrams. Screenwriting credits were shared by Scott Richardson and Eszterhas, though there's no doubt that Richard Marquand also had a hand in the shooting script.

'I'd got the script to a point where I was very happy with it,' Marquand recalled. 'I'd put it through a very very expensive and major rewrite, and come up with this very important character Billy Parker who, as you know, represents an older American rock star who retired from the music scene about ten years ago… And when I had the script at that point, I was obviously starting to think that this was a movie that I wanted to make…'

Marquand negotiated a deal with American company Lorimar Pictures and got the go-ahead to shoot the movie at Shepperton Studios in England, and on location in Hertfordshire, Bristol and Canada for the American scenes. Now all that needed to be done was assemble a cast.

Take Four – Enter Molly Maguire

The leading lady role, Molly Maguire, was the first to be filled, and by a relative unknown singer, Fiona Flanagan, who had dropped her surname, calling herself simply Fiona.

Born in New Jersey in 1961, Fiona had turned down a scholarship for the Drama Department of the New York University in order to become a rock singer. She signed to Atlantic Records in 1982 and made an album called *Beyond The Pale*. As a result of the videos made to support some of the tracks on the album she was persuaded to resume her career in acting.

'I was being solicited; I didn't go after them. I decided that, since opportunity was knocking, I should get serious and see if I had any talent. It was a personal challenge.'

Her first role was in TV's *Miami Vice*, which led to her being offered the part of Molly in *Hearts of Fire*. Iain Smith found her '…a very interesting girl… It's an extremely difficult role because basically the film is a rite of passage - it's about her going from childhood, in a way, to adulthood. Growing in maturity, growing into success...'

The choice of Fiona's character's name in the movie is an interesting one and considering Eszterhas' former political inclinations, it is highly possible that he had a hand in choosing it. The original 'Molly Maguires' were a secret society of Irish miners in the anthracite mining fields of 1870s Pennsylvania. At a time when unionisation was forbidden, the Maguires used industrial action and acts of violence against the mine owners in order to secure their rights. Though they were ultimately infiltrated by the Pinkerton Detective Agency and their revolt crushed, their name still lives on in labour circles around the US. A movie was even made documenting their struggle, Jonathan Ritt's *The Molly Maguires* starring Sean Connery as the Maguires' organiser.

In addition to her name, *Hearts of Fire* gives a number of other intimations of Molly's bona fide, blue-collar credentials. To begin with, Molly comes from the outskirts of Pittsburgh, where the film, like Eszterhas' *Flashdance*, is set. More tellingly, at one point when she and the male lead, James Colt, are driving through her hometown and Colt says what a dump it is, against a backdrop of smoking chimneys and foundries, Molly replies that it's beautiful because it's real, a line that harks back to Eszterhas' blue-collar obsessions so evident from his early career.

Take Five – Enter The Young Actor

Two years older than Fiona, Rupert Everett was a graduate of the Central School of Speech and Drama in London. By the mid-1980s he was becoming an established young male lead in finely crafted British films such as *Another Country* (1984), *Dance With A Stranger* (1985) and *Duet for One* (1986) when he got the call for *Hearts of Fire* to take the part of jaded Pop star James Colt. Generally cast as an upper-class, aristocratic type, Everett was a surprising choice. In fact, Marquand had originally wanted either Sting or David Bowie for the role – both of whom would have at least been able to draw on their own experiences in the music business. Everett did not slip easily into the part. During filming he was concerned that people would think his adopted all-purpose 'street accent' sounded phoney. But he had other worries too.

'Rupert was scared, as all good actors will be with any part,' Iain Smith recalled, 'but he was particularly scared about the role he was playing – James Colt. Here he was dealing with what he was contriving and creating out of himself, and here was Dylan who absolutely *was* this, who *could* stand up in front of 50,000 people and make them wait, and who knew what it's like at big rock concerts. So I think Rupert found it difficult to deal with Dylan...'

According to reports from the set, things between Dylan and Everett gelled a few weeks into the movie, though the scenes between them in the movie show a very wary Dylan skirting round the young English actor's decadent mannerisms. Maybe they both felt put off by each other's professionalism in their individual fields of expertise. And one should always be wary of 'reports from the set.'

Take Six – Enter Billy Parker

After more or less finalising the script, Marquand went on the look out for his Billy Parker, a retired rock star who takes Molly under his wing. Just as with his initial preferences for James Colt, Marquand wanted Billy to be played by a real musician.

'... I started to meet one or two contemporary American rock stars of the younger generation who might be interested in playing this role,' Marquand remembered, ' but also in a way, people who I was interested in meeting just to find out what it's like in the '80s to be a big American rock star.

'And it was at that point that I got a phone call from Bob's agent and friend... in Los Angeles... And she phoned me up and said, "Richard, had you thought of Bob for the role of Billy Parker?" I said, "No, of course not, how could I possibly? On the other hand, my God! Do you think for one second that it might be possible?" And she said, "Well it's more than possible, he's read the script and he's very interested in talking about it...'''

The agent invited Marquand to a preliminary meeting at Dylan's house in Malibu. After negotiating the security at the gate and heading up the driveway to the main building, Marquand was ushered into Dylan's inner sanctum.

'And he's sitting in his kitchen,' Marquand recalled, 'rather like, I guess, I sit in my kitchen. It's full of today's papers and yesterday's papers and a bottle of wine and wine glasses, piles of letters and cassettes everywhere, and a guitar propped in the corner, and somebody washing up in the back...'

Marquand and Dylan spent the rest of the day drinking Cabernet Sauvignon and discussing the Parker character. During the meeting, Dylan was apparently impressed by Marquand's capacity for wine, even mentioning it at the London press conference.

Later, Marquand steered the discussion round to Dylan's involvement in Peckinpah's *Pat Garrett and Billy The Kid*:

'I made a point ... to try and find out what happened, because very often, unless you're careful, a director can judge an actor's performance wrongly in another film where they may have been bad, and come to the conclusion that the actor is bad. Not that Bob was bad. In fact I thought he was rather interesting in that role, and I think in a way Sam Peckinpah had cast him quite carefully as a sort of icon...'

By the end of the day the two men appeared to be in agreement. Marquand would set up a short screen test for Dylan. He would shoot it on video, possibly even fly Fiona in from New York to take part, then let Dylan privately see the results. No one would know about it, and if Dylan didn't like what he saw he could pull out, and the same would go for Marquand. In fact, when the two men subsequently viewed the footage, they both liked what they saw.

Take Seven – Let Shooting Commence

While agents were contacted and contracts drawn up, back in England Iain Smith began sorting out the logistics of the various shoots. In addition to the usual production issues such as budgets and timetables, locations, catering, accommodation and processing, Smith had one particularly challenging duty: he had to make sure that Dylan was co-operative, on time and happy.

'It was my duty to make it clear to Richard that he had to make damn sure that Dylan was even capable of mastering the technical requirements of acting,' Smith explained. 'Was he, for instance, fully compos mentis? Was he emotionally, intellectually interested enough to do the work, the hard work you need to have? Did he for instance identify a future in films sufficiently for him to work hard with us, or was he just going to play with us?… And then once we'd sorted it out we had to convince the people who were putting up the money… If they're paying millions of dollars, throwing it out into an enterprise which hinges on the quality or otherwise of performances, they want to know they're getting something…'

Still, it was Marquand who had the more delicate task of easing Dylan into the role – essentially having to train him how to act. Dylan had spent all his life singing his own words (and, yes, on occasion singing others' words when they particularly meant something to him) and Marquand sensed that this was because those words represented a reality to Dylan. There was no perceived 'falseness' about them. Now he had to try and get Dylan to act, to play a part, be someone else, naturally. It wasn't going to be an easy task as the director explained:

'So what would happen that would be quite interesting was that he would stumble on certain lines. And I always used to be conscious because there has to be a psychological reason why an actor can remember a whole series of lines and then can't remember a certain line – it's just like psychology really, isn't it? And so I'd pick up on it immediately… and I'd say, "Well, what was it about this?" And he would usually be able to figure out that the line had the wrong rhythm or was slightly phoney – it's not exactly what Billy Parker would say. It would just be written wrong.'

Once Marquand began to understand the nuances of Dylan's performances he took to coming on set earlier just so he could go through things with Dylan and ensure that the 'feel' of the lines was right. One of the problems, of course, was that Dylan has an instinctive mechanism that drives him, constantly to adapt and rearrange. This is challenging and invigorating in a musical context where Dylan's performances of his own songs are modified every time he performs them. However, to adopt a similar approach to acting in front of a camera could clearly be problematic. In the theatre and on film, actors talk of 'the beat', that is, the internal rhythm of the text being performed. A director will suggest an actor pause for 'a beat' before delivering a line. What Marquand noted about some of Dylan's delivery was that it was placed on the off beat. The curse of being a musician perhaps. A dialogue coach, Harold Guskin, was brought in to help develop Dylan's skills.

WELCOME TO THE FILM

HEARTS OF FIRE

Below is a brief outline of the shooing day.

The day will consist of 2 SCENES as described below.

SCENE 48   INT CONCERT HALL NIGHT

The hall is full - PEPPER WARD and BAND are on stage doing a song "FEAR, HATE, ENVY, JEALOUSY" PEPPER WARD waves and encourages the audience to sing along - they do and obviously love the number.

SCENE 49   INT CONCERT HALL LATER

'BONES' another member of PEPPER WARDS BAND is on stage introducing a Rock and Roll Legend - 'BILLY PARKER' the lights come up and there he is! There is loud applause 'MOLLY' the only female member of the BAND stands across from him. 'BILLY PARKER' intruduces the hard rousing Rock song "I HAD A DREAM ABOUT YOU BABY" and goes straight into the number.

The back-up band are not very good but "PARKER" doesn't seem to care - he carries on exaggerating his every move, the crowd cheers. 'MOLLY' suddenly can't handle it anymore and joins 'PARKER' singing and gives it everythign she's got. This encourages 'PARKER' and the number winds up to a full scale climax. The crowd goes wild.

Attached are copies of the Lyrics for the two songs that we will be filming. Please look over them so that you can join in the singing.

A Film Extras day can be both long and difficult, a book or other form of entertainment certainly helps during periods of rest while the crew set up the different shots.

PLEASE ARRIVE PROMPTLY at the specified time indicated by the colour on your ticket:-

BLUE, GREEN, PURPLE - PLEASE ARRIVE AT 7.50AM

WHITE, YELLOW, BROWN - PLEASE ARRIVE AT 8.20AM

When you arrive you will be given a pay slip which MUST be kept on your person at ALL times. Attached to this slip will be a set of cloakroom tickets (again colour coded to the same colour on your ticket) one of which will be collected by the caterers at each meal - Breakfast, Lunch and Tea.

Once you have collected your slip look for the catering station which relates to your colour where you can have a roll and coffee. A Lunch box and Tea will be served in the same way, so make sure you have your pay slips and tickets.

You should be prepared to be able to stay quite late approx. 500 people may be required for extra shots. If you are one of these people you will receive a supliment of £5.00 and something to eat.

Shooting of the film is dependent on a lot of people. In order to achieve the best possible result in the given time it is important that everyone does their job well.

Finally may we welcome you among our extras and hope you will have an enjoyable day.

'Dylan often had problems understanding the pacing of a line and the motivations behind the line,' says Smith. 'Guskin's function was to work that through with him, go through the script and to do with him what a professional actor would do within himself... all these things that actors have to work through, Guskin was providing Dylan with, and at some points that confused Dylan, because he's a guy who does his own thing, he speaks his own words, and here he was having to deal with another writer's words. He wasn't forgetting lines – he's not a forgetful person. It's very complex all of that.'

Shooting began at Shepperton in late August 1986, mainly occupied with interiors. Sets that were built included a pub (later cut from the final release print), Molly and Parker's hotel room, a recording studio and several rooms in Colt's mansion.

At the end of the month Dylan went into the London Townhouse Studio to cut the 'live' music tracks for use in the film's concert sequences. Among the musicians booked for the recording were Eric Clapton and Ron Wood.

It's not unreasonable to assume that the producers hoped for a soundtrack album to tie-in with the movie. The problem was that Dylan, at the time, was suffering from writer's block and hadn't written anything of significance for several months. At the press conference he was asked about the half-dozen songs he was supposed to have written for the movie. Dylan admitted that they weren't written yet, but said that he hoped to finish them while filming. As the studio session was booked for ten days hence this was rather pushing it. As a result, by the time he got into Townhouse all he had were the rather weak sounding, 'Had A Dream About You Baby' and 'Night After Night'. He was forced into the position of covering two tunes by other writers, John Hiatt's, 'The Usual' and Shel Silverstein's wonderful, 'Couple More Years'. The incidental music was written by veteran British movie-scorer, John Barry.

In September the production went on location. Concert sequences were filmed at London nightclub Heaven and at Bristol's Colston Hall, where, in 1966, Dylan had been roundly booed for playing with an electric guitar. More concert footage was filmed at London's

Electric Ballroom in late September. Three further days' filming took place in Wales: at Dunraven Beach, Southnerdown, Bridgend and at Rhoose Airport in Cardiff.

In October the location shooting moved to Ontario in Canada for the American sequences, common practice in the film industry then, as now, because the cost of shooting in the USA is prohibitive by comparison. Hamilton doubled for Pittsburgh and another concert sequence was shot at the Canadian General Electric Warehouse in Toronto. Dylan's involvement finished at the end of October and editing began in the New Year with a summer 1987 release in mind.

Take Eight – Billy, Molly and, er, James

The narrative of *Hearts of Fire* is fairly straightforward. Molly works in a toll booth by day and fronts a bar-band at night. One evening, Billy Parker, a retired rock star who owns a chicken farm outside of town, turns up to watch her play. Their relationship grows and when he's invited to play at an 'oldie's show' in England she travels over with him.

In London, Molly meets rock superstar James Colt, an old friend of Billy's. Together they are invited to Colt's country mansion. It soon becomes clear that Colt has designs on Molly's body and her career. Parker warns her about the pitfalls of stardom and goes back to his chickens. Molly goes on a tour of America with Colt and eventually realises that Parker was right. I guess it's supposed to be an updated rock and roll slant on the old eternal love triangle.

Take Nine – The Fiddler Now Speaks

Hearts of Fire opens with a version of Gloria Jones' 60s' hit 'Tainted Love' (Soft Cell's style, but with a new vocal by Everett) playing over images of tollbooths on an American highway. The track goes from dominant to sub as we see it's a cassette being played by Molly Maguire as she works in one of the booths. The name on the cassette cover says, 'James Colt'.

We then get our first sighting of Dylan – only we don't because although he tells Molly that the music 'sucks', he never actually raises the visor on his motorbike helmet, so we never get to see his face.

This 'teaser' shot is designed to build up our anticipation of seeing Dylan properly. Unfortunately, the trick is repeated the next time he appears on screen, which is overdoing the mystique approach a little bit.

That next screen appearance is at 'Woody's Club', a local bar, where Molly and her band are grinding out Rock standards such as 'Proud Mary'. This time we get a low tracking shot of Dylan's booted feet moving through the club and up to the bar. He orders a drink and we finally get to see his face in a profile shot.

Alan Hulme, the cinematographer, really does an outstanding job when showing Dylan on screen. Throughout the movie he uses a variety of lighting positions to make the most of Dylan's craggy features. Often he'll place him in a half-light with just a shaft of main-light illuminating a portion of Dylan's face.

In the scene that follows, Dylan's acting is fine. It doesn't appear strained and he seems quite natural. Marquand and Guskin's coaching appears to have paid off.

It's a scene that relies heavily on close-ups – one of the hardest things for an actor to do on film. You have absolutely nowhere to hide in a close-up, the camera will reveal the slightest thing: one wrong eye movement, or twitch of the lip, and the whole scene can be ruined. Marquand was extremely happy with some of Bob's close-up work.

'And then you go to the cutting room and see this stuff cut together and it's... wonderful!' the director enthused. 'I mean, really wonderful... Or I'd watch the rushes and I'd see this close-up of Bob, which after all cinema is about close-ups – it is for me anyway – and I'd see things happening in close-up that I hadn't actually seen watching it live...'

A couple of scenes where Marquand manages to capitalise on this style of shooting take place in Colt's mansion. After lunch Molly is watching a video of Parker in his glory days – actually Dylan's appearance in the *Concert for Bangla Desh* movie. Parker angrily turns it off and asks Colt, who is manfully swigging from a bottle of vodka, how long it is since he last wrote a song? Parker then delivers a speech about the pitfalls of stardom. Dylan does this rather well and Marquand sensibly sticks to his idea of magnifying Dylan's performance with big close-ups.

The first on-stage music sequence featuring Dylan is shot competently, but has two rather jarring features. One is Dylan's never ending problem coming to terms with lip-synching, his vocals mysteriously continue when he's turned his head away from the mike, and the second is the lighting on this scene.

The establishing shot, that is, the one that sets the scene, is a standard long-shot of the entire group on stage. The main shots, which are then edited in, are cut-aways and close-ups of Dylan. Hulme and Marquand use a standard classical Hollywood lighting trick of having two different set-ups. If you look closely you'll see the difference between them. The establishing shot is lit 'naturally', that is, made to look as natural as possible. The close-ups are lit 'expressionistically', that is, light is manipulated to create an effect – a system of lighting developed in Hollywood during the 1930s, partly inspired by German Expressionist filmmakers who'd fled there from Nazi Germany. Equally inspirational in its influence on this form of lighting were paintings by artists like Rembrandt and Vermeer. Art-directors would often carry books of their work around with them for on-set inspiration.

The trick is to make the transitions from each set-up as seamless as possible. Great directors like Rouben Mamoulian could use sixteen different set-ups in a two-minute sequence of a Garbo movie and you'd never notice. Marquand singularly fails to do this with Dylan.

When we cut from the establishing shot to a close-up, Dylan is often in a slightly different position, standing to the side of the mike rather than facing it. The difference in lighting is also too noticeable and the overall effect is awkward not cohesive. The same can be said for the live footage shot at Bristol's Colston Hall and elsewhere. Marquand fails to capture the atmosphere of a live gig, presumably because the imperatives of a dramatic film dictate that the musical numbers have to be interrupted by sections of plot line. For instance, in the scene when Dylan is going down badly in front of a punk-rock audience (an interesting enough concept anyway), Molly takes to the stage and straps on a Fender guitar, revitalising his performance by showing him how it should be done. The cutaways of Molly looking anguished and then finally deciding to go on stage to save the day are ineptly shot and they interfere with the performance. Other directors, such as Oliver Stone in his movie bio-pic of Jim Morrison, *The Doors*, avoid the pitfall by skilful and imaginative use of camera and editing.

No matter how clichéd the camera angle, though, there is no denying Dylan's on-stage charisma. This is his arena and it's to his credit that he carries this through all his scenes in the film. But sadly, the moment Dylan is off screen the whole movie fizzles out. We see Molly and Colt make love and his lost muse is magically restored. Yawn. We see Molly and Colt tour America. Yawn, yawn.

Everett's musical numbers look like some sort of Neo-Nazi music festival: people marching up and down, dry ice and spotlights. He is rigid in front of the microphone displayings all the on-stage charisma of a soap dish. I could go on, but the film does that for itself. However, one bit worth mentioning for its sheer idiocy is the sequence when a blind girl, who turns up at all Colt's gigs, pulls a gun on him, threatening to shoot him. A blind girl with a knife I could understand, but a blind girl with a gun is just so illogical. Possibly figuring that being blind she might miss Colt she turns the gun on herself and blows her brains out all over his shirt.

Towards the end of the movie, Molly turns up at Parker's and tells him he was right and that the music business is all shit. Dylan is excellent in this scene, his close-ups are terrific and he actually does sound as if he believes what he's saying to Molly. He potters around his cluttered-up kitchen offering her eggs – he has thousands – toying with a kettle and making coffee. Anybody who thinks Dylan can't act should watch this one scene to check out what we've been missing all these years. And of course, he does sing too. In a beautifully lit scene, Parker comes into the barn where she's sleeping and plays Shel Silverstein's 'A Couple More Years' to her on an acoustic guitar.

There are several other poignant moments in the movie. A scene that takes place on a Welsh clifftop overlooking the sea also allows us a glimpse of what could have been. Shot from a high angle it takes in the whole vista of sunset, seashore and rocks, perfectly framing the aging rock star and the young female ingénue. Dylan's dialogue is delivered in a tenderly, but world-weary, manner as he tries to persuade Molly that the music business is a trap. The subtext here, and it does come across, is that Parker himself is in love with her but feels too inadequate to express it. If the movie had been constructed around their relationship, it might just have worked. Both Fiona and Dylan have an on-screen rapport that is pointedly missing from her scenes with Everett.

Take Ten – 'Get Rid Of The Pussy – Jump The Rhythm And Tune It Up'

One of the principal reason's the film is so flawed and has such jumps and unexplained changes of direction in the narrative is because so much of the sub-plot was removed in the editing stage. For instance in one scene near the beginning of the movie, Molly leaves Woody's bar in tears and goes out into the street where van loads of cops are rousting people. It's clear that an incident has just taken place. Dylan appears and hustles her away –

Parker – *You don't want to go to jail do you?*

As they drive off down the main street they pass a cinema. On the marquee is that night's feature – *Pat Garrett and Billy The Kid*. (I presume they couldn't resist the temptation.) Now, what we've seen is a trifle mystifying. Quite a lot is made of the cops running around and there's a sense of urgency about Parker trying to get Molly out of there, but nothing is developed from it, nothing is explained.

What's actually happened is that Parker has a sideline in being a bit of a Robin Hood character. Later in the movie he introduces himself to James Colt under that name. In the original script he's just robbed a Burger King. He is the one the cops are looking for. The robbery scene was even shot, as was a scene where he robs Molly's triumphant home-coming gig. For some inexplicable reason this whole side to the Parker character was cut out of the finished film, leaving some strange continuity gaps. Perhaps Richard Marquand cut them because they simply didn't work. What seems more likely is that the cuts were ordered by Lorimar, the film's investors, who wanted a straightforward ninety-minute feature, with no awkward plot lines.

Another scene that would have added more to the characterisation and the plot line of the narrative also found itself on the cutting-room floor. This was a nude love scene between Parker and Molly that has now become legendary in Dylan fan circles as a glorious example of 'What if ...'

We don't know how Dylan felt about shooting this scene – certainly earlier on in the movie, when there was supposed to be a nude skinny-dipping scene with Fiona, he resolutely kept his clothes on, though hawk-eyed observers will notice that, though he jumps into the lake with his motor-cycle boots on, when he comes out of the water he's wearing white socks. To be fair, this scene was Dylan's first scene shot for the film.

'Poor Bob, poor Fiona...' Richard Marquand recalled. 'we'd shot the skinny-dipping scene, which we shot in appalling cold in Black Park Lake, just outside Pinewood. And admittedly Bob didn't have to take his clothes off, but it was his very first dramatized scene... Oh God it was cold! But he didn't have to go in the water, so that's all made up. Fiona was the brave one because she had to go in – and that was incredible. She took her clothes off and – pish! – in she went.'

However, when it came to the proper love scene Dylan did strip. In an interview for the *Daily Express* in 1987, Fiona explained 'There was lots of tumbling about and cuddling. I really enjoyed doing it though, but I'm not sure Bob did.' Was this because he was nervous about the scene, or, as Fiona concluded, because '...he likes buxom blondes and I'm certainly not that.'

Another scene cut out beggars belief. Imagine a busy London pub and a conversation about rock and roll taking place between Bob Dylan and Cockney rock-legend Ian Dury. Hovering about around them is Woodstock veteran Richie Havens. Well, you will have to imagine it because it's another example of the wasted opportunities in *Hearts of Fire* – Dury is an engaging character whose persona is as large off-screen as it is on. He and Dylan together should have made for compelling viewing. And in the BBC documentary *Getting To Dylan*, Dylan himself speaks very highly of Dury.

Take Eleven – Snatching Defeat From The Jaws Of Victory

Hearts of Fire was premiered in the UK in London in October 1987. Dylan didn't attend even though he was in town at the time (see Appendix Two). Perhaps he sensed what was coming. The reviews were so universally appalling that Lorimar withdrew the film after one week in the cinema, and all plans for a US cinema release were hastily dropped. *Hearts of Fire* would not even be released on video in America until 1990. Its reception probably scuppered any more plans Dylan had of involvement in filmmaking. The big question now of course is, is it really that bad?

The simple answer is, yes. How it could have failed so horrendously is difficult to say. The crew were first-rate, Richard Marquand was a proven, workman-like director, with a modestly impressive CV behind him. The script, though very much a re-working of the *A Star Is Born* concept, could have been a lot worse. What made it so risibly bad has much to do with Lorimar's interference with the footage shot by Marquand – making a mockery of certain scenes and themes. The idea of Parker carrying out robberies for kicks isn't quite so far-fetched as it appears on paper and it might have added another dimension to the character. Certainly, as previously mentioned, the absence of the robbery scenes left plenty of continuity problems. Also, the cutting of scenes between Dylan and Ian Dury took away much of the rock'n'roll authenticity that the film so desperately needed.

LORIMAR
MOTION PICTURES
and
Twentieth Century Fox
cordially invite you
to the
World Gala
CELEBRITY PREMIERE
of

Hearts of Fire (15)

at the
ODEON Marble Arch W2
on Friday, October 9th 1987
at 8.30pm
(doors open 7.30pm)

DRESS INFORMAL   *ADMIT ONE*

The other key problem was miscasting. Contrary to the opinion of many critics who singled out Fiona for particular blame, she's not that bad – though sadly her career would never recover from the poor notices and this would be her only starring role.

Perhaps Fiona does overplay the young girl naivete, but she brings a credible innocence to the part. Rupert Everett, on the other hand, is woefully wrong as Colt. It's impossible to believe for one minute in his performance. All the way through the film he looks awkward and ill at ease, even nervous. His mannerisms are stilted and stiff. He is acting in the manner he thinks a musician will act. But we are all to aware in his scenes that Everett is not a musician – there is not a moment when we are able to suspend this belief. Everett may well be a gifted actor in other roles, but in *Hearts of Fire* he's simply embarrassing. Worse still, there's absolutely no chemistry between him and Fiona. Their relationship doesn't develop, it just happens because it's in the script. There is a spark between her and Dylan, though, even if he does give the impression of perceiving it as more fatherly than sexual. In interviews Fiona describes Dylan as 'a great guy. He was always teasing me ... he was always standing behind the camera pulling faces at me, trying to make me laugh.'

Which brings us, naturally enough, to Dylan's role in the movie. He is the only reason to sit through the film. His acting, while a little quirky or unorthodox, is something of a revelation. He brings the role off with a quiet dignity and watching him in *Hearts of Fire* just makes you want to see more of this side of his talents.

'Well in *Hearts of Fire* I think he's arguably the best thing in the film,' Iain Smith would reflect. 'It's not because he's a great actor, it's because Richard has worked very hard to bring out, by cutting and editing Bob's material, what is in the man, which is his natural charisma and graciousness... he's not stodgy, he's funny and quirky and strange and you watch him on the screen and you think, Well, he's not acting – you can see that – but, and it's a bit odd, he's very watchable. You just want to watch him. And it's a totally indefinable quality. But it's a real quality.'

The film's director, Richard Marquand, sadly died after completing the editing of a promotional trailer for *Hearts of Fire*, just a week before the premiere. His associate producer, Iain Smith, has gone on to work on seven more feature films, including the highly acclaimed *The Fifth Element* (1997) and *Seven Years in Tibet* (1997). Rupert Everett, after several years in the wilderness, re-focused his career during the 1990s with starring roles in *The Comfort of Strangers* (1990), *Pret-A-Porter* (1994), *The Madness of King George* (1995) and became an established Hollywood star with *My Best Friend's Wedding* (1997). Fiona has had a less illustrious film career since her involvement in *Hearts of Fire*, only appearing as the Fog Groupie in *The Doors* (1991). Currently she works for Danny Sugarman, formerly Jim Morrison's manager.

Reel Six
Cameos, Guest Slots & Promos

An artist of Dylan's stature is bound to attract offers to make cameo appearances in movies. For Dylan, in spite of his averred interest in cinema, these have usually been musical ones.

Take One – *Festival*

Festival, a movie about the Newport Folk Festival, directed by Murray Lerner, is the first in a trilogy of films that would climax with *Woodstock* (though some may see *Gimme Shelter*, the Altamont flick as completing a quadrumvirate, I prefer to consider this a postscript, or aftermath). The second is D.A. Pennebaker's *Monterey Pop*. All three are focused around large-scale, open air, musical events and represent high points in American popular culture. Dylan is the link between them all, even though he only appears in the first. In *Monterey Pop*, his unspoken presence is given form by Jimi Hendrix's version of 'Like A Rolling Stone'. For the film *Woodstock*, the Woodstock festival organisers tried desperately to book Dylan for the three-day event; instead he chose to go to the Isle of Wight in the UK, horrified at the thought of 250,000 people landing on his doorstep. Ironically, he'd originally retired to Woodstock after his motorcycle crash to recuperate away from the glare of the spotlight and the pressure of the music scene.

'Then came the big news about Woodstock' Dylan explained ruefully, 'about musicians goin' up there and it was like a wave of insanity breakin' loose around the house day and night... It was really dark and depressing... we *had* to get out of there. This was just about the time of the Woodstock Festival, which was the sum total of all this bullshit...'

The days of the Newport Folk Festival, however, were younger and more innocent. Having been staged originally as an off shoot of the older, Newport Jazz Festival, the Folk side of things had grown and grown as the Folk Revival had taken hold of young people's imaginations. Its rise, in a way, reflected the growth in Dylan's own popularity.

Festival, which received its premiere in 1967 was a compilation of Newport highlights from the years 1963 to 1966, and featured a dazzling array of different talents. Peter, Paul and Mary figure very prominently, as does Joan Baez and Johnny Cash, while Howlin' Wolf, Son House, Sonny Terry and Brownie McGhee are amongst the Blues' contingent. The performances, drawn from hundreds of hours of film shot by Lerner and his crew, represent a unique moment in musical history, and none more so than when Dylan plays electric guitar in front of an audience for the first time since his schooldays.

The first time we see Dylan in the movie, however, was shot on the afternoon of Saturday July 24th 1965, when he performed at a Songwriters' Workshop away from the main performance area. Dylan was by now so popular that his appearance threatened to overshadow all the other events taking place around the festival.

'The crowd around the Songwriters' Workshop was so immense that it was swamping the other workshops,' Joe Boyd, a young record producer and future Witchseason chief, remembered. 'People were complaining: "Turn up the Dylan one because we're getting bleed from the Banjo one on the other side! This was very much against the spirit of what the Festival was supposed to be about...'

The idea of workshops was that a small audience of a hundred or so could get in close proximity to an artist and watch them do their thing. At Newport there were banjo workshops, dulcimer workshops, line dancing and *a cappella* singing workshops. The intimacy of the situation was supposed to result in people gaining an insight into the production of Folk-Art. Dylan drew thousands.

In *Festival*, we see Dylan performing at the workshop in 1965, while what he hear is an amalgamation of his 1964 and 1965 renditions of 'All I Really Wanna Do'. When the camera pans over the crowd the music track cuts to his 1964 appearance.

He looks happy and smiles away at the people gathered in front of him. Lerner's camerawork tends towards tight close-ups, with just one or two framing shots added to give depth. At one point though there is a precursor of the 1976 shot from *Hard Rain* that was used for the back of the album cover (see Reel Four). The camera goes behind Dylan and we see his back, centre frame, whilst the audience look on. The panning shot across the crowd is informative and delightful. Here they are, gathered together in their thousands to see Dylan, sitting quietly on the grass, taking in the balmy afternoon sunshine, while he strums away for them. The next day couldn't have been more different, both musically and cinematically.

Dylan had decided to use his Sunday night appearance to unveil his new electric sound in front of a live audience. Rehearsals had taken place at a mansion near the festival site, with Al Kooper, Barry Goldberg and three members of the Paul Butterfield Blues Band, who were also appearing at the festival. Dylan was scheduled for the middle section of the closing concert.

Before reaching Dylan's Sunday segment we get a number from Peter, Paul and Mary, and 'I Walk The Line' from Johnny Cash. The film then cuts to two elderly ladies who talk about how 'children' today just want rock'n'roll. It then cuts to another elderly lady, who this time we can identify as Traditional singer Almeda Riddle, making a remarkably astute observation.

'*I don't know though*,' she muses, '*what we call Folk now, two or three hundred years ago was possibly Pop... You see, we change.*'

Lerner dramatically cuts to a side shot of Dylan, dressed in black leather with a Fender guitar strapped across his chest launching into 'Maggie's Farm'. The monochrome film stock heightens the dramatic impact of the scene, its stark black and white chiaroscuro lending itself perfectly to the charged atmosphere.

Using a basic two-camera set-up, Lerner edits from one tight close-up to another. Very occasionally one of the cameras pulls out sufficiently to allow us a glimpse of Mike Bloomfield playing lead guitar. One of the Irish-American singing group The Clancy Brothers, Liam, was there:

'I was actually filming at the Newport Festival that year. I was up a twelve-foot platform, filming with a telephoto lens, so I could zoom in close. And Dylan came out and it was obvious that he was stoned, bobbing around the stage, very Chaplinesque really.'

When 'Maggie's Farm' finishes, the soundtrack mixes in the barrage of booing that greeted Dylan's first live experiment with his brand of electric 'mathematical music'. The film then cuts to Dylan standing at the microphone with an acoustic guitar. He starts strumming the chords of 'Mister Tambourine Man' and then realises that he hasn't got the correct harmonica.

'Does anybody? Has anybody got a harmonica? An "E" harmonica? Anybody? Just throw them all up.'

At this request, a hail of harmonicas is hurled at the stage, a missile barrage that quite possibly frightened Dylan more than the booing! Dylan fits one into his harmonica holder and goes into the song, of which we're sadly only treated to a fragment.

As well as these three numbers Lerner also shows fragments of the Sunday afternoon soundcheck interspersed with comments from the elderly ladies. Dylan, resplendent in his polka dot shirt, jams on the organ with Sam Lay or Jerome Arnold, while Joe Boyd and others scuttle round trying to get the sound balanced.

Festival is a delight to watch, the artists performing in it are uniformly good, the atmosphere, until 'Maggie's Farm' anyway, relaxed and intimate. It's a perfect document of Dylan on the cusp of a change that will rock the world of music. The film's use of dialogue from artists and crowd as punctuation make it a refreshing encounter between movies and music. The film was recently re-released in America (1998), and will hopefully be shown in Europe soon.

Take Two – 'A Friend Of Us All'

In the summer of 1971 the music press was abuzz with talk of an unusual concert that was scheduled to take place in New York's Madison Square Gardens that August. Former Beatle, George Harrison, was putting together a benefit concert for Bangladesh, a country torn apart by war and famine. He'd been asked to do this by his sitar teacher Ravi Shankar. In retrospect, what Harrison did in calling on his musical friends to play the benefit with him, was create the template for Live Aid and all other such subsequent charity

Advertising block for the film of the concert for Bangla Desh

The Greatest Concert
Of The Decade'
NOW YOU CAN SEE IT
AND HEAR IT...
AS IF YOU WERE THERE!

THE
CONCERT FOR BANGLADESH
U

apple presents
THE CONCERT FOR BANGLADESH
ERIC CLAPTON · BOB DYLAN · GEORGE HARRISON · BILLY PRESTON
LEON RUSSELL · RAVI SHANKAR · RINGO STARR · KLAUS VOORMANN
BADFINGER · PETE HAM · TOM EVANS · JOEY MOLLAND
MIKE GIBBONS · ALLAN BEUTLER · JESSE ED DAVIS · CHUCK FINDLEY
MARLIN GREENE · JEANIE GREENE · JO GREEN · DOLORES HALL
JIM HORN · KAMALA CHAKRAVARTY · JACKIE KELSO · JIM KELTNER
USTED ALIAKBAR KHAN · CLAUDIA LENNEAR · LOU McCREARY
OLLIE MITCHELL · DON NIX · DON PRESTON · CARL RADLE · ALLA RAKAH
Directed by Saul Swimmer · Produced by George Harrison and Allen Klein
Music Recording Produced by George Harrison and Phil Spector

Technicolor*
apple / 20th century-fox release

concerts. Much of the press speculation about the gig centred around two rumours – firstly that the Beatles might reform for a one-off appearance, and secondly, that Bob Dylan might emerge from his self-imposed exile and perform there.

Both the afternoon and evening shows were recorded by the legendary Phil Spector for release as an LP, and a film of the event was directed by Saul Swimmer.

Instead of a Beatles' reunion, the audience got Harrison, Ringo Starr, Leon Russell, Eric Clapton and Billy Preston. Ravi Shankar also performed, as did, much to everyone's surprise, Bob Dylan.

'Right up to the moment he stepped on stage I wasn't sure if he was going to come,' Harrison recalls of Bob's appearance. 'So it was kind of nerve-racking. I had a little list on my guitar and I had a point after 'Here Comes The Sun' – it just said 'Bob' with a question mark. So it got to that point, I turned around to see if Bob was there, if he was going to come on. Because the night before when we went to Madison Square Garden [to soundcheck] he just freaked out, he saw all these cameras and microphones and this huge place. He was saying, "Hey man, this isn't my scene. I can't make this"... So on stage I just looked around to see if there was any indication if Bob was going to come on or not, and he was all ready. He was so nervous, he had his harmonica on and his guitar in his hand, and he was walking right on stage, like it was now or never.'

Harrison announced him simply:

'Here's a friend of us all... Bob Dylan!'

To ecstatic audience applause Dylan ambled on stage wearing a denim jacket and khaki chinos. If he was nervous he didn't look it as he moved straight into 'Hard Rain', accompanied by Harrison on bottle-neck, Leon Russell on bass and Ringo on tambourine.

The film is very simply shot. Harrison was aware of how disturbing it could be to the atmosphere of a show if the stage was swarming with a film crew, so he directed Swimmer to keep the filming as low-key as possible. The lighting too was unobtrusive, mostly based around a single spotlight on Dylan that occasionally filled out to illuminate the other people on stage.

Employing little more than a two-camera set-up somewhere in the balcony, and one camera closer to the stage, the results are somewhat reminiscent of Dylan's style of direction during the concert sequences of *Renaldo and Clara*. The camera, generally speaking, concentrates on Dylan, occasionally making use of a slow, gentle zoom to open up the image. About two-thirds of the way through the opening number the film cuts to a very tight close-up filmed from the side at a slightly lower level. This will remain the basic camera work throughout Dylan's set. Unsubstantiated reports were published in the underground press at the time of this film's release that Dylan had demanded final say in the editing of his sequences. If this is true, it sheds a new and interesting light on Dylan's concepts of how he should be presented on screen, taken to its logical extension in *Renaldo and Clara*. This style of representation works by filling the screen with an enormous close-up of the performer. The lack of any other visual input or movement concentrates the mind of the viewer on the lyrics of the song. Nothing else is allowed to intrude. Its impact is undeniably effective. Former Buzzock's manager Richard Boon reports that at the film's screening in Sheffield, people rushed to the front of the cinema to look more closely at Dylan – to be engulfed by Dylan and subsumed into his music, as it were.

During the second number, 'It Takes A Lot To Laugh', Harrison fills in around Dylan's harmonica breaks with some nice guitar licks, as Leon Russell plays gently away in the background. The close-ups get tighter and tighter until Dylan's face fills the entire screen.

To another round of ecstatic applause Dylan goes into 'Blowin' In The Wind'. His vocals, which were criticised at the time as being too thin and reedy, sound remarkably versatile and melodic, Dylan adopting a lilting modulation that breaks a single note of the melody into three or four. It's almost a return to his pre-Nashville voice.

Commented Phil Spector, 'When he broke into "Blowin' In The Wind", it was a great surprise. We didn't expect him to do it... [At the meeting with Harrison] George said to Bob, "Do you think you could sing... 'Blowin' In The Wind' – the audience would just love it" ... And Bob looked at him and said: "You interested in 'Blowin' In The Wind'?... Are you gonna sing 'I Wanna Hold Your Hand'?"'

After fumbling around in the breast pocket of his denim jacket for a capo, Dylan starts strumming the intro to 'Just Like A Woman'. Harrison and Russell harmonise with Dylan on the choruses drawing applause from the audience each time. The whole thing sounds relaxed, more like a bunch of friends jamming together than a group of superstars in front of an audience of thousands.

At the close of the number the film fades to black before cutting to a rapturous audience.

The Concert for Bangladesh is currently available on video.

As a short aside, one of the most amusing sequences in the movie takes place during Ravi Shankar's set. The New York rock'n'roll audience enthusiastically applaud the first thing they hear him doing on his sitar. Drolly looking up from where he's sat on the floor of the stage he says:

'Thank you. If you applaud the tuning so much, I hope you will enjoy the playing more.'

Take Three – Fare Thee Well

Dylan's next guest role in a movie came at the end of the *Rolling Thunder Revue*, just before he began work on editing *Renaldo and Clara*. His old backing group from the Sixties, subsequently successful in their own right, The Band, had decided to call it a day after sixteen years on the road and were holding a farewell concert in San Francisco. Though The [mostly Canadian] Band would be forever associated with Woodstock in upstate New York, and more specifically the house they rented there, 'Big Pink,' in which they recorded the legendary *Basement Tapes* with Dylan, they had moved to the West Coast in 1972 and now resided in a house-cum-studio on Malibu Beach, which they named 'Shangri-La'.

The event was christened 'The Last Waltz' and was to be put on at the Winterland Ballroom by legendary concert promoter Bill Graham and filmed, for a concert movie of the same name, by one of Band guitarist Robbie Robertson's closest friends, the celebrated movie director, Martin Scorsese.

While Scorsese – best known for bleak dramas like his auteur debut, the critically revered Italian-American low-life tragedy, *Mean Streets*, which made stars of the young Robert De Niro and Harvey Keitel, and the highly charged, nihilistic and extremely violent Vietnam-vet picture, *Taxi Driver* (written by Paul Schrader, who went on to make one of Dylan's favourite movies, *Mishima*) – may have seemed an odd choice for a music movie; he had earlier worked as an editor on Michael Wadleigh's *Woodstock* and Warner Brothers' *Medicine Ball Caravan* (directed by Francois Reichenbach, 1971). Also, one of the defining characteristics of *Mean Streets* was its stunning use of a contemporary Rock soundtrack.

Scorsese had first met Robertson at Woodstock back in 1969 – The Band had performed, though they did not feature in the movie – and had immediately hit it off. It was this friendship, and some would also say Robertson's desire to become a bona fide movie star, an ambition he may have felt could be fulfilled through an association with the acclaimed film maker, that led to Scorsese being invited to direct *The Last Waltz*.

Take Four – 'For Thine Is The Wigdom!'

With Scorsese at the helm, it was obvious that *The Last Waltz* would not be a run-of-the-mill concert flick, cobbled hastily together to make a fast buck. Scorsese already had a firm grasp of the politics and etiquette of Rock. He was, in other words, 'hip to the gig'. He was also a radically different director than, say, Pennebaker or Swimmer, in that he was concerned with the aesthetics of film and, as a former professor of film studies, had a deep understanding and appreciation of film history. *The Last Waltz* would not be a 'cinema-verite' presentation, where the 'truth' emerged with minimal control and editing.It would be both a'production' and a

celebration, utilising juxtaposition and montage as the framing devices for telling both the story of the concert, and the story of the long musical road that had led The Band to the Winterland on that valedictory night.

With six weeks to go before the concert, Scorsese, in conjunction with Robertson, set about planning his movie. First, he hired ace cinematographer Michael Chapman. Next, in direct contrast to Dylan's more improvisational approach to concert filming, he sat down and wrote a three-hundred page shooting script that keyed in every single camera shot to synchronise with the lyrics and chord changes in the thirty-seven songs to be performed on the night. Scorsese was determined to do his best for the movie in all possible ways, visually and aurally – and it was the first music film to be recorded on a 24-track sound system.

Meanwhile, Bill Graham was taking equal pains to ensure that the live concert audience would experience a night to remember. To make the Winterland look even more opulent he hired the set of *La Traviata* from the San Francisco Opera Company. In keeping with Thanksgiving Night, he also arranged for every single member of the 5,000 audience to be fed on turkey and salmon, while being serenaded – before The Band came on to play – by the Berkeley Promenade Orchestra performing a selection of waltzes. Ironically, much of the evening's tension would come from conflict between the Graham and Scorsese camps, as Graham tried to ensure the film crew didn't spoil the show for the live audience, while Scorsese insisted the movie should take precedence.

By the evening of 25th November, all Graham's preparations were in place and Scorsese had assembled his forty-five man film crew, and set up his seven camera locations inside the ballroom. Everything was ready for the show to go ahead.

Aside from Dylan, the guests performing that evening with The Band included: Joni Mitchell, Eric Clapton, Dr John, Ronnie Hawkins, Van Morrison and Paul Butterfield. Scorsese also later shot studio footage of Emmylou Harris and The Staples Singers, which he cut into the finished film. The latter's version of The Band classic, *The Weight*, forever associated with Dylan and the Big Pink, is not only one of the movie's high points, but also one of the most powerful performances of a rock song ever committed to celluloid.

Take Five – Lord, Be The Fire Next Time

Dylan was the final guest star of the evening and the film shows us his set from mid-way through. It starts with a black screen and the camera panning down to reveal Dylan in a polka dot shirt and a large white pimp-style hat. He begins by leading The Band into a slow, stately version of 'Forever Young', Dylan's song for his son Jakob. The camera work and angles reflect the sombre mood of the delivery. Indeed Barney Hoskyns points out how, during the tentative opening chords, 'the camera pans down dramatically onto Dylan's head as though consecrating him.'

In fact Dylan's appearance on stage represented the first point at which Robbie Robertson was supplanted from centre spot of Scorsese's camera – up till this point, regardless of who shared the stage with The Band, or who was actually singing, Robertson generally remained in focus at the heart of the lens. During Dylan's set, shots tend towards medium close-ups, pulling out occasionally to reveal the interaction between Dylan and Robertson during the guitar breaks. But, even when Robertson goes into another blistering guitar solo, Scorsese's camera, in the main, keeps its gaze fixed resolutely on Dylan. It is as if Dylan's overriding charisma has suddenly transfixed a director who, up till this point, was clearly in love with the image of the lead guitarist.

As the song comes to an end, there is a remarkably dramatic shot that hints at some of the behind-the-scenes tension of the evening. The camera is on Band drummer and vocalist, Levon Helm who stares hard at Dylan watching his every move, looking for clues as to when they'll switch into the next number. Without pause, Dylan goes straight into a reprise of 'Baby Let Me Follow You Down' – the unfilmed song he'd opened his set with – exploding the reverent atmosphere with a series of raucous power chord riffs. It's a deliberate harking back to the heady days of the 1966 tour when he and The Hawks, as The Band were then known, faced hostile audiences around the world with their electric performances. The delivery here is good, raucous fun, with Dylan grinning and mugging for the cameras, shot in an extremely tight and professional manner.

At the close of the song, all the guests troop back on stage to surround Dylan and The Band for the final number, 'I Shall Be Released'. Individual shots of Ronnie Wood and Ringo Starr are cut into the film as Dylan, accompanied by the star-studded ensemble, sings the first verse of the song. Van Morrison and Robbie Robertson join Dylan on the choruses, and Richard Manuel takes the second verse. Dylan finishes up the number as back tracking shots reveal some of the scope and magnitude of the affair.

The film ends with Robertson telling Scorsese about The Band's reasons for calling it a day as we cut to shots of Dylan and the cast leaving the stage to triumphant applause. Then *The Last Waltz* segues into one final Band instrumental – shot in the studio.

When the time came to edit the movie, Robbie Robertson was living at Scorsese's Mullholland Drive house – growing ever more keen to carve out a career in pictures. With both men separated from their wives and families, they embarked on a six-month bender of drugs and booze, watching movies on Scorsese's projector throughout the night and sleeping intermittently in the day. Somehow, in the middle of all this madness, they managed to supervise the movie's completion.

'[Scorsese and Robertson] would call the editor of *The Last Waltz*, Yeu-Bun Yee, in the middle of the night with ideas,' Jonathan Taplin, the movie's producer recalled. 'They were so stoked up they thought everyone else was up all night too.'

Still, whatever the conditions under which the editing took place, the end result is a truly remarkable movie– one that has stood the test of time far better than most celluloid rock hagiographies. The *Village Voice's* reviewer Terry Curtis Fox, was bowled over by the film's scope and impact, but also made it clear who the real star was:

'While ostensibly… about The Band, Scorsese's editing makes no bones about how much a Dylan event it became… Everything else disappears behind his presence. Scorsese… does nothing to hide or minimise this effect. It is not merely the best rock-concert movie ever made; it is as intensely personal as anything Scorsese has ever done.'*

Curtis Fox's comments become even more interesting when we learn that the film itself nearly wasn't made and that Dylan's

---

*Still, Scorsese himself certainly did not consider the movie a high point.

'It hit me finally, when I was watching the end credits crawl of The Last Waltz *at the Cinerama Dome, that I didn't enjoy it anymore,' he confessed to journalist Peter Biskind in 1996. 'There was nothing left. I knew why I broke up the second marriage – I had a child, I knew I was not going to see the child for a while – but I always had a bottom line: the work, and felt good about being able to say something in a movie, but this one day, it was like rock bottom. I thought, I've lost my voice.'*

involvement was even more precarious. Warner Brothers only agreed to put money into it when they heard that Dylan was going to be appearing. However, as show night approached, Dylan became increasingly reluctant to allow his section to be filmed. Howard Alk, who was editing *Renaldo and Clara* with Dylan, kept telling him that it would detract from the value of their movie. Even when the gig started, Dylan still hadn't made up his mind if he was going to allow Scorsese to film him.

'With Dylan's Socratic way of existing, he claimed he knew nothing about the show being filmed,' Dylan's tour publicist Paul Wasserman recalled. 'That was not exactly a Pentagon-Chernobyl secret. He *knew* there was a movie. I had discussed it with him... He *knew*. He was told there would be a movie...'

During the intermission Robbie Robertson and David Braun, Dylan's attorney, came to see Bill Graham, and told him that Dylan had changed his mind and wasn't going to appear in the film. Aware that Warner Brothers had only agreed to fund the movie on the understanding that Dylan would be in it, Graham and others pleaded with the recalcitrant musician.

Finally, about five minutes before he was due on stage, Dylan reluctantly gave permission for two numbers to be shot. But, as Graham walked towards the stage to introduce him, Dylan apparently changed his mind again and one of his entourage, Lou Kemp, was stationed at the side of the stage to make sure none of the cameras were rolling.

'We had to turn the cameras away from Bob to prove that we weren't secretly filming him,' Taplin later explained, 'and the guys had to get down from all their stands for the first two numbers...'

Bill Graham thought, 'Oh fuck it!' and ordered the crew to be on stand-by. 'Let's just shoot,' he told them, 'I'll *make* it happen.'

' ...Lou Kemp was standing right there stage left next to Bill Graham,' Taplin continued, 'Near the end of the second song, we said, "Okay. Everybody get ready. Put your headphones back on." He went into the third song and we started filming. And it was going great. He went into his fourth song and that was going great too...'

Dylan, as fox-like as ever, seemed to be completely aware that he was being filmed, and immediately reprised the first song he'd performed again. Taplin and Graham shouted at the film crew to keep rolling. Lou Kemp threw a fit and tried to get the cameramen to stop.

'Bill Graham grabbed Lou Kemp,' Taplin recalled, 'and said, "You *don't* stop! You motherfucker, get off the stage. *Don't* stop!"

'I stuck my finger in his face and I said, *"Back off*. You roll that fucking camera. Just *roll"*' Graham explained in his autobiography. 'I went to the other side of the stage and yelled the same thing at the top of my voice.'

Not surprisingly, Kemp backed off and let the crew film.

'Of course, it turned out that this was what Bob wanted,' Taplin reflected. 'For us to keep going to get that one because he thought it was his best tune.'

In fact Scorsese later claimed that Dylan's people had always kept to the promise that he could shoot two songs and that some kind of signal – though nature unspecified – would be given him to indicate which two.

'[From the beginning] Bill Graham was next to me shouting, "Shoot him! He comes from the same streets as you, don't let him push you around."' Scorsese told Barney Hoskyns, 'But I didn't want to press it.'

Still, somehow it seemed Scorsese got his cues right and filmed the correct two numbers (plus the bonus reprise of 'Baby Let Me Follow You Down'). Scorsese's account makes sense, as it was only during the filming of the unscheduled reprise that Kemp tried to stop the filming. The final word however, should go to Robbie Robertson.

'For some reason, in my mind,' the Band guitarist later reflected, 'I never thought we were *not* going to shoot Bob. I thought, "Oh, we'll go through all this bullshit and in the end, we'll shoot it." I knew the game very well. Thank God for Bill Graham. In the end it *was* shot. And it looked staggering. He looked amazing in the film, Bobby Dylan. Almost like a Christ figure. A Christ in a white hat. I mean, what *more* could you ask for?'

Take Six – Mama, Take This Video Offa Me

Before looking at Dylan's forays into the world of 'Rock-Video', I'd like to attempt a definition of the term. Way back in the good old days there were 'promo-films' (see Reel One). With the arrival of affordable domestic video recorders and the rise of MTV throughout the 1980s, the promo-film mutated into what has become known as 'the Rock video'.

It's become a generally perceived truism, certainly up until lately, that for an act to break big, particularly in America, they need exposure on MTV or VH1, through the medium of specially produced video-promos. If not Dylan, then certainly his record company, Sony Columbia, became increasingly aware of this, and over the years have tried to get a hit video out of him. That they and Dylan have met with so little success isn't necessarily Dylan's fault. For an artist who's so aware of the visual arts, and who, albeit with mixed results, has pursued film enterprises, his relationship with the electronic media has been singularly disappointing.

Dylan has spoken about trying to come to terms with the new format:

'I'm not quite sure I know what a video is except that the market for video is new, but the form has always been there. Yeah, [they view] "Subterranean Homesick Blues" as a video. I don't know if it was a video. We didn't think of it as a video at the time, we just needed a piece of film to go at the beginning of a movie...I really haven't found anybody that really thinks a certain way that needs to be [done], like the German film-makers, the English film-makers. In the States there aren't people like that. They just don't exist...I visualised "Neighbourhood Bully"... there were certain segments which I just wrote down one night which I though would look really great on film and it would look like a Fassbinder movie...'

Take Seven – Through A TV lens Darkly

Once upon a time Bob Dylan appeared to trust only two people: himself and Albert Grossman. How strange it is that in the 1980s when confronted by the relatively new phenomenon of MTV and Rock videos, he allowed himself to be put into the hands of a variety of el quicko TV wunderkind, fellow rock stars and a succession of sycophants.

Arguably this lack of televisual success is mirrored by an uneasiness of direction in his songwriting. 1983's 'Sweetheart Like You' doesn't remotely approach the splendour and stature of his earlier output. Nor do songs like 'When the Night Comes Falling From The Sky' or 1985's double bill, 'Emotionally Yours' or 'Tight Connection To My Heart', match up visually or musically with what one had come to expect from Dylan.

The whole sorry saga of Dylan and video is perhaps best summed up by the one produced for the song, 'Unbelievable'.

'Unbelievable' was directed by one Paris Barclay, and was shot in the Mojave Desert. Its washed out colours and 'teen ambience' make this video look more like an advert for jeans than a Bob Dylan video, but by 1990 Dylan was probably desperate.

The video opens as a thoughtful looking youth in jeans and a T-shirt leaves his house and jumps into an open topped car. As he drives along he passes a large, black limousine that is being driven by Dylan in full chauffeur's uniform. As if that isn't unusual enough, Dylan's passenger in the back seat is a large pig with a ring through its nose.

Next we see a lot of people's legs and the pig being taken for a walk on a leash, while Dylan sits on a car bonnet playing his guitar. The young guy goes into a diner where he meets Molly Ringwald, the iconic teen queen veteran of John Hughes' 80s 'Bratpack' movies like *The Breakfast Club* and *Pretty in Pink*. A friendly black, short-order chef smiles happily at the couple as they make friends.

Suddenly the peaceful calm is shattered by the arrival of three juvenile delinquents who waste no time at all in beating up the young guy. He's saved by Molly and the short-order chef and he and Molly escape, and jump into his car. They drive off through the desert followed by Dylan and the pig. They stop and the laughing Molly runs off into the desert. After a harmonica solo they book into a sleazy motel run by Dylan's long-time girlfriend, Sally Kirkland (whose acting career began as a member of Andy Warhol's Factory stable) along with another of Dylan's muses, Edie Sedgewick (see Appendix Three).

Molly and the youth go to bed together, but fortunately aren't joined by Dylan and the pig. While he sleeps, Molly steals his belt and wallet. The kid wakes up just in time to see her drive away. Sally Kirkland looks lustfully at him. He hitches a ride and who should stop but Dylan (couldn't see the pig, but I bet it was there somewhere). Dylan has the kid's belt and wallet. They laugh. The car drives away and we see the number-plate – 'LSD'.

Unbelievable, eh?

So why did he place himself in the hands of such disparate people who could produce rubbish like this? Dylan himself said in a 1985 interview, 'Videos are out of character for me ...' This is reasonable enough to see and understand. When he has ventured into the world of moving images it has always been on a far vaster scale than the short burst of digitised images presented in the video format.

If Dylan felt out of touch with the world of video and was under pressure from his record company to 'produce the goods' then would it be natural for him to turn to other people for assistance? In the grand scheme of things – no, but during this period we're dealing with a Dylan emerging from the consequences of the total upheaval of his life over the previous decade, a Dylan now approaching middle age, no longer a young lion and not yet a venerable 'old man' of music. Perhaps this is a Dylan suffering from the pangs of self-doubt, for the first time in his life unsure of how to handle a new medium? So, reluctantly, he turns to others for help.

For his first proper foray into the promo-video world he chose a professional director, Mark Robinson. Unfortunately Robinson falls into the usual trap we've come to associate with Dylan and video, that of what Michael Gray has termed 'overinterpretation'.

Shot in LA by Mark Robinson featuring an elderly cleaning lady who was mistakenly thought by many fans to be Dylan's mother, Beattie.

'We were ... about to do a simple club scene where one woman's face was every woman's face,' Robinson explained, 'and we had thirty extras ... lined up ready to shoot. But while we were setting up the club with upturned chairs on table tops, there was someone sweeping up the cigarette butts... I went to Bob and suggested we take an old lady and have her sweeping up, with it all coming from her point of view.'

The fairly gentle mood of the song is reflected in the relaxed style of the video. What spoils it though is Dylan's obvious unease at lip-synching the vocal track and the occasional cut-aways to the elderly cleaning woman who Dylan is supposed to be aiming the song at. Still, it's better than Robinson's original concept.

Even when working with seemingly sympathetic partners, Dylan's videos have been mired down in a bog of cliché and overkill. Take for instance his collaboration with Scorcese screenwriter and director in his own right, Paul Schrader. Dylan had been highly enthusiastic about Schrader's film biopic of the life of right-wing Japanese poet Mishima. So Dylan thought that Schrader might be just the person to translate his vision into video form and after a series of meetings commissioned him to direct a video for the song 'Tight Connection To My Heart'. The two of them flew to Tokyo and it was downhill from there. Dylan was extremely uncommunicative during the shooting, leading Schrader to comment that the video was 'a little piece of eye candy I shot in Tokyo. It means as little as it looks it means.'

It really is a tragedy that the video fails to live up to the promise of these two talented artists. In washed-out colour, it flips through a series of stock American abroad spy-school cinema shots, occasionally bordering on the pretentious, but more often than not on ineptitude masquerading as inability.

After the Robinson debacle, next Dylan employed the services of fellow rock star Dave Stewart as executive producer and, though more successful than the Schrader collaboration, the Stewart-produced videos for 'When the Night Comes Falling From The Sky' and 'Emotionally Yours' still fall well short of the expectations of his fanbase.

Visualised as episodic and designed to be shown consecutively on TV, the two numbers were handed over to the video director team of Markus Innocenti and Eddie Arno.

'We were simply told by Dave Stewart that black and white were required,' the directors explained. 'We weren't told why. In fact we wished that Dylan had talked directly to us earlier because we learned that Dylan wanted it to look like an old Japanese movie.' – like Paul Schrader's *Mishima* in fact!

Shot in a church in Sunset Boulevard in Los Angeles, the 'When the Night...' video featured a performance of the song by Dylan and his band that is actually quite well shot but marred by a series of negative flashes that are randomly placed throughout. Whether this is supposed to suggest nuclear blasts or is simply a cheap gimmick, the overall effect adds nothing to what is a quite reasonable scene.

Tacked onto the beginning of the video is an effective hand-held sequence shot on a bus and featuring Dylan and the band on their way to the gig. Quite unnecessary though is the sudden appearance in the crowd at the gig of actress Jill Hollier playing the part of Dylan's estranged girlfriend. While one can see what Dylan is suggesting in a narrative sense it now looks like a superfluous intrusion. His performance and exuberance throughout the video was enough.

However, we have to bear in mind that the girl represents some form of continuous reality within Dylan's mythologising and that she is also central to the video 'Emotionally Yours' that was made the next day, shot in black and white. An overhead spot illuminates a simple take of Dylan sat on a stool gently playing his guitar. The overall effect is moody and atmospheric, fitting the feel of the song. The use of subtle editing and straightforward camera angles add nicely to the video. Then the whole thing is ruined by a series of flashback shots, the kind of thing that has been sent up countless times in satirical movies like *Hot Shots, Part Deux* and *Naked Gun*. In slow motion the 'Buckskin Girl', as she's called in the shooting script, swings from a tree, runs down a street and appears to be rotating on a cake stand while cut-away shots show Dylan looking moody and introspective.

I mentioned earlier that both videos were supposed to run consecutively, but the programmers at MTV couldn't, or wouldn't, see why that was necessary. As a result they were shown weeks apart, losing any impact they might have had as an episodic sequence. Once again, Dylan and video just didn't work out.

Happily, Dylan and Stewart have also collaborated on what, to me, was the highly successful 1993 video 'Blood In My Eyes'. Here, former Eurythmic, Dave Stewart, has finally discovered the essential missing component for getting Dylan across to the people, and it works brilliantly. Its success is maybe due to the choice of song, or the location, London's Camden Town. Certainly, everything comes together in this masterful video, shot plainly in black and white on a mainly hand-held camera. There are no contrived story-lines imposing their narrative yokes on the video, just a sequence of simple shots of Dylan walking around Camden interacting with ordinary members of the public, with the occasional bit of lip-synching as he intones the song's chorus.

The essentially plain presentation of Dylan comes across superbly, simply because he has such an enormous presence. In cinematic terms it has been remarked on since the days of *Dont Look Back*, and this video, in a strange way, has strong echoes of Pennebaker's original documentary, the top-hatted character loping through the streets of London in Stewart's video is, after all, the same one, only older now.

If Surrealism is, as Andre Breton stated in *The Surrealist Manifesto*, the chance meeting of a sewing machine and an umbrella on a dissection table, then seeing Bob Dylan in a top hat walking through Camden must rank pretty close. The unbelieving stares of tourists and inhabitants bear witness to his alien-like appearance. Even though it's shot in real time, the atmosphere is one of slow motion, the almost grainy monochrome footage paying homage to the sinister hyper-reality of Luis Bunuel's *Un Chien Andolou* or Rene Claire's *L'Entracte*.

To my mind, the most successful of Dylan's video promos is 'A Series of Dreams' (1991), produced at Windmill Lane Studios in Dublin. Released to coincide with the *Bootleg Series* CD set, this brilliantly conceived and executed montage draws slightly on the 'Jokerman' video, directed by Larry Sloman and George Lois in 1984, but with the use of digital technology carrying it light years ahead of its predecessor.

Utilising footage from a bewildering variety of sources this is a whirlwind trip through decades of Dylan. Dylan pensive, Dylan playing, Dylan typing and Dylan singing, all combined together to produce a flood of images, flowing easily into one another and merging to form a complete moving portrait of the man.

Added on the top of the montage are some breathtaking morphing sequences – Bobby Neuwirth's head expanding and leaping forward like some crazed acid vision. Words leap out of the screen at the viewer, appearing and disappearing, dissolving and shattering, a swirling metamorphoses of images clutching at our senses. The whole piece is edited at a frantic pace, bringing to life the speed and fury of Dylan's creative processes.

It is an outstanding piece of work, but sadly, it came too late in Dylan's career to have much bearing on the MTV audience, whose tastes and opinions have been formed in the preceding years by an endless diet of Aerosmith, Phil Collins and Michael Jackson. For the audience and the programmers, Dylan no longer figured in the reckoning, if he ever had at all. While near-contemporaries, such as the Rolling Stones, had caught the video boat, Dylan was left forlornly on the quayside.

It was a while before Dylan made another promo video, 1997's 'Not Dark Yet', a pleasing enough, though totally unsurprising, video to promote the single from his album *Time Out Of Mind*. The song itself heralded the renaissance of Dylan, but regrettably, so slick is the packaging, the video is more suited to the style of Mick Hucknall appearing on the Des O'Connor show.

Nothing would ever surprise me about Dylan and I'm certain that one day he will amaze us by producing a video that lives up to our expectations. The promise of the music on *Time Out Of Mind* seems to lend itself perfectly to visual representation in one form or another. We would love to have had videos for *Blonde On Blonde* or *Blood On The Tracks*, but those were created in a period before the format existed. Now we'll just have to wait and see. (See Appendix One).

Take Eight – An Artist And His Friends

In 1988, Dylan agreed to return to cinema acting in Dennis Hopper's, *Flashback* (also known as, *Backtrack*). The movie was about a young woman who witnesses a gang-land killing. Jodie Foster plays the young woman and Dennis Hopper is the Hit-Man sent to kill her who gradually falls in love with his prey. It also starred Vincent Price, John Turturro and Joe Pesci.

Dylan played a typically eccentric role, that of a chainsaw artist, called, in the official credits, 'Artist'. He appears only in one scene, and is his usual bewildering self – either brilliant or completely awkward. Dylan is on screen for less than twenty seconds, the first four or five of those wearing a welder's mask so his face is obscured. When he looks up and raises the mask from his face it's to tell Dennis Hopper that he doesn't know where Jodie Foster's character is. It's as simple as that.

Dylan agreed to appear in the film as a favour to his old friend Hopper and his appearance is a perfect example of his bizarre and contradictory nature – what Michael Gray would call an example of his 'undiminished, playful waywardness.' The film itself, based on a reasonable narrative, sadly disintegrated for reasons unknown. Dennis Hopper had his name taken off the directorial credits and replaced with the Hollywood pseudonym for a film that nobody wants to be associated with, 'Alan Smithee'. In one of those strange convoluted twists of circumstance, Joe Eszterhas' latest movie to date is called *Hollywood's Burning, A Film By Alan Smithee*, the irony being that the director had his name removed and replaced with that of Alan Smithee.

Dylan was also one of the guests on BBC TV's *Arena* special on Van Morrison, broadcast in 1991. Dylan and Van Morrison were filmed singing together on a hill overlooking the Acropolis in Greece, in June 1989. The tunes and their performances are outstanding, Dylan harmonising on 'Crazy Love' and 'One Irish Rover', then contributing harmonica on 'Foreign Window'. The idyllic setting and the glorious weather, the obvious camaraderie and close musical kinship make this a formidable viewing experience, despite Dylan's occasional failure to remember Van's lyrics.

Finally, in 1997, Dylan upped his profile with the hip MTV crowd by making a guest cameo appearance in someone else's promo-video – Wyclef Jean's 'Gone Til November'.

The young rap star had been an admirer of Dylan's for years and when he realised he was on the same label as Dylan put feelers out to see if he would be willing to make a special appearance in one of his videos. Dylan agreed and appears with Wyclef, sitting on a bench at LA International Airport. A strange and yet delightful scene.

Reel Seven
Talkin' TV Blues

For approximately two thirds of this century the dominant image has been the big screen. But for the final third, beyond a doubt, television's small screen has transformed the world, and not of course always for the better.

As American comic Lord Richard Buckley so aptly put it,

'Now I know why they call television a medium – because it's very rarely well done!'

He was talking with a savvy far ahead of his time. In a sense, the way Dylan has handled television can also be perceived in the same light. Most other performers of his generation and beyond have seen television as the way forward in advancing their careers. Dylan, on the other hand, has treated it very much in the same way as we might treat something we find stuck to the bottom of our shoe.

His appearances have been limited, sparse and regulated with the kind of overseeing eye that has levelled caution, with brevity. It certainly wasn't lack of offers that kept him off the television screen. D.A. Pennebaker credits Albert Grossman for recognising Dylan's worth very early on and protecting him from the damage that inappropriate television coverage or overexposure might have brought:

'He refused to let him go on any rinky-dink TV shows, refused to let Columbia do bullshit things with him...'

Take One – Do The Right Thing

It's not the intention of this chapter to provide an exhaustive account of all of Dylan's TV appearances. Instead I'd like to dwell upon a selection of his TV highlights.

One of Albert Grossman's earliest coups, and one within keeping with his policy of 'no rinky-dink' stuff, was getting Dylan contracted to fly to England to appear in a major BBC television play, way before he'd ever appeared on American TV.

The Madhouse on Castle Street

Left to right: Bob Dylan, Maureen Pryor, James Mellor, Ursula Howells and Reg Lye

Dylan had been spotted singing in a club called Tony Pastor's Place on West 4th Street in Greenwich Village by the play's producer/director, Phillip Saville.

Saville had started his television career over on the UK's then only other channel, ITV, producing their prestigious drama series *Armchair Theatre*. The play he wanted Dylan to appear in, Evan Jones's *The Madhouse On Castle Street*, was the author's third play for the BBC. Jones also wrote film scripts for blacklisted American film director Joseph Losey who was living and working in Europe at the time, the most famous of which was the biker movie *The Leather Boys*, starring Oliver Reed.

Grossman negotiated a particularly impressive contract for his new, young client. Dylan was to be flown to London, provided with top-class hotel accommodation and paid a reasonable fee. Not bad for an artist who was virtually unheard of in the UK, and not much better known than that in his own country. Also, considering that his part in the production was fairly minor, the contract was quite a managerial coup.

Dylan duly landed in London just before Christmas 1962 and arrived at the Mayfair Hotel, but, as he wasn't comfortable there, he immediately switched to the more down-market Cumberland. (By 1964 his tastes had changed and for his subsequent trips to England he would stay at either the Mayfair or the Savoy!)

When Dylan started rehearsing for *Madhouse* it became immediately apparent to Saville that he was incapable of delivering his lines properly. Dylan accordingly begged Saville to change his part simply to that of a singer. Dylan was probably nervous, having never acted before and obviously felt more secure behind a guitar and, of course, to Dylan the point about doing the play was to get the chance of making contacts in the UK folk world on an all expenses paid trip to England.

'...Dylan played the role of a beatnik, I played his sidekick,' actor David Warner remembered. '...the first day he came into the studio nobody paid him any mind. During rehearsals he was withdrawn and shy. I'd have to say such lines as, "*Sing it buddy!*" which he'd do, marvellously. He seemed to come to life then. Everybody has something which makes him come to life – brings him into focus... I thought what a desperate angry poet he is! He's so angry he has to express his vision!'

Before shooting, Dylan spent several nights at Saville's house where he played him 'Blowin' In The Wind'. Saville immediately decided to use it over the opening credits.

Recording of the play commenced on 30th December 1962 and finished on 4th January 1963. When it was broadcast in February the 'modernist' work wasn't what one might call a resounding hit with the critics. *The Listener* bemoaned that,

'Each character seemed to take it in turn to explode any attempts to label Evan Jones's script...Bob Dylan, a young American folksinger said to have been brought over for the play, sat around playing and singing attractively, if a little incomprehensibly...'

The *Daily Express'* reviewer went even further:

'It [the play] was a confused, bitty, talk-about-nothing, irritated by Saville's abrupt flashbacks. While on the stairs, nasal-voiced young Bob Dylan – whom the BBC flew specially over from New York – provided a constant unspirited blues dialogue...'

9.0
SUNDAY-NIGHT PLAY
The Madhouse
on Castle Street
by EVAN JONES
starring
URSULA HOWELLS
MAUREEN PRYOR
with DAVID WARNER
and introducing BOB DYLAN
Produced by Philip Saville
Bobby.............................BOB DYLAN
Mrs. Griggs.............MAUREEN PRYOR
Martha Tompkins...URSULA HOWELLS
Lennie.......................DAVID WARNER
Bernard.......................JAMES MELLOR
Susan Taylor.........GEORGINA WARD
Rev. Spooner...................IAN DALLAS
Walter Tompkins.............REG LYE
Music by BOB DYLAN
Designer, John Cooper
See page 13

With typical foresight, the BBC wiped the recording of *The Madhouse On Castle Street*. The only thing to survive is a recording of Dylan's musical contribution. Critic Rory McEwen later summed up Dylan's first dramatic appearance rather succinctly in *New Society* magazine:

'When [Dylan] arrived, it was soon discovered that he did not respond to the idea of speaking anyone else's words, and he ended up making a very brief appearance in his one and only role of Bob Dylan, bard, singing, among other of his own compositions, "Blowin' In The Wind" considerably before it became a hit over here. His performance was excellent, but virtually unnoticed and he became known in the BBC as, "the most expensive screen credits in history", the credit titles being rolled over most of the shots of him playing and singing.'

Take Two – From Ed Sullivan To
The Streets Of London (Again)

On 12th May 1963 Dylan was booked to make an appearance on *The Ed Sullivan Show*, one of America's most popular TV variety shows. Exposure to a mass audience was guaranteed, an unheard of thing for an artist from the Folk genre at that time. This was the show that had presented Elvis Presley to the nation in the 1950s, and that would break the Beatles to a nationwide TV audience a few months later. For Dylan and Grossman it would be a supreme moment.

But it was never to be. Earlier in the week, Dylan had played his choice of material to Ed Sullivan and the show's producer Bob Precht. The song they agreed to let Dylan perform was his satire on the quasi-fascist political group, the John Birch Society, 'Talkin' John Birch Society Blues'. On the day of the programme, Dylan ran through the song at the dress rehearsal. Stowe Phelps, editor of CBS-TV programme practices, burst into the studio and said the song couldn't be used because it was potentially libellous. Sullivan tried to smooth things over and told Dylan he could sing any other song he wanted, but Dylan was furious at the censorship and stormed out.

The incident became a minor cause-celebre in New York. Both the *New York Times* and *New York Post* wrote articles critical of CBS's handling of the situation. Dylan himself felt angry enough to pen a letter to the Federal Communications Commission, demanding a public inquiry. In the long run, walking off the show probably raised his kudos more than if he'd done it. To the majority of left leaning Folkniks he was a hero because he'd made a stand and hadn't sold-out.

However... during the year Dylan made one other appearance on a more Folk oriented programme entitled *Freedom Songs*, on New York's educational channel, WNEW. It would be January 1964 before he set foot in a TV studio again, this time in Canada.

The Canadian Broadcasting Company (CBC) had booked Dylan for a thirty-minute special. One would assume that the normal way of going about this would be to put Dylan in front of an audience of young people and then let him sing. This is what the BBC would do a year later, but it's not the way TV director, Daryl Duke, saw things. He had a vision. A way of making the most exciting talent to have emerged in contemporary music for years look even more exciting. He would put him in a fake log cabin with a group of fake-looking roughnecks.

Dylan, in his best *Times They Are A Changin'* outfit of work shirt, jeans and boots, would wander around the cabin serenading the rough and rowdy men of the Rockies. Whilst he sang, they would play cards, smoke pipes, gaze longingly at photos of loved ones and write letters back home. And this is what he did.

Watching this footage now, with all the benefit of hindsight, one is amazed that Dylan agreed to go through with the charade. He was notoriously against this kind of thing, the falseness, the pretence and yet, here he is, playing along with it. At times it even looks as though Dylan is miming. Sound in those days was still quite primitive, and yet here is Dylan walking around, sitting down, playing continually, without the slightest drop in sound levels. No mikes are in sight and yet everything is crystal clear.

The choice of numbers, though, is perfect, the delivery assured and well carried out. He starts with 'The Times They Are A-Changin'', and moves easily into 'Talkin' World War 3 Blues', 'Lonesome Death of Hattie Carroll', 'Hard Rain', 'Girl From The North Country' and finishes evocatively with 'Restless Farewell'.

Even the dramatic appearance of a man with a hook for a hand, blowing cigarette smoke furiously, doesn't put Dylan off his stride, and the end credits roll over a nice silhouette shot of him strumming away and playing the harmonica.

After Canada, Dylan must have been wary of how producers envisaged portraying him on TV, and one suspects that he complained to Albert about how they were making him jump through hoops. Presumably his manager raised this with the directors of Dylan's next British TV appearances. The result was that these were more guarded affairs. Consequently, within a couple of months of the *Quest* show, we have Dylan in Manchester, England, refusing even to do a rehearsal for the *Hallelujah* show for ATV*.

Even so, when he appeared on BBC's *Tonight* programme, the director couldn't resist putting him in front of a twee, 'folksy' backdrop, trees, a farm house and leading with a wonderfully 'plummy' introduction by Cliff Michelmore.

Take Three – What Johnny Hamp Missed

Before moving on to Dylan's BBC TV specials from June 1965, a quick mention of the *Les Crane Show* on WABC-TV, which was broadcast live in February 1965. Dylan performed two numbers, 'It's All Over Now, Baby Blue' and 'It's Alright Ma, I'm Only Bleeding', on which he was backed by Bruce Langhorne on electric guitar.

This show is of even much greater interest because instead of slipping quietly into the background after each number, Dylan is part of the chat show host's contingent of guests on the couch for the evening. The dialogue and repartee that Dylan engages in present a wonderful new side to his character – witty and sophisticated, sure, but charming and engaging too.

'I saw the *Les Crane Show* and will never forget it,' Peter Stone Brown, musician and writer, enthused. 'Aside from it being Dylan's first and only late-night talk show appearance [not counting the Steve Allen afternoon show], it was a preview of what was to come. Not only was Dylan backed by Langhorne playing a Martin with a pick-up, starting off with the obviously rock and roll-influenced, 'Baby Blue', but he had dramatically changed his appearance too. Gone were the suede jacket and blue-jeans [his standard performing uniform] I'd seen him wear at the Philharmonic Hall only a few

---

*See Like The Night, *by this author, for the complete story.*

months before. He was wearing a suit, perhaps the very suit from the cover of *Bringing It All Back Home*, or perhaps the clothes he recorded that album in [judging by Daniel Kramer's photographs of the sessions], complete with snap-tab collar. I remember my brother saying that night before we went to sleep, "He'll make a great rock and roll star."

'But the thing was, he was hysterically funny! *"I'm digging the yellow of the carpet, Les." "Well I'll tell ya, Les – I buy a lot of ashtrays."* It was the real deal, but not the old folk Bob Dylan. This was the about to be rock and roll Bob Dylan – a once-in-a-lifetime occurrence.'

At the end of his 1965 British tour, Dylan was booked by the BBC to make two thirty-five-minute programmes. After a short bout of illness had caused the shows to be cancelled, Dylan went into the studio on June 1st even though he was still quite sick. The shows were to be screened on 12th and 24th June.

Once again, the BBC have wiped the tapes for these programmes. (Upon hearing recently that they have also managed to wipe all their live coverage of the 1969 moon landing, I find myself wondering if they ever keep any material at all?) Audiotapes and contemporary reports exist, however, so we can rebuild an approximation of the recording.

Tito Burns said at the time, 'there is a possibility that British artists may guest on one or both the shows.'

This didn't come to pass though there is a press report that Dylan had asked singer, Paul Jones from the group Manfred Mann to act as

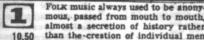

1 10.50 FOLK music always used to be anonymous, passed from mouth to mouth, almost a secretion of history rather than the creation of individual men and women. But mass media—records, radio, TV—have changed the process. Singers like Woody Guthrie and Ewan MacColl are two examples of folk artists who have composed their own material.

Another of this new breed of folk singers and writers is Bob Dylan, who can be heard and seen tonight in the first of two programmes he recorded while in London recently. Dylan has fused two separate strands of American folk-music—Negro blues and white country music—and made this the vehicle for his own blend of vivid imagery and social comment.

Bob Dylan grew up in Hibbing, Minnesota, but at ten he ran away—the first of several similar jaunts—to Chicago, where he bought a guitar. By the time he was fifteen he could also play the piano, autoharp, and harmonica, and had written his first song. Then off he went rambling his way through New Mexico, Kansas, South Dakota, and California. Soon afterwards, in the spring of 1962, he began taking New York's Greenwich Village by storm.

Today Bob Dylan is probably the most adulated of all folk singers, for the boom in folk music has put his records in the Top Twenty.

RADIO TIMES, JUNE 1965

compere. Moves were also made to book Martin Carthy and John Mayall's Bluesbreakers, but either all of them had prior commitments, or the BBC fought shy of spending any more money, so Dylan had little choice, sick as he was, but to go it alone.

The original producer, Stewart Morris, was replaced by Yvonne Littlewood, and she was put in charge of presentation, perhaps because Littlewood was a friend of Tito Burns? On the day of recording, Dylan ran through a number of tunes, but avoided the rigours of a full dress rehearsal.

Phil May of The Pretty Things was in the studio:

'We were there all afternoon watching him rehearse and he never sings a song the same way twice,' May recalled. 'It was a complete joy to hear him do 'Boots Of Spanish Leather' three or four times, and the nearest he got to doing it the same way as on his LP was at the actual taping... We didn't stay long because he didn't look very well, and we could see the strain on him.'

Dylan appeared on the studio floor around 8 o'clock dressed in his standard black leather jacket that he'd worn throughout his UK tour. Penny Valentine, a journalist for the now defunct *Disc Weekly* commented on how pale and thin Dylan looked, no doubt a result of his illness. The studio audience applauded his entrance and he wandered over to a bright red leather-topped stool and began tuning up. Overhead, for some inexplicable reason, five monitors showed an image of a girl on a beach. Dylan paused for a moment and called Bobby Neuwirth over.

'Hey, wait a minute. I can't see those cue cards ... I've got bad eyes,' Dylan joked to Neuwirth who brought them up closer to the stool. But the studio lights had affected his strings again and Dylan had to re-tune once more. When Neuwirth remarked that the guitar sounded fine to him, Dylan looked up and grinned, 'Well it doesn't to me. I've got bad ears too.' The banter was enough to break the ice with the audience and Penny Valentine noted, 'Some sort of magic seems suddenly to have hit the entire proceedings with Dylan's grin and joke. We all laugh.' Penny Valentine also reported that Dylan rehearsed an acoustic version of 'Maggie's Farm', but later dropped it.

Throughout the two shows, artist Felix Topolsky sat sketching

Dylan. However, members of the audience and crew who were hoping to pick up a drawing were disappointed at the end when Topolsky stashed them all away in his bag! In the mid-1980s they were apparently being sold at auction for over £300.

The performances themselves were a bit perfunctory, but considering Dylan's state of health at the time this was hardly surprising. Also, the numbers were very much those that he'd just played on the tour.

In terms of presentation, a little bit of camera gimmickry was used during 'Mr Tambourine Man' when Dylan's fingers were merged with the image of a fairground spinning wheel but essentially the producer let the songs come to life through Dylan's performance alone. No lumberjacks in checked-shirts here.

At the end of the session Dylan crouched down by a monitor and watched the final credits roll. He then thanked everybody including the audience and went home.

'I thought his voice sounded perfect,' Phil May reflected. 'The way he picks out one person in the audience to aim the verse at, and then times that verse for them, knocked us out... At one part I thought, if he knocks the mike with that harness once more it'll be the end. There was such an atmosphere of perfection that one more tiny mistake and you could feel the thing might collapse and he'd stop and never start again.'

Take Four – The Man In Black

Before moving on to what I consider Dylan's second major TV event of the 1960s, his appearance on the Johnny Cash special, it's worth mentioning a non-musical, but still highly entertaining piece of material that was televised in 1965.

San Franciscan educational channel KQED taped an entire Dylan press conference which was broadcast on December 3rd 1965. It has since been repeated several times in the Bay Area over the years.

This is vintage Dylan at his cocky best. Wearing a Mod-suit and chain smoking, he sits grinning like a Cheshire cat parrying questions from the likes of Allen Ginsberg, George Lucas and Ralph J. Gleason, who hosted the affair. In the audience are Bill Graham and members

of The Family Dog Troupe. This is the beginning, dare we say first flowering, of the emerging Underground scene, and Dylan looks delighted to see so many freaks in the assembled crowd of straight journalists. At one point Allen Ginsberg raises his hand to ask Dylan the question, '*Can you ever envisage being hung as a thief?*' He follows up immediately with another, '*Can you think of a word that rhymes with orange?*'

Dylan's answers to the press were no less surreal.

Journalist – *What poets do you dig?*

Dylan – *Rimbaud… WC Fields… the trapeze family… in the circus… Smokey Robinson…Allen Ginsberg… Charlie Rich…*

Journalist – *For those of us over thirty, could you label yourself and perhaps tell us what your role is?*

Dylan – *I'd sort of label myself as well under thirty. And my role is… to just stay here as long as I can…*

Journalist – *What's your new album about?*

Dylan – *All kinds of different things… rats, balloons.*

And so on for fifty-one glorious minutes.

But that was in the past. By 1969 the playful young jester had given way to a more thoughtful kind of family man.

Dylan had been in a kind of self-imposed seclusion since his motorbike accident in 1966. However, despite his apparent reclusiveness, Dylan had been busy recording in the basement at Big Pink. He'd also spent time in the Columbia studios making *John Wesley Harding* and, by February of 1969, he was in Nashville recording *Nashville Skyline*. Johnny Cash joined him in the studio for two days and one track featuring a Cash duet, 'Girl From The North

Country', ended up on the album. It was presumably at these sessions that the idea for Dylan to appear on Cash's upcoming TV series was discussed.

Towards the end of April, Dylan spent several more days in the studio in Nashville, looked around for some real-estate and on May 1st went along to the Ryman Auditorium, then home to Country Music's spiritual centre, The Grand Ole Opry, to take part in *The Johnny Cash Show* for ABC TV.

Cash was riding high at the time, his personal difficulties of the mid-1960s behind him and his TV series was watched by millions. Budgeted at $150,000 per show it featured guest artists of the calibre of Dusty Springfield, Joe Tex, Ray Charles, Glen Campbell and Joni Mitchell, who was second guest on the Dylan edition of the programme.

Dylan was asked by reporter, Red O'Donnel, from *The Nashville Banner* why he was doing Cash's show when he was known to have turned down the chance to appear on many others. Dylan told him that it was because it was the best TV show around. He politely declined an interview with O'Donnel but offered to provide him with a list of things he felt important. O'Donnel was never sure if they were a put on or not –

'I love children. I love animals,' Dylan told him, explaining his personal credo. 'I am loyal to my friends. I have a sense of humor. I have a generally happy outlook. I try to be on time for appointments. I have a good relationship with my wife. I take criticism well. I strive to do good work… I try to find some good in everybody.'

O'Donnel reported that Dylan seemed very shy and restrained and his first appearance on screen reflects this. Dylan had asked that there be no scenery behind him and he's shot against a simple black background. Dressed in a black suit with an open necked white shirt, the effect is to emphasise his vulnerability. The shots, starting off with a long shot, fading to medium close-up, gently merging into one another as Dylan sings 'I Threw It All Away'. He looks fit and lean, though the tan on his face could be real or panstick, and as the song finishes and he looks more at ease, you can almost see a weight gently slipping off his shoulders.

Dylan must have been nervous. Here he was, a Sixties' counter-cultural hero, in the hallowed halls of Country, appearing as a guest of one of the genre's biggest stars. It had been years since he'd appeared on TV, months and months since he'd been on stage, and now he was facing an audience of millions with a set of brand new numbers that represented a total departure from anything he'd done before.

Looking less apprehensive, though still cautious, he lets himself be carried gently by the backing band (who we never get to see) into 'Living The Blues'. Compared to the Dylan of 1966, he has almost completely changed, not just in appearance but in vocal style as well. Gone was the nasal, almost whining voice that characterised his early official recordings. His voice is now more mellow, more 'opened out'. Peter Stone Brown has pointed out the similarities between his Nashville voice and the one of the young Bob Dylan on the Bonnie Beecher tapes, made before he hit New York. In an interview with Jann Wenner for *Rolling Stone* later in the year Dylan claimed:

'When I stopped smoking, my voice changed... so drastically I couldn't believe it myself. That's true. I tell you, you stop smoking those cigarettes (laughter)... and you'll be able to sing like Caruso.'

At the end of his second number the audience applause is full and welcoming, the screen fades to black for a second and then cuts to Cash's set, which is designed like a kind of ranch house living room with a stone, circular seating area in the middle. Cash greets Dylan with a handshake and they both sit down with their guitars, strumming gently. For the first time since the show began Dylan allows himself a smile.

Their duet on 'Girl From The North Country' is superbly played and sung – delicately understated and emotional. Dylan takes the first verse and then looks over at Cash who delivers the second in his rich distinctive style. There is a magic about the performance. So, this was two old friends who'd both seen some hard times and got through to the other side, sitting together and just doing what they do best, playing music together. The mutual rapport was clearly visible. Cash, however, was more sanguine about the rapturously received duet.

'That's something everybody else sees but I don't,' the puzzled Country veteran mused. 'We've done it dozens of times just foolin' around. But everybody here said that "North Country" was the most magnetic, powerful thing they ever heard. Just raving about electricity, magnetism. And all I did was sit there hitting G chords...'

Still, the show was unanimously acclaimed in the US. Sadly, we'll never know what the British reaction would have been, because despite buying all the other programmes in the series, the BBC declined the Dylan guest show, on the grounds that his performance was inferior!

Still in Country Music territory, Dylan made a special guest appearance in a Public Broadcasting Service (PBS) documentary, later aired by NBC, entitled *Earl Scruggs Performing With His Family & Friends*. The Dylan segment of the film has a very 'down-home' feel to it, nice and easy, and was shot in the New York home of Thomas B. Allen., artist and album-cover designer. Scruggs, accompanied by his son, jams with Dylan on 'Nashville Skyline Rag' as the opening credits roll. Then Dylan duets with Scruggs on 'East Virginia Blues'. The performances are laid back and lack any of the tension that accompanied Cash's show. Dylan seems perfectly at ease with the other musicians, and himself, perhaps because there was no audience present.

Take Five – The Two Hard Rains

In September 1975, Dylan and the nucleus of what would become the *Rolling Thunder Revue* band, Rivera, Stoner and Wyeth, flew to Chicago to appear on a televised tribute to John Hammond Sr, on PBS TV. They performed three songs, 'Oh Sister', 'Simple Twist of Fate' and a blistering version of 'Hurricane', which was subsequently shown on BBC TV in the UK.

The next major TV project of significance was the *Hard Rain* TV special filmed in 1976. Dylan's star had risen to almost epic proportions the preceding year. *The Rolling Thunder Revue* had been a major artistic and critical success, though the *Renaldo and Clara* footage was in the can waiting to be edited. *Desire* too had been a triumph. In order to retain artistic control over the completion of *Renaldo and Clara*, Dylan needed to raise enough cash to produce it properly, so consequently he wheeled out The Revue for a second tour, this time away from the north-east.

After presenting a 'Night of the Hurricane II', at the Houston Astrodome, the tour properly got under way in April. Dylan pitched the idea of a TV special and three major networks put in bids for it. NBC won.

There are two *Hard Rains*. Before focusing on the one that eventually made it onto TV screens around the world, we'll look

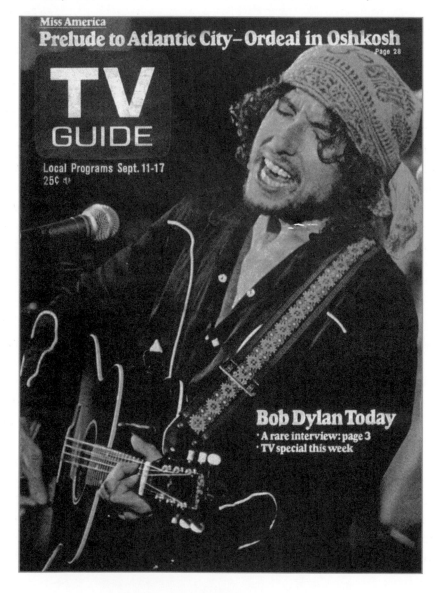

briefly at the first version, a one hour TV special recorded in the ballroom of the Bellevue Biltmore Hotel, Clearwater, Florida on April 22nd for 'The Midnight Special' – a fairly dull and conventional late night series featuring contemporary rock acts.

'It's a straight concert, no crap,' Stan Harris, the show's producer/director told *Rolling Stone* in the May 1976 issue.

Bert Sugerman was in charge of 'The Midnight Special''s production outfit. When he and his crew arrived at the Biltmore, the first thing they did was construct a set for the band to perform on. Seeing the set now, you realise how little distance TV stage design has come over the decades. Scaffolding platforms were erected around the ballroom's stage and the audience positioned on various levels, just as had been done on every teen TV Rock show since the beginning of teen TV Rock shows. The cameras were mounted, allowing for two things – one, a clearly delineated sequence of shots according to a pre-arranged shooting script, and – two, a complete lack of spontaneity.

Sugerman's crew shot two concerts in total, one matinee and one in the evening. From the repertoire of the Revue they selected a reasonable cross-section of material – the band was on form despite previous lacklustre rehearsals.

'The rehearsals sucked in that place ...' drummer Howie Wyeth remembers. 'It just wasn't happening... Then we did the concerts and they were filming it and it happened. That was the first day that the music started feeling right again. Bob did a really hip version of 'Like A Rolling Stone'. He did some tunes that he hadn't done at all.'

According to all accounts, Dylan behaved with a level of professionalism that surprised some of the people on the tour. He spent considerable time ensuring that the tuning was correct and insisted on second takes when he felt that the performance hadn't been tight enough. Even when he turned in two allegedly stunning versions of 'Visions of Johanna', he insisted on junking both because he wasn't quite satisfied. Other numbers that failed to make the final film included, 'Leopard Skin Pill-Box Hat', 'One More Cup of Coffee' and 'Romance In Durango'.

Numbers that did make it included, a riveting Baez duet on 'I Dreamed I Saw Saint Augustine', and a Baez solo performance of 'Diamonds And Rust', her poignant ballad about her 1960s' relationship with Dylan.

As good as the music is, and it is *very* good, the accompanying concert film is just not up to the dynamism of the music and the interaction of the band members. Still, it is perfectly adequate TV: cliched and unadventurous. The most cringe-making moment is during 'Just Like A Woman' when the camera cuts during the chorus from a woman to a little girl. This was obviously not an approach that would go down well with the mercurial Dylan.

'Well, Bob got into a fight with [one of] the guys that were doing [the Clearwater special]' Howie Wyeth explains… 'He got into a big argument with the guy over the dinner table one night after we'd already done half of it. And then he said, "No! We're not going to do it. Fuck it!" So he decided that wasn't the way we were going to do it, and then they decided to record it at the end (of the tour).'

An insider told *Rolling Stone* that Dylan hated the finished TV show, 'Evidently, it wasn't what he was looking for. Dylan felt it looked like every other "Midnight Special".' Dylan subsequently shelved the footage and contacted another television company, TVTV, to shoot his imminent 23rd May concert at Hughes Stadium in Fort Collins, Colorado. Dylan was already familiar with TVTV as the company employed several of the *Renaldo and Clara* camera crew.

TVTV stood for 'Top Value Television,' which this concert film

BOB DYLAN
10:00 ⑩ ④

A RARE TV APPEARANCE

Special: A concert headlined by a famous singer-songwriter.

Bob Dylan performs with Joan Baez and The Rolling Thunder Revue (a backup group featuring singer-guitarist Roger McGuinn) in a show taped last May at Colorado State University in Fort Collins.

There is no commentary about Dylan; for that, see Neil Hickey's interview on page 3. Instead, what the hour offers is a portrait of the man through his music — a multi-faceted view that reflects the words of biographer Anthony Scaduto: "[Dylan] has been interpreted and acclaimed as a teacher, revolutionary, firebrand, messiah, mystic, prophet." (60 min.)

The program . . . "A Hard Rain's A-Gonna Fall," "Blowin' in the Wind," "Railroad Boy," "Deportees," "I Pity the Poor Immigrant," "Shelter from the Storm," "Maggie's Farm," "One Too Many Mornings," "Mozambique," "Idiot Wind," "Knockin' on Heaven's Door."

was considering Dylan paid for the whole of the production out of his own pocket. His prior association with TVTV employees and knowledge of their ability must have put him and his fellow performers at ease as the crew prepared to film the concert. Dylan even arranged a little bit of R and R for the Revue – the only problem was that at such extremely short notice, it was difficult for the Revue members to know what to do.

'All of a sudden they said we got four days off before we do Fort Collins and the record,' Howie Wyeth recalls. 'They said, "You're gonna love this. We got you in this dude ranch up in the mountains." And it was raining so you couldn't go riding and it was up in the mountains so you couldn't breathe. There was nothing to do. And we were all stuck up there… For four days we had nothing to do. And it was raining. It was dreary…'

With very little to do up in the mountains Revue members resorted to a limited number of pastimes to wile away the hours in the rain. All of them drank too much. Dylan committed adultery.

The marriage had not being going well. Away from Sara and with audience figures at the concerts down, Dylan was going through some changes.

'I don't know what the fuck came over him…' says bassist Rob Stoner. 'It was a big void in his life. The marriage was falling apart and this thing which had seemed so exciting and promising – Rolling Thunder – that wasn't [working] and he couldn't figure out why, I don't think… It was like a mid-life crisis. He was confused and he was searching. He tried a lot of chicks; he tried one chick; he tried [every] kind of chick.'

Dylan's personal life came to a crisis point on the morning of the tele-recording, when Sara turned up at Fort Collins with his children and mother. Dylan was in their hotel ballroom 'rehearsing.'

'Sara showed up late in the tour,' Baez recounted, 'wafting in from a plane looking like a mad woman, carrying baskets of wrinkled clothes, her hair wild and dark rings around her eyes… Bob was ignoring her, and had picked up a curly headed Mopsy who perched on the piano during his rehearsals in a ballroom off the main hotel lobby. Sara appeared airily at the front door dressed in deerskin, wearing her emerald green necklace and some oppressively strong and sweet oils. She greeted me with a reserved hello and talked distantly about nothing in particular, all the while eyeing the closed door to the ballroom.'

Meanwhile, it had continued to rain and rain. The conditions were far from ideal for performing, never mind shooting a concert film. Still, it was the penultimate show of the tour and virtually the last chance to make the TV special. Dylan was caught on an emotional roller-coaster, yet even as Sara berated him in the hotel parking lot in the pouring rain, a decision had to be made about the filming. He gave the word to go ahead.

Take Six – Shelter From The Storm

'Everybody's soaked,' Rob Stoner recounted at the time, 'the canopy's leaking, the musicians are getting shocks from the water on the stage. The instruments are going out of tune because of the humidity. It was awful. So everybody is playing and singing for their lives...' It was to be the longest set played anywhere on the tour.

This time the cameras aren't still. Though TVTV employ rostrum-mounted cameras placed strategically at the side and front of the stage, they also use a hand-held. The editing isn't slick like the Clearwater show, it's roughhewn and emotional. Though the camera often lingers for extended periods on close-ups of Dylan, head swathed in an Arab headdress, his curls sodden with the rain, looking for all the world like a character from an Old Testament movie, it isn't afraid to strike out on its own. For once, this is really like being on stage with a band. We see people hanging around at the side of the stage, climbing scaffolding, children gazing on, musicians late for their entrances and an audience that, though damp, is ecstatic in their rapture.

There are no long tracking shots taking us slowly to the focus of our attention, just immediacy and involvement. This is direct video, even the image itself seems to be grainier, more real somehow than the classically lit Clearwater set.

At one point, during 'Maggie's Farm', one of the cameras goes directly behind Dylan to frame a shot that allows us to see his back and then the audience, all 25,000 of them, peering back at him through the drizzle. It's such a successful image that it was used for the back cover of the *Hard Rain* album.

'I think it was Howard Alk's suggestion,' Joel Bernstein explained. 'Anyway, they wanted to have some shots of Bob from the video of

Craig Stereo
invites you to a
Bob Dylan concert,
"Hard Rain."

Presented by
Craig Powerplay
Car Stereo and
Craig Series 5000
Audio Components.

Bob Dylan's live album
on Columbia Records and
Tapes coming soon in
your local record stores.

Bob Dylan posters
are available at your Craig Dealer.

TONIGHT
10.00 PM NBC-TV 104

Fort Collins for the LP sleeve and I had come up with this technique of photographing from video using still frame... I'd shot a lot from the front, but the background was very cluttered with all the scaffolding and the paintings... The shot from the back just happened to be the one that I stopped at. I never thought it would be used.'

Dylan and Bobby Neuwirth had painted a bright, garish backdrop of Arabs, Red Indians and pirates, magical symbols and stars to go behind the stage, and the *Rolling Thunder Revue* curtain was used at the front. It rolls up at the beginning when the band is playing 'A Hard Rain's A Gonna Fall'. This number was actually the second encore, but its placement at the top of the show seems logical as the working title for the video production was 'Hard Rain' and it was pouring down at the time.

When Joan Baez joins Dylan for their duets, 'Hard Rain' enters a whole different dimension. For their opening number they sing the obligatory 'Blowin' In The Wind', but the magic really kicks in when they start on the old Buell Kuzee banjo song, 'Railroad Boy' – a number off Harry Smith's *Anthology Of American Folk Music* that deals with a young girl's unrequited love and suicide. The pair of them attack the song with breathtaking pace. Baez clawhammers the banjo riff on her six-string while Dylan thrashes the relentless Em/C chord changes as the song reaches its tragic climax. The penultimate note of the melody is held as if forever, drawing cheers from the audience and smiles of wonder from the other musicians.

By complete contrast, the next song, 'I Pity The Poor Immigrant', is delivered in a jaunty, sprightly Calypso style. On the duetted line, *'He fills his mouth with laughing'* Dylan can't resist throwing in a quick, *'Ha Ha!'* which gets a wry smile from Baez.

The subsequent 'Shelter From The Storm' even features Dylan on raucous electric slide guitar, while he shouts the lyrics exuberantly, just as he does on 'Maggie's Farm', which follows.

This number becomes the virtual equivalent of a strip-tease routine with Dylan dragging out the length of an *'Ooooh!!'* on the next to last words in the verse, almost to breaking point. With each verse the gap gets longer and longer until Mick Ronson's guitar solo stretches it to breaking point – screeching the same notes over and over again.

Gradually things get more serious as the bands move on through 'One Too Many Mornings', 'Mozambique' and a particularly angst-ridden 'Idiot Wind'. Then comes the final number of this unique performance, 'Knocking On Heaven's Door'.

The Revue players give it their all. Roger McGuinn throws in a wonderful new verse beginning, *'Mama take this twelve string off of me'* and everybody joins in the chorus as the credits roll. Amongst the people graced with 'special thanks' are the poets Peter Orlovsky and Arthur Rimbaud. Musicians thanked included, Robert Johnson and Woody Guthrie. A very special thanks is extended to Woodstock resident Bobby Charles, who wrote 'See You Later Alligator'.

Take Seven – 'an anti-special'

While *Rolling Stone* was initially tentatively encouraging in its reception of *Hard Rain* – 'a documentary of the concert with so many raw close-up shots of Dylan and company in front of 25,000 fans that "You kind of feel that you're right there on stage",' – the mainstream press reviews were a foretaste of what Dylan was to get with *Renaldo and Clara*. Critics' verdicts ranged from 'painlessly artless' to 'a mess' and 'a debacle'. But what had made them so furious?

Well, presumably they had expected something more polished and conventional along the lines of the Clearwater 'Midnight Special' footage that Dylan had so disliked. *Hard Rain* by contrast was raw, rough and too contextualised. The TV reviewers clearly preferred their entertainment sacharine sweet, safe and bland.

The underground press on the other hand were delighted by *Hard Rain*. One writer in particular, Steve Levy of Philadelphia's *Free Times* was so incensed with its mainstream reception that he wrote a kind of review of the reviews:

'So for one night, everybody becomes a television critic. With a mind filled with false ideas, images and distorted facts, the United States of America tuned into NBC on the fourteenth of September…[everything] seemed to give everybody something to complain about. He didn't talk! The songs were too intense for television! His Rolling Thunder band all looked like Arabs – with those turbans and all!… Television, they decided, had proved kryptonite to the superman of popular music… Dylan had misunderstood the nature of television. He hadn't realised that when you're a visitor in the living room of America, you have to make small talk, keep your hands on your lap, and not make threats... He had not realised that slickly-done, recognisable versions of his songs ... would pacify his fans, educate the curious ... you need middle-of-the-road production values... All this is an insult to Bob Dylan...'

Perhaps even more importantly, the film was a big hit with Dylan fans watching in their living rooms, around the world.

Take Eight – Through The Cathode Eye

In October 1979, now a committed born-again Christian, Dylan presaged his forthcoming 'Gospel' tour with an appearance on the decidedly un-godly long-running comedy show *Saturday Night Live*. Introduced by former Monty Python man Eric Idle, Dylan and his back-up band sang three numbers from his recently released album, *Slow Train Coming*.

The songs were delivered in a sombre manner by a stern-looking Dylan. Not often given to smiling on stage anyway, his dark and brooding face peered out into the hinterland of America as he spread his apocalyptic message.

Three months later he reprised one of his *Saturday Night Live* set-list numbers, 'Gotta Serve Somebody', on the coast to coast prime-time TV Grammy Awards Ceremony. Dylan, in full evening dress, blistered his way through the song lyric's check list of leaders, gurus, saints and sinners, ideas and nightmares, for over six minutes before accepting the award for 'Best Male Rock Vocal Performance of 1979'. In his acceptance speech he thanked – *'The Lord, Jerry Wexler, and Barry Beckett... Who believed.'*

It wasn't until March 1984 that Dylan would return to the world of late-night television with a guest-spot on *Late Night With David Letterman*. When the TV offer came through he asked drummer Charlie Quintana to put together a band for the gig. Quintana had a three-piece outfit called The Cruzados (previously known as The Plugz and often referred to mysteriously as a 'Punk' band) with guitarist Justin Jesting and bassist Tony Marisco. For such a young band they knew their chops and at times, though their sound was very different, they were reminiscent of Dylan and The Hawks – rough, positive and energetic, with just the right amount of youthful arrogance. And they needed arrogance a-plenty for playing on Letterman.

Their major problem was that they barely knew any Dylan numbers.

'Well, we rehearsed at the TV soundcheck and we'd rehearsed the night before,' Quintana remembered. 'But the night before we went through fifty fucking songs we didn't know! At the soundcheck they sealed off the studio and all the NBC top brass were there 'cos it's Bob, and we'd never start '1, 2, 3...', he'd just start strumming and we'd just jump in and follow it, and it would end the same way – he'd just stop playing...

'And it was five minutes before we were supposed to go on and I'm asking Bill Graham, saying, "Jesus Christ, we're shitting bricks over here! Can you please go in and ask Bob what songs we're gonna to do?" And he'd come back and say, 'He's not sure yet'.'

At 6 pm they trouped into the studio to record the broadcast. Dylan, wearing a black suit, black shirt and pencil-thin white tie, was clean shaven and looking great. A delighted Letterman introduced the band and Dylan immediately went into a growling version of Sonny Boy Williamson's 'Don't Start Me Talkin'' – possibly an ironic choice seeing as this was a chat show!

Watching it now you'd never realise that, according to Quintana, not only was this not one of the 'fifty fucking songs' they had rehearsed, the band had never even heard the tune before.

The sound is ragged but determined. Dylan, legs astride, shoots out a powerful delivery of the lyrics, while Justin Jesting wallops out a series of electric twelve-bar licks that fit perfectly with Dylan's clawhammer technique. At the end of the number, Letterman walks up to Dylan and shakes his hand, asking if they'll stick around and do more numbers later in the show.

After the break, Dylan and The Cruzados walk their way into 'License To Kill'. As with the rest of this show it's one of the finest Dylan performances on video. He's confident and assured. There's a swagger to the way he moves around the stage. The Cruzados just don't seem to be able to put a foot wrong as Dylan's backing band, even when he takes his guitar off and stalks around the set looking for a harmonica. (He finds it and brings the song to its conclusion with a phenomenally riveting harp break.)

After another commercial break, Dylan returns for his final number, a performance of 'Jokerman' quite unlike the album version. His vocals are superb and the band grinds along behind him. Then comes an almost hilarious moment – once again Dylan unstraps his axe, hands it to a roadie and searches for his harmonica. He finds one, starts playing it and realises that it's in the wrong key. The band keep on playing the riff, not looking in the slightest bit phased as Dylan keeps looking for the lost harp.

'Maybe if we'd rehearsed a song from beginning to end, it would have fallen apart,' Quintana later reflected. 'But because we were used to not knowing what was happening, when he was fumbling around for the harmonica I was just able to keep tapping it out - a couple of verses, a chorus. It seemed like ten years! The cameraman got so bored he actually did a close-up of me!... The director must have been screaming, 'Guitar player! Bass player! Guitar player! Bass player! Alright... Let's try the drummer!' Hahahaha!'

After being handed the harp Dylan blasted a magnificent coda to 'Jokerman' and that was that.

Take Nine – Distant Electric Visions

In early 1985 Dylan was part of a video feature chronicling the recording session for the 'We Are The World' single – America's version of Bob Geldof's pop-stars-for-African-famine-relief Band Aid project. This was followed in July by his performance at the US leg of the subsequent fund-raising concert, Live Aid, at Philadelphia's JFK stadium.

In front of an estimated global audience of over one billion, accompanied by Ron Wood and Keith Richard, Dylan gave one of the worst performances of his life. Most people watching thought he'd blown it because he was too out of it – Keith Richards certainly looked that way. Dylan insisted afterwards that the problems were down to technical difficulties.

'They screwed around with us. We didn't even have any monitors out there. When they threw in the grand finale at the last moment they took all the settings off and set the stage up for the thirty people who were standing behind the curtain. We couldn't even hear our own voices, and when you can't hear, you can't play; you don't have any timing. It's like proceeding on radar.'

Apparently, many of the people behind the curtain waiting to come on were practising their vocal parts for the final number, 'We Are The World'. Still, there is no escaping the fact that Dylan and his cohorts were more than somewhat alcoholically challenged that day. Several reliable backstage sources have maintained that he was far gone even when he arrived at the stadium.

Dylan also antagonised a large section of the audience by calling for some of the money raised for emergency African famine relief to be given to American farmers to help them pay off their mortgages. If this really was a cause that Dylan felt deeply about, he had not chosen a good moment to bring it to the attention of the world. His comments were deemed inappropriate at least, scornful of the starving Ethiopians at worst. Still, many Americans sympathised with what they saw as a genuine plea for a disadvantaged group. Willie Nelson and Neil Young certainly took Dylan's comments to heart and in September of that year a benefit for US farmers took place, entitled, a little unimaginatively, Farm Aid.

For all the contemporary criticism of Dylan's Live Aid performance, the dust soon settled and by 1986, his stage show had been reinvigorated by the presence of a band he'd originally teamed up with at the Farm Aid concert – Tom Petty and The Heartbreakers. How well they meshed is obvious in an HBO special that was later turned into a video release, *Hard To Handle*.

Shot over two nights in Sydney, Australia, by Gillian Armstrong, the filming rights cost HBO a reputed $500,000. What they got for their money is a chunk of good, mid-period Dylan, while The Heartbreakers are definitely one of his best backing bands. However, the show is not striking enough, visually or musically, for it to be called a classic.

Take Ten – The Kosher Cowboy

In 1983, Dylan began visiting an Hasidic Jewish group called Chabad Lubovitch, who are based in Brooklyn and run a series of national programmes for the rehabilitation of drug addicts and alcoholics. The Lubavitchers placed great emphasis on the importance of music as a powerful, spiritual healing force. Dylan's association with them would result in appearances on three *Chabad Telethons*. Telethons are a peculiarly American invention. For a whole evening, and sometimes longer, a TV station gives over its airtime to a worthy cause. A succession of celebrity guests appear and appeals are made for donations. The total sum raised so far is regularly displayed as people phone in their pledges.

Dylan's first appearance on Chabad was in 1986 with Tom Petty And The Heartbreakers, performing an old Hank Williams song, 'Thank God', in a prerecorded clip. Dylan also appeared in a filmed insert:

'This is Bob Dylan, I'm in England right now working, so I can't be with you tonight, but I'd like to say that Chabad is a worthy organisation helping people in need. Helping to get them free from the misconception and devastations that are destroying their lives from within. Of course, this is the first battle, for those responsible for poisoning the minds and bodies of America's youth are reaping great profits - If you can help Chabad to help others who've fallen victim through the lies and deceits of those who are much more powerful. Do so.' (sic).

So far, so good. A strong musical number and a heartfelt plea, par for the course on a telethon. For his next appearance for Chabad, in September 1989, Dylan's approach would be a little more complex.

1989 was the 25th anniversary *Chabad Telethon* and Dylan agreed to perform live from their studio in San Francisco. When the announcer said – *'We have a fantastic surprise tonight…,'* he couldn't have been more right, though perhaps not in the way he envisaged. Accompanying Dylan was his son-in-law, Peter Himmelman, and actor Harry Dean Stanton. They introduced themselves as 'Chopped Liver', and Himmelman introduced his father-in-law as Moishe Rubenstein. Dylan, wearing a black suit, white shirt and yarmulke, was carrying a flute instead of a guitar, and looked more like a rabbi than the rabbi who was running the show. Dylan hovered on the sidelines while Himmelman got the first number, 'Einsleipt Mein Kind Dein Eigalach', underway. Throughout the doleful Yiddish song, Dean Stanton and Himmelman strummed away on their guitars while Dylan made a racket on his flute, occasionally finding the right notes, but sadly in the wrong places.

During the second number, 'Adelita', Dylan harmonised with Harry Dean Stanton and switched to recorder with much more success than the flute. To make things more interesting, it was a Mexican song sung in Spanish.

At the end of the number an enthusiastic bear of a rabbi came on and hugged everybody. Himmelman asked him what 'Hava Nagilah' meant, to which the beaming rabbi replied: *'Let's be happy because God is good to all his children throughout the whole world!'*

And off went Chopped Liver into a frenzied version of the unofficial Jewish anthem.

Dylan made his, so far, final appearance on a *Chabad Telethon* in 1991. He began by joining the rabbi again in an appeal for the former Soviet Union to return a library of looted Jewish sacred texts. Later on, he stands by looking slightly bewildered as an ex-junkie tells how Chabad saved his life. At the end of this monologue the rabbi thanks him and begs for the audience to send in their donations. *'Bob! Tell them what to do!'* he extols Dylan. Thrust into the foreground, Dylan tells the viewers to, *'call and call and call again...'*

Later in the show, the rabbi introduces Dylan and Kinky Friedman, the 'Texas Jewboy,' possibly most famous for having written that old Country classic, 'They Don't Make Jews Like Jesus Anymore'.

Anybody expecting a duet would have been sadly disappointed. Kinky manfully sings away against a strange noise emanating from beside him. Dylan had chosen to play lead guitar. This would have been all well and good if Dylan had chosen to play lead guitar on the same tune as Kinky, but for reasons best known to himself he didn't, and happily chugged along on his own musical agenda.

At the end of the number while removing his guitar, Dylan knocks off his cowboy hat to reveal his yarmulke underneath. It seems rather incongruous with his pale blue anorak and hood, but then Dylan has never been one to appear orthodox, even on a Jewish charity show.

Take Eleven - Documentary Season

Since the mid-1980s, Dylan has featured in two BBC TV documentaries: *Getting To Dylan*, by Omnibus director Christopher Sykes in 1986, and *Tales of Rock & Roll: Highway 61 Revisited*, in 1993.

Getting To Dylan was ostensibly made to promote the movie *Hearts of Fire* – director Richard Marquand was a former *Omnibus* alumnus and the documentary crew were accordingly given unprecedented on-set access to location shooting in Wales, Bristol and even Ontario, Canada.

The documentary shows some interesting footage of movie scenes as they were shot, including sequences that never made it to the final version. However, from the beginning [and of course in accordance with the title itself], the director's main objective appeared to be to pin down Dylan for an exclusive interview. Sykes makes much of Dylan's evasive tactics, starting off by showing extracts from the *Hearts of Fire* press conference, and commenting on Dylan's legendary reticence in giving straight answers to interviewers.

Much is also made of the film crew trekking towards the door of Dylan's caravan only to be politely rebuffed. Eventually though, in Canada, Dylan agrees to talk to Sykes, though he begins by telling him, *'If you're looking for revelation, it's just not gonna happen'*.

However, oddly, it does, despite Sykes's awkward style, who was no doubt unsettled by the fact that Dylan sketched his portrait throughout the interview. This wouldn't be so bad for the hapless BBC man, except that Dylan was using the back of Sykes' list of interview questions as a sketchpad. Sykes grows more uncomfortable when he tells Dylan that there's a woman in his hotel claiming to be Dylan's sister. Sykes believes that she might be dangerous. Dylan asks him why he hasn't called the police then? Sykes doesn't know.

Still, for all the occasional awkward moments, Dylan comes across as intelligent, private, fairly down to earth and quite charming.

He genuinely tries to help Sykes through the difficult bits, and even though some critics have maintained that Dylan is putting him on all the way through, Dylan is acting in a more than co-operative manner. As a documentary about the making of *Hearts of Fire*, it's not much to talk of, but as a documentary about Bob Dylan it's essential viewing because of the remarkable candour of the interview and the footage peripheral to the making of the film. For instance, a sequence in a Canadian car-park, where Dylan meets a group of his fans, is a touching insight into the workings of his mind.

The second BBC documentary, *Highway 61 Revisited*, is an altogether different animal. Made for the *Arena* series of arts programmes, it traces the cultural history and importance in American popular culture of Highway 61 – the road which snakes its way from the north to the south of the United States, and has attained a kind of mythical status, particularly with black and white musicians. Elvis Presley lived just off it, Bob Dylan did too. Bessie Smith died along it and many Blues players have written songs about it. The programme, produced and directed by James Marsh, uses Dylan as a kind of chorus around which to tell the tale. What makes the documentary unique is the participation of Dylan's childhood friend, John Bucklen, and the use of Bucklen's 1958 home recordings of him and Dylan trying out songs on guitar and piano, and talking about Rhythm and Blues.

In fact, all the Dylan material used is archival, examining his career up to his arrival in New York in 1961. Anyone hoping for a retrospective overview of his entire professional life will be disappointed. The film's strength lies in its ability to make clear what influenced the young Zimmerman and how he came to become Bob Dylan, because, as John Bucklen points out, the person he knew will always be Bob Zimmerman and he barely knows Bob Dylan at all.

Perhaps it was so successful because the documentary was made with the assistance of John Bauldie, the late and much lamented founder of Dylan magazine, *The Telegraph*.

Take Twelve – Dealing With The MTV Generation

In the early 1990s somebody at MTV had the bright idea of inviting established artists to come onto the station and perform their set acoustically. The show was to be named *MTV Unplugged* and it became one of the most successful ventures the company has embarked upon. Artists who have made critically acclaimed appearances include Nirvana, REM and Eric Clapton. In November 1994, Bob Dylan succumbed to the allure of 'Teen TV' and began rehearsals at Sony's New York Studios for his MTV in concert debut. In November 1993 Dylan appeared to have had a stab at recording his own equivalent TV special at New York's Supper Club. Four sixty-minute shows were filmed, the performances being hailed by those present as his best in years. The resultant concert film, however, has never been seen, except for two tracks on the *Highway 61* CD Rom. These promise much but deliver little by dint of the constraints imposed by the thumb-nail screen. Once again, Dylan is referring to his past cinematic representations by utilising a simple two-camera set-up with the mainframing on silhouettes of himself performing 'Queen Jane Approximately' and 'One Too Many Mornings'. Once again, for some inexplicable reason, Dylan decided to slam the lid on the TV special and so, for now, that's the only tantalising glimpse we have of the performances.

With his own project now pushed firmly under wraps, Dylan appears to have succumbed to the blandishments and wallets of MTV. On the evening of November 17th, Dylan and his regular touring band of John Jackson, Tony Garnier, Winston Watson and Bucky Baxter, augmented by Brendan O'Brien on keyboards – entered the TV studio to record a programme for the music channel. From the start Dylan was ill at ease with the proceedings. The set was claustrophobic and the audience hand picked. Very few of them looked over twenty-three. In fact, the MTV floor managers asked anybody with grey hair or who looked over thirty to move to the back of the studio. The socially cleansed 'wunderkinds' applauded the start of every song and gave standing ovations at the end of every number. Occasionally, led on by the floor manager, they would burst into 'spontaneous' applause at the beginning of each separate verse of a particular tune. However, MTV were unhappy with Dylan's one-hour set.

Surprisingly, in an unprecedented act of magnanimity, Dylan agreed to go back to the studio the following night and redo the concert. This time he presented much more of a 'Greatest Hits' package.

When it came to editing the two shows together to create a seamless TV special, Dylan kept away from the grafting and crafting, though he did retain final say over the finished product. 'Like A Rolling Stone' had taken almost two minutes before he abandoned the take and reverted to a more up-tempo version. On the broadcast programme, the extended false start is edited down to a few seconds. It's one of the only times that Dylan allows himself a smile.

Dylan and the band are generally on top form and the set is lively on the whole, though occasionally they appear to be strolling through some of the numbers. However they are let down by clichéd and unoriginal camera work direction – jarringly reminiscent of the Clearwater, 'Midnight Special' debacle. The audience 'interaction' is cloyingly embarrassing – their interpolated applause becomes nauseating. And you just sense that Dylan, feels that way about it too.

It was a show that brought him to a much younger audience.

Take Thirteen – Kissing The Pope's Ring, Amongst Other Things

In 1991, a suitably 'emotional' Dylan was presented with a 'Lifetime Achievement Award' at the Grammys, by a suitably 'emotional' Jack Nicholson. Following a brief video summary of his life and career Dylan chose to sing an acerbic version of 'Masters of War' to an audience that was gorging itself on an orgy of televised Gulf War footage from CNN. He then did something that he hasn't done on stage very often, outside of his 'Born Again' period, which is make a relatively lengthy acceptance speech. It's worth repeating here in full:

'Thank you … well … alright …yeah, well, my daddy he didn't leave too much … you know he was a very simple man and he didn't leave me a lot, but what he told me was this … what he did say was…

son … he said, uh … (long pause)…he said so many things you know … he said, you know it's possible to become so defiled in this world that your own mother and father will abandon you, and if that happens God will always believe in your ability to mend your ways. Thank you.'

At the end of this remarkable piece of wisdom the audience of music big-wigs stood up and gave Dylan a standing ovation.

It's hard to come to any other conclusion but that Dylan is sending up the hypocrisy of the gathering in this delivery of a down-home piece of country hokum, rather in the manner of James Stewart in *Mr Smith Goes To Washington*, with its 'aw gee, shucks' homily and cracker-barrel pontification. I wonder if anybody took him seriously, if they thought he was talking about himself. It's one of the personas that Dylan adopts – that of the country boy in the big city, counterpoised with the 'nice Jewish boy at a party' schtick that he also occasionally draws on.

Before bringing this chapter to a close, it's worth taking a look briefly at two more TV events: Dylan's appearance before the Pope in Bologna, 1997; and his 'dance with destiny', at the 1998 Grammy awards.

Broadcast on Italy's RA1 TV, the Papal Youth Congress in Bologna is of significant interest because it was Dylan's first TV appearance after his near-fatal heart condition earlier that year. In front of a huge crowd, Dylan and the band turned in a reasonable performance. Every now and then the camera would cut to John Paul II, resplendent on a raised dais at the side of the stage. Sadly, Il Pape appeared to be dozing gently through Dylan's set. Eventually, Dylan was ushered up the steps to meet the Pontiff. As Dylan leaned forward to have a quick word with the Pope, it was hard not to wonder what they were talking about.

Finally, at the 1998 Grammy Awards Ceremony, at New York's Radio City Music Hall, Dylan was nominated for a handful of awards. He had also agreed to sing 'Lovesick' off his new album *Time Out of Mind*. Two things stand out: firstly the performance. Everything was going perfectly well. Dylan and the band were nicely slotted onto the Radio City stage, surrounded by a hired group of adoring young people. It must be pointed out that this was not Dylan's idea. It had been foisted onto him by the Grammy director. Suddenly, about half way through a very charismatic version of 'Lovesick', one of the on-stage audience, a performance artist, tore off his shirt, revealing the words 'Soy Bomb' written in magic marker on his chest, and leapt to the front of the stage to join Dylan. Not losing his cool for a second, Dylan carried on singing as if nothing was going on. But the situation highlighted the dangers facing performers. It took a good few minutes before other members of the audience, *not* security, bundled the gyrating offender off the stage. Later on, in his acceptance speech for the 'Most Outstanding Record of 1998', Dylan made no mention of the invader. He did however, much to the consternation and bafflement of many, thank Buddy Holly for his contribution towards the recording of his magnificent album *Time Out Of Mind*. (An amusing footnote to this is that about six months later 'Soy Bomb' himself was more than a trifle angry when a small group of Dylan fans invaded the stage at one of his own performances in New York City. He claimed they were 'interfering with his artistic integrity!')

Bringing the millennium to an end was one of Dylan's strangest decisions when he appeared on the highly popular American sitcom *Dharma and Greg*. The show, about a young couple, Dharma (played by Jenna Elfman) and Greg (played by Thomas Gibson), bases its fairly lean premise on her having been brought up as a hippie, he as a straight, and the wacky situations this brings to their marriage. They are, in effect, the culturally 'odd couple'. Almost universally reviled by the critics when it was first screened, the show has defied all the odds to become one of the most popular programmes in America. It's nothing exceptional as comedy, but for some reason Elfman's bubbly vivacity has struck a chord with the TV-viewing public. In an episode entitled *Play Lady Play*, screened in October 1999, Dharma is trying to 'find herself' by trying out as a drummer for a local high school/garage band. Just before the show's conclusion she auditions for one more group that, to everyone's surprise, is fronted by Dylan, accompanied by, amongst others, T-Bone Burnett.

Two questions arise: why did he do it and how did he do? In answer to the first one, it appears that he did it for fun, as a favour to Eddie Gorodetsky, a writer on the show who'd been friendly with Dylan since he released a CD entitled *Christmas with Eddie G* on a Dylan-sponsored label. There certainly doesn't appear to have been any attempt by Dylan to capitalise on the show's popularity. In fact, he specifically asked for a ban on all pre-publicity, with ABC TV refusing to confirm his appearance even hours before the episode's airing.

How did he do? Well, wonderfully considering he is on screen for only a few minutes and is not required to do anything other than be himself. He does reveal, however, a perfect sense of comic timing when Jenna Elfman asks, *'Do I get the job, do you want me to play some more so you can decide?'* Dylan pauses for a second before answering totally deadpan, *'Er, no.'* Throughout the scene he appears to be absolutely delighted to be on camera, mugging away directly to the lens and cheerfully laughing at all the right moments.

There have been many other TV appearances by Dylan that could have been included in this section. Sadly there isn't enough space to do them all justice, but all known ones are listed and commented on in a separate appendix at the end of this book. Stay tuned!

Reel Eight
Sand In The Mouth Of The Movie Star

Bob Dylan's screen ventures have been as complex and idiosyncratic as the man himself. In between recording and performing some of the most important music of the latter half of the twentieth century, he has found time to feature in one ground-breaking documentary, conceive and edit another, make an impressive acting debut in one of legendary director's Sam Peckinpah's greatest Westerns, direct an accomplished, if avant garde, feature, and take the lead role in a mainstream Hollywood-style movie. He has also featured in some of the most compelling music television – both in terms of live performances and guest appearances.

While the feature Dylan directed, *Renaldo and Clara*, may have been only partially successful, he brought a truly individual, and quite ambitious, vision to both that movie and his mathematically constructed documentary *Eat The Document*.

For all the criticism of Dylan's much derided last feature *Hearts of Fire*, in terms of his acting, the key question is not how successful each movie or television show in which Dylan appears is, but how successful Dylan is in each movie and television show. There can be no doubt that he made a major impression in all three of his major acting roles. While he didn't always get the best lines, what shines through in all of his screen appearances is his sheer personal magnetism. There is no denying that Dylan has a unique charisma. To watch something like the San Francisco press conference from 1965, or *The Les Crane Show* from earlier that same year, we can understand why film producers were so eager to sign him up for a movie deal.

Dylan grew up surrounded by images of Hollywood – in the early 1950s he would sit entranced for hours in his uncle's Hibbing cinema – and we know for certain he consciously adopted the poses and mannerism of James Dean. However, close examination of his screen work reveals that he assimilated the characteristics of another celluloid deity too. Over the years many observers have remarked on his 'Chaplinesque' stage presence – consisting of gestures and movements and impeccable comic timing. Dylan himself said of Chaplin in 1962, 'He influences me, even in the way I sing. His films really sank in. I like to see the humour in the world. There's so little of it around. I guess I'm always conscious of the Chaplin tramp.'

Michael Gray, for one, has remarked how clearly this influence can be seen as late as 1987 in Dylan's appearance on the *Chabad Telethon*. There are echoes too in *Pat Garrett and Billy The Kid*, when Dylan performs his business with the baked bean cans, peering and peeping and fiddling with his spectacles.

While the role of Alias in *Pat Garrett* may initially have seemed a poor choice, typically it wasn't the kind of part anyone would have expected Dylan to have taken – rumoured roles such as angry young rebel Holden Caulfield or Dylan's Folk idol Woody Guthrie would have been far too obvious. Also, the decision to work with a genuine master like Peckinpah showed a real interest in discovering more about the filmmaking process. As we have seen, though, it was a mixed blessing. While *Pat Garrett* gave Dylan an affirmation of his abilities in front of the camera – and contemporary film critics weren't unkind in their comments about his acting prowess, more surprised at how little his obvious on-screen persona was utilised – the main thing Dylan learnt about Hollywood during and after the shoot was a confirmation of his fears about letting control get out of his hands. His appetite for movies had been whetted, but he would ensure his next venture would circumvent any of the hassles Peckinpah had had to put up with.

Based on what we know of Dylan's personality and creativity it was inevitable that he would embark on a brave experimental work like *Renaldo and Clara*. However, for all its redeeming features, there's no denying that it was a huge critical and commercial failure. We'll never know the actual extent of how hurt Dylan was by the public mauling he received for *Renaldo And Clara*. But, it wasn't long before he received more criticism for another visual foray when his groundbreaking *Hard Rain* TV special, now hailed as a classic, was derided by both critics and general public alike. Not surprisingly, by the 1980s Dylan was less inclined to rise to the challenges of either the large or small screen. His appearances – limited to a televised European concert here, a late-night talk show there – became more perfunctory.

Pushing the boundaries of the visual media no longer seemed important. Which makes it even more surprising that in the mid-1980s Dylan put out feelers to see if there was a major film role that might suit him. Now this was not something he had to do. He no longer had anything to prove. So, his decision to take a lead role in *Hearts of Fire*, (significantly a British film, not a Hollywood one) was both baffling and tantalising. But then this was a man in his mid-forties who had been told all his professional life that he should be in the movies.

As it turned out, he acquitted himself well considering the odds stacked against him, though the movie of course was a critical and commercial catastrophe. Still, Dylan may not have chosen his script well, but the fact that he chose one at all tells us that he was still willing to take artistic chances.

If *Hearts of Fire* was not the success Dylan had hoped for, neither was he having much luck in the video format that was dominating the early 1990s music industry. The man who virtually invented the music video found himself completely flumoxed by the MTV generation.

All in all Dylan's experiences in film and television have been somewhat mixed, but never dull. The key defining characteristics of these forays have been that Dylan has never shied away from experi-mentation. He has always taken on new challenges in spite of the expectations of his fans and critics, and he has always tried to break new ground. He may not be a technical master craftsman in video and celluloid – and how could he be with no training and precious little experience? – but is clear that the distinctive vision he unleashed in such breathtaking epic songs such as 'Desolation Row' and 'Idiot Wind' is also present in the ambitious mathematical constructions of *Eat The Document* and *Renaldo and Clara*. Likewise, the icon behind era-defining anthems like 'Blowing in the Wind' and 'Like a Rolling Stone,' is captured as definitively in *Don't Look Back*, *Pat Garrett and Billy the Kid* and *Renaldo and Clara's* time-arresting bullets of light.

In February 2000, D.A. Pennebaker told an Internet chat room, '[Dylan is] absolutely determined that he will make the longest film that's ever been made'! Brilliant.

Appendices

Appendix One

This is a list of what I consider are Dylan's most significant TV and movie appearances over the years. It is therefore not a complete listing. For instance I've chosen to leave out his Travelling Wilburys' videos because I wanted to concentrate on Dylan as a solo performer. Similarly, I have also left out a number of televised press and TV interviews and, likewise, certain TV 'specials', either because I found them unremarkable, or I felt that they effectively duplicated material I have covered.

1963 – **January** – *Madhouse On Castle Street*, BBC TV, UK – directed by Phillip Saville – Dylan as 'Bobby', an American Folksinger. His first properly televised appearance.

1964 – **February** – *Quest*, CBC-TV – directed by Daryl Duke – Dylan sings six songs with a bunch of lumberjacks.

1964 – **February** – *The Steve Allen Show* – CBS-TV, USA – Dylan performs 'Lonesome Death of Hattie Carroll'.

1964 – **May** – *Tonight* – BBC TV, UK – Dylan sings 'With God On Our Side'.

1964 – **May** – *Hallelujah*, ABC TV, UK – Dylan sings, 'Don't Think Twice' and 'Chimes of Freedom'. A partial audio tape exists, but this show was never broadcast.

1965 – **February** – *The Les Crane Show*, WABC-TV, USA – Dylan sings, 'It's All Over Now, Baby Blue', and 'It's Alright Ma', accompanied by Bruce Langhorne on electric guitar. He also chats for a long time with the show's host. An extremely amusing and informative show. An audio tape exists, unfortunately the video has been wiped.

1965 – **June** – *Bob Dylan*, BBC 1, UK – Two 35-minute concerts in front of a specially invited audience. As usual, the shows have been wiped but there are audio tapes in existence of both shows.

1965 – **July/August** – *Fifty Fantastic and Fifty Personalities*, USA – Three minute screen-test for Andy Warhol. Never shown.

1965 – 'Subterranean Homesick Blues' – promo film released to TV stations in the USA and UK.

1965 – **December** – KQED-TV, San Francisco, USA – A fifty-one minute long press conference that has to be seen to be believed. The full press conference has been shown on Bay Area TV over the years, and is available on an audio CD.

1967 – **May** – Premiere of *Dont Look Back* – directed by D.A. Pennebaker – groundbreaking 'Direct Cinema' documentary about Dylan's 1965 UK tour. Is available on video and DVD in the USA.

1967 – Premiere of *Festival* – directed by Murray Lerner – Fine documentary, covering three years of the Newport Folk & Blues Festival. Includes Dylan's 'going electric'. Has been shown on European TV fairly regularly, and is allegedly available on video in the USA.

1969 – **March** – *Johnny Cash, The Man & His Music*, WNEW-TV, New York, followed by a theatrical movie run and subsequent video release – directed by Robert Elfstrom – A documentary about Johnny Cash in Nashville, it features Dylan and Cash dueting on, 'One Too Many Mornings'.

1969 – **June** – *The Johnny Cash Show*, ABC-TV, USA – Dylan as Cash's special guest.

1971 – **January** – *Earl Scruggs Performing With His Family & Friends*, WNEW-TV, New York, followed by video release. The video, which was available in Europe and the USA, is currently out of circulation. Features Dylan and the Scruggs boys performing 'East Virginia' and 'Nashville Skyline Rag'.

1971 – **February** – Premiere of *Eat The Document*, Academy of Music, New York, subsequently shown on PBS TV, and in various cinemas in the USA in 1998/9 – directed by Bob

Dylan and Howard Alk. The aborted TV special of the 1966 European tour.

1972 – Premiere of *The Concert For Bangladesh*, theatrical cinema release, currently available on video in the USA – directed by Saul Swimmer – George Harrison's charity concert, featuring a set by Dylan.

1973 – Premiere of *Pat Garrett & Billy The Kid*, theatrical cinema release. Re-edited and re-released in 1988 – directed by Sam Peckinpah – Dylan in his first proper professional acting role, as 'Alias', Billy The Kid's sidekick.

1975 – **CBS TV** – *The World of John Hammond* – TV special featuring a selection of people who'd been signed to CBS Records by John Hammond. Dylan, accompanied by Stoner, Wyeth and Rivera performed 'Hurricane', 'Oh Sister' and 'Simple Twist of Fate'.

1975 – 'Tangled Up In Blue' (shot 1975, released 1978) – Taken from *Renaldo and Clara*, the cine footage for this song was transferred to video and sent out to TV stations as a promo for the film.

1976 – **April** – *Clearwater* – Original, shelved version of *Hard Rain*.

1976 – **May** – *Hard Rain* – Broadcast version from Fort Collins, Colorado.

1976 – 'Maggie's Farm' – Taken from the Fort Collins, *Hard Rain* footage, this was later used as a promo item on USA TV.

1976 – Premiere of *Renaldo and Clara*, directed by Bob Dylan.

1979 – **October** – *Saturday Night Live* – NBC TV USA – Introduced by Eric Idle, the 'born again' Dylan premieres, 'Gotta Serve Somebody', and two other numbers.

1980 – **February** – *The Grammy Awards*, USA TV – Prime-time broadcast – Dylan wins an award for 'Best Vocal performance of 1998'. He also sings, 'Gotta Serve Somebody'.

1981 – 'Shot of Love' – Filmed on stage in Avignon by long-term collaborator Howard Alk.

1981 – 'Heart of Mine' – Ditto.

1983 – 'Sweetheart Like You' – Promo video featuring an elderly

cleaning lady often mistakenly thought by fans to be
Dylan's mother Beattie.

1983 – 'Don't Fall Apart From Me Tonight' – Promo video shot by
Dave Stewart in a New York studio.

1983 – 'License to Kill' – ditto

1984 – **March** – *Late Show With David Letterman*. NBC TV –
With The Cruzados. Despite a bizarre rehearsal, Dylan
turns in superb performances, featuring 'Jokerman',
'License To Kill' and 'Don't Start Me Talkin''

1984 – 'Jokerman' – Promo video shot by Larry Sloman and
George Lois – slightly more successful than earlier Dylan
videos.

1985 – **July** – Live Aid – live, world-wide broadcast. Dylan, with
Ron Wood and Keith Richard, gives succour to the starving
masses.

1985 – 'We Are The World' – The American pop equivalent of Live
Aid's 'Do They Know It's Christmas'.

1985 – 'Tight Connection To My Heart' – Promo video directed by
Paul Schrader, filmed in Tokyo.

1985 – 'When The Night Comes Falling From The Sky' – Promo
video directed by Markus Innocenti and Eddie Arno.

1985 – 'Emotionally Yours' – Ditto, shot the day after.

1985 – 'Sun City' – Promo video in the style of 'We Are The
World', attacking apartheid and artists work in South
Africa.

1985 – **October** – *20/20*, ABC-TV, USA – An unusually intelligent
profile of Dylan and his career, consisting of archive
footage and a contemporary interview with Bob Brown.
Dylan appears to be quite revealing in his answers. Also
contains scenes of Dylan rehearsing with the Heartbreakers.

1985 – **November** – *Old Grey Whistle Test*, BBC 2 TV, UK – A
brief, unrevealing interview with Andy Kershaw.

1986 – **January** – *Martin Luther King Birthday Celebrations*, NBC-
TV, USA.

1986 – **February** – *Hard To Handle* – An HBO pay-per-view that
went onto video release. Currently available.

1986 – **July** – *Farm Aid 2*, VH1, USA – Dylan with Willie Nelson and Tom Petty and The Heartbreakers.

1986 – **August** – *Chabad Telethon*, USA – Dylan, with Tom Petty and The Heartbreakers singing 'Thank God'.

1987 – **March** – *Gershwin Gala* – Multi-cast around the world, Dylan sings an astonishing version of Gershwin's 'Soon'.

1987 – Premiere of *Hearts of Fire* – Directed by Richard Marquand.

1988 – **January** – *Rock and Roll Hall Of Fame* USA TV – Multi-cast induction of Dylan into the archives of oblivion. Bruce Springsteen presided over the ceremony.

1988 – **Summer** – *Flashback* (aka Backtrack) Movie, USA – Dylan has a cameo role in a Dennis Hopper movie playing an artist who 'creates' with a chainsaw!

1989 – 'Political World' – Promo video, produced by musician John Cougar Mellencamp.

1989 – 'Everything Is Broken' – An unauthorised promo video produced by CBS France.

1989 – **September** – *Chabad Telethon*, USA. TV – Dylan, his son-in-law Peter Himmelman and actor Harry Dean Stanton, go crazy on Jewish charity TV.

1990 – **February** – *Roy Orbison Tribute* USA TV – Dylan appears on stage with The Byrds and sings on 'Mister Tambourine Man'. He also plays guitar on 'He Was A Friend Of Mine' and 'Only The Lonely'.

1990 – 'Most Of The Time' – There are two versions of this video, one directed by Dylan's son Jesse, and one by a Tony Curtis (not the actor).

1990 – 'Unbelievable' – Promo video – Dylan, Molly Ringwald and a pig in the desert – unbelievable!

1991 – **February** – *The Grammy Awards* USA TV – Dylan receives the Grammy Lifetime Achievement Award. See separate section in Reel Seven.

1991 – 'Series of Dreams' – Promo video put together at Dublin's Windmill studios – One of Dylan's best.

1991 – **September** – *Chabad Telethon* USA TV – Dylan plays 'lead guitar' for Kinky Friedman.

1991 – October – *Guitar Legends*, European TV – Dylan performs along with a cast of thousands.

1992 – January – *Late Night With Letterman* NBC TV – A reluctant Dylan performs 'Like A Rolling Stone' on Letterman's 10th Anniversary show.

1992 – October – *30th Anniversary Show*, USA, Pay-per-view TV, and later video release. Dylan appears at the end of this tribute featuring a star studded cast.

1993 – January – *A Country Music Calendar* CBS TV USA – Duet with Willie Nelson on 'Heartland'.

1993 – April – *Willie Nelson's Big Six - 0* – USA TV – Dylan again duets with Nelson on 'Pancho & Lefty' and solos on 'Hard Times'. Essential viewing.

1993 – May – *Arena – Highway 61* – BBC 2 UK TV – A documentary about America's Highway 61, features recordings made by John Bucklen in 1958.

1993 – 'Blood In My Eyes' – Promo video shot on the streets of London by Dave Stewart – possibly Dylan's most successful video to date.

1993 – November – *Late Night With Letterman* – NBC TV – Dylan performs 'Forever Young'.

1994 – May – *The Great Music Experience*, Japanese TV – Dylan performs three numbers backed by the Tokyo New Philharmonic Orchestra. Outstanding.

1994 – August – *Woodstock 2 Festival* – HBO, USA TV – Dylan goes through a reasonable set for the MTV generation.

1994 – November – *Unplugged* – MTV USA – Dylan goes through a very good set for the MTV generation.

1995 – November – *Frank Sinatra's 80th Birthday Tribute* – USA TV – Dylan sings 'Restless Farewell' for the other 'Old Blue Eyes'.

1996 – June – *Prince's Trust* – HBO – Dylan plays Hyde Park in London. Reasonable.

1996 – August – *House of Blues* – USA TV – A hastily arranged gig for the Olympics. A very good show from Atlanta's

House of Blues.

1997 – **September** – *World Eucharist Congress* – RA1 TV Italy – Dylan performs in front of the Pope. Interesting in a bizarre kind of way.

1997 – 'Not Dark Yet' – Promo filmed in the New Daisy Theatre, Memphis.

1998 – **February** - *The Grammy Awards* – USA TV – Dylan performs 'Lovesick' and is joined on stage by Soy Bomb, a 'performance artist'.

1999 – **October** – *Dharma and Greg* – ABC TV USA – Dylan makes guest appearance on this popular sitcom.

2000 – 'Things Have Changed' – Promo video shot by Curtis Hanson for the Michael Douglas movie *Wonderboys*. Marvellous stuff, Dylan dances and lip-synchs with Michael Douglas.

Patrice Hamilton is an artist who lives in the West Country, in England. The story of her involvement with *Hearts of Fire* is an interesting one and complements the artefacts she has loaned for this book. Here's Patrice's tale in her own words –

'Early in 1986, I did a drawing of Bob Dylan. Shortly before I'd heard that he was coming to Shepperton Studios in Middlesex to make a film called *Hearts of Fire* ... I went there and gave one of the PA girls a print of the drawing that she said she'd definitely pass on to Bob for me...

'A couple of days later I was summoned to the phone at work, to be told that a certain Susan D'Arcy of Shepperton Studios was on the line and wanted to speak to me ... she said, "Mr. Dylan has seen your drawing and loves it. He wants it to be blown up into a poster and used in the film... We need to obtain your permission to use it."

'The rest of the conversation was a bit of a haze, all to do with written confirmation, the fact that the drawing would be enlarged and "Parker" would be put at the bottom, as that was the name of the character in the film. With that, she brusquely announced that she'd be in touch.

'... I didn't get to meet Bob that time, but some good things came out of it ... One – I got a signed copy of the poster that was to appear in the film. Also, a signed photo of Bob, one of a hundred sent out to people who'd helped on the movie ...

'The second thing was that I was invited to the premiere of *Hearts of Fire*. It was held at the Astoria, Charing Cross Road ... I got out of the taxi to be greeted by a huge crowd and press photographers who were just clicking away regardless – I could have been the cleaner for all they cared – it was all rather bizarre. As I was going in I noticed Sandie Shaw, most of the cast of *Eastenders*, perhaps they were a block booking? Nina Carter, the model, Kevin Godley of 10CC... The face that surprised me the most was Des O'Connor with tan and trenchcoat. A closet Dylan fan perhaps? ...

'But I wasn't pleased when I heard that Lorimar had bought the rights to the film and for some bizarre reason cut out large chunks of the film, including all of Bob's love scenes with Fiona. In particular, a bedroom scene where my poster was on the wall. The love triangle advertised in the film didn't exist, just Fiona and Rupert with Dylan on the sideline. Iain Smith told me it a great shame because a lot of really relevant scenes had been hacked out of the film.'

Appendix Three
Napoleon In Rags Meets The Creep

Warhol was important to me. He was before his time. He busted through new territory. Andy Warhol did a lot for American cinema. He was more than just a director. I think his 'Empire State Building' is more exciting than Bergman. I liked Warhol a lot.

Bob Dylan in Bockris' 'Warhol'

In the seething cultural cauldron of mid-1960s New York, Warhol and Dylan represented two sides of the same coin. Both of them were leading lights in their own particular field, Andy Warhol as an artist and 'underground' film maker, Dylan as the electric pied piper of popular music. It was inevitable that they would meet, and meet they did, for the first time, in 1965. The catalyst for this encounter was Edie Sedgewick who at the time was considered the leading 'star' of Warhol's Factory studio system, but was gradually being wooed over into Dylan's camp.

Bobby Neuwirth had become her lover and introduced her to Dylan at a nightclub called 'Arthurs'. Some kind of relationship grew between them and Edie started making visits to Albert Grossman's Woodstock retreat with Dylan and his entourage. Edie began to tell any one who'd listen that she was going to be managed by Grossman and cut a record with Dylan. Grossman was going to put her in the real movies.

None of this went down too well at the Factory, Warhol and his crew began calling Dylan 'the Creep', Dylan and his in-crowd accusing Warhol of stringing Edie out on drugs. Many commentators have drawn significant allusions to Edie's story and the lyrics to Dylan's massive 1965 hit, 'Like A Rolling Stone'. Warhol believed that 'Napoleon in rags' was a reference to himself. What we have to bear in mind that both these groups were representative of the hippest, coolest avant-garde scene in the world, and yet were polar opposites – Warhol's entourage, generally homosexual and into amphetamine; Dylan's, heterosexual and into amphetamine and acid. Both groups despised each other.

Gerard Malanga – *They were like oil and water. There was just bad friction. Dylan immediately hated Andy and Andy thought Dylan was corny.*

Warhol claims to have met Dylan for the first time at a party thrown by art dealer, Sam Green -

Warhol – *At Sam's party Dylan was in blue jeans and high-heeled boots and a sports jacket, and his hair was sort of long. He had deep circles under his eyes, and even when he was standing he was all hunched in. He was around twenty-four then and the kids were all just starting to talk and act and dress and swagger like he did. But not many people except Dylan could ever pull that anti-act off – and if he wasn't in the right mood, he couldn't either...*

Always obsessed with fame and celebrity, Warhol wasted no time in inviting Dylan along to the Factory for a screen-test.

In late July, or early August 1965, Dylan travelled uptown in a station wagon, from the Village to East 47th Street, and climbed into the rickety lift that would carry him and his crew up to the Factory, Warhol's silver painted studio.

Victor Bockris – *Andy took his usual refuge in the humble position of the fan, chewing his fingernails and squealing, "He's here! He's here!" when Dylan, foreshadowed like a Presidential candidate by his advance men and accompanied by bodyguards and a film crew, swept in, in the opinion of several onlookers, high on amphetamine and blotter acid. He was jiving with the Factory's resident poet Gerard Malanga and bouncing off the walls and there was an immediate standoff between the two camps...*

According to reports, Dylan prowled around the studio looking at Warhol's famous screenprints, scowling and making put-down comments. Eventually, after fifteen or twenty uncomfortable minutes, he agreed to sit down and be filmed.

One of Warhol's pet projects at the time was a succession of filmed portraits entitled, *Fifty Famous & Fifty Fantastic Personalities.* Anybody of importance who visited the Factory was asked to sit for the camera. Warhol sifted through the footage as well as the gossip columns to decide who would make it to the final cut (Donovan did Dylan didn't!). His sequence was shot on two cameras simultaneously:

Gerard Malanga – *...it was three minutes of stillness and silence, 100 feet of film. It was shot on a Bolex and Dylan had to look in the camera wearing his sunglasses... I have a colour reel also, besides the black-and-white, of Dylan I shot the same day...*

According to Bockris, Dylan also shared a ritual toke on a joint with Warhol and Malanga while shooting took place.

As soon as it was finished, Dylan stood up and walked over to one of Warhol's prints of Elvis Presley, announcing that he was taking it as payment for allowing himself to be filmed. Apparently Warhol was furious but too stunned to be able to say anything. With that, Dylan and his entourage left the building. The last Warhol saw of his Elvis picture was Dylan and Neuwirth struggling to strap it on top of the station wagon. In later years he was annoyed to hear that Dylan was using it as a dartboard, but this wasn't true.

In fact, Dylan had shown it to Albert Grossman, complaining that he didn't like it. Grossman offered to take it off his hands and Dylan agreed swapping it for a sofa that Grossman had in his office. Years later, when the value of the picture had risen into five figures, Dylan and Warhol were having dinner together in London when Dylan admitted what he'd done and said to Warhol, *'But if you ever gave me another one, Andy, I wouldn't make that mistake again....'*

Dylan's screen-test for Warhol now resides in the archives of the Museum of Modern Art in New York. There are no plans for it to be shown.

Notes on Reels

Aside from the thirty-plus hours of footage that I've usually enjoyed watching, I've drawn material from a variety of sources for this book, including interviews with other writers and several participants in the man's life.

Reel One – Dont Look Back

Anybody interested in finding out more biographical details of D.A. Pennebaker should look at *Microsoft Cinemania* CD Rom, *Corel ALL MOVIE GUIDE* CD Rom, and *Cinema – A Critical Dictionary*. Interviews with Pennebaker are from *The Telegraph, Isis, Who Threw The Glass?* an Australian fanzine, and two on-line chats that Pennebaker has given.

Background information for *Dont Look Back* came from Chris Cooper and Keith Marsh's, *The Circus Is In Town*, and *Images and Assorted Facts* by Gavin Diddle. The Ballantine paperback transcript of *Dont Look Back* proved a very handy document to have around.

Other material is drawn from Heylin's and Shelton's biographies, and, of course, D.A. Pennebaker's movie *Dont Look Back*.

Reel Two – Eat The Document

Shelton and Heylin were useful for background information, as were the magazines *Who Threw The Glass?* and *The Telegraph*. The privately published, *Endless Road – A Dylan Magazine,* provided a useful guide to *Eat The Document*.

Information about filming on the tour is drawn from several conversations with Mickey Jones, who also allowed me access to his home movies from that period.

A full transcript of the Dylan/Lennon car journey was published in *Mojo* in November 1993, as were Lennon's quotes about the film.

Details about the New York premiere of *Eat The Document* are from *Rolling Stone,* March 1971.

Further details from a privately published volume by Gavin Diddle, entitled *Images & Assorted Facts*.

Plus, there is the recently re-released *Eat The Document*.

Reel Three – Pat Garrett and Billy The Kid

Garner Simmons's, *Peckinpah – A Portrait in Montage*, provided really good biographical information about the maverick movie director and his involvement with *Pat Garrett and Billy The Kid*, as did Clinton Heylin's article in *The Telegraph* #37.

More information about Peckinpah's career was taken from *Microsoft Cinemania* CD Rom, and *Corel ALL MOVIE GUIDE* CD Rom, David Weddle's, *If They Move – Kill 'Em*, and Stephen Prince's, *Savage Cinema*.

Food for thought came from articles by Stephen Scobie in *On The Tracks* Vol 7 #1, and Kim Newman and Richard Combs in *Sight & Sound Magazine*. Biographical and background historical material about Billy the Kid came from Garrett's ghost written memoirs *The Authentic Life of Billy The Kid*.

Not to mention the two film/video versions that have been circulating in their released and newly released forms.

Reel Four – Renaldo and Clara

Material for Reel Four came from a number of interviews published in *The Telegraph,* principally with Joel Bernstein and Allen Ginsberg who interviewed Bob Dylan himself.

Heylin and Shelton biographies provided much useful background information as did Sam Shepard's *Rolling Thunder Logbook*. An idea of what the tour must have been like came from material drawn from Larry Sloman's *On The Road With Bob Dylan*.

Some handy hints and useful facts came from Marshall Crenshaw's *Hollywood Rock,* and *The Bob Dylan Companion,* edited by Carl Benson, supplied contemporary source material. Joan Baez's, *And A Voice To Sing With*, is a highly recommended read. Several threads came from conversations with Paul Williams, author of many highly acclaimed book and articles on Bob Dylan.

Thanks to Channel Four UK for the broadcast version.

Reel Five – Hearts of Fire

Press conference accounts came from a variety of sources, but the most amusing was Patrick Humphries' in *Oh No – Not Another Bob Dylan Book!*, co-written with John Bauldie. Iain Smith's and Richard Marquand's quotes are from *The Telegraph*. The biographical information and critical reviews come from *Microsoft Cinemania* CD Rom and *Corel ALL MOVIE GUIDE* CD Rom. Anybody interested in the aesthetics of film production should study *How to Read A Film* by James Monaco, and Bordwell and Thompson's highly acclaimed, *Film Art, An Introduction*. Background information comes from interviews with Patrice Hamilton, Mark Makin and Ian Dury's manager, Andrew King (sadly, none of them publishable) and also from Robert Shelton and Clinton Heylin. Not forgetting the BBC's, *Getting To Dylan* documentary.

The video version of *Hearts of Fire* is currently unavailable, but the movie itself recently surfaced on Channel Five UK.

Reel Six – Cameos and Guest Slots

Festival: Background information came from Joe Boyd in the *Telegraph* #37, Robert Shelton and Clinton Heylin and *The Telegraph*.

Concert for Bangladesh: The George Harrison interview was broadcast on BBC Radio 1, in 1976. Phil Spector and Bob Dylan material is from *Rolling Stone Magazine*.

The Last Waltz: Source material was provided by, *Microsoft Cinemania* CD Rom, Robert Shelton and Clinton Heylin, *Scorsese on Scorsese, Bill Graham Presents*, Hoskyn's, *Across The Great Divide*, and Peter Byskind's, *Easy Riders and Raging Bulls*.

Promo-video information came from Robert Shelton and Clinton Heylin, *The Telegraph* and *Tangled Up In Tapes*.

Festival, Concert For Bangladesh and *The Last Waltz*, are available on NTSC video, the latter two are also available on laser disc.

Reel Seven – TV Talkin' Blues

Quotes were drawn from a variety of magazines and periodicals, *The New Yorker*, *Disc Weekly* (now defunct), *TV Guide*, *The Telegraph*, *Rolling Stone*, *The Radio Times*, and Philadelphia's *Free Times*. The Heylin and Shelton biographies were also useful.

Of great help in sourcing trivia were, *Images and Assorted Facts*, and *The Circus Is In Town*. Obviously viewing the TV shows themselves is the best way of getting information, and two in particular were of great assistance, both made by the BBC, *Getting to Dylan* and *Tales of Rock n Roll*, *Highway 61 Revisited*.

Finally, conversations with Peter Stone Brown who allowed me to access the database in his head.

Reel Eight – Sand In The Mouth Of The Movie Star

Is a distillation of my thoughts on Dylan's acting career and relevant TV appearances.

Bibliography

Baez, Joan, *And A Voice To Sing With*,
    Summit Books, 1987

Bauldie, John, (Ed), *Wanted Man: In Search of Bob Dylan*,
    Citadel, 1991

Benson, Carl, (Ed), *The Bob Dylan Companion: Four Decades of*
    Dylan Commentary,
    Schirmer Books, 1998

Bockris, Victor, *Warhol*,
    Penguin, 1990

Bordwell, David & Thompson, Kristin, *Film Art: An Introduction*,
    Alfred A. Knopf, 1987

Byskind, Peter, *Easy Riders And Raging Bulls*,
    Bloomsbury, 1999

Cook, Pam & Bernink, Mieke, (Eds), *The Cinema Book*,
    BFI Publications, 1999

Cooper, Chris & Marsh, Keith, *The Circus Is In Town*,
    (Privately Published)

Crenshaw, Marshall, *Hollywood Rock*, Plexus, 1994

Diddle, Gavin, *Images And Assorted Facts: A Peek Behind The*
    Picture Frame,
    (Privately Published), 1983

Graham, Bill & Greenfield, Robert, *Bill Graham Presents: My Life*
    Inside Rock And Out,
    Doubleday, 1992

Gray, Michael, *Song And Dance Man III: The Art of Bob Dylan*,
    Cassell, 1999

Helm, Levon, *This Wheel's On Fire*, Plexus, 1994

Henderson, Dave, *Touched By The Hand of Bob*,
    The Black Book Company, 1999

Heylin, Clinton, *Bob Dylan: Behind The Shades*,
    Penguin, 1991

Heylin, Clinton, *Bob Dylan Day By Day: A Life In Stolen*
    Moments,
    Book Sales Ltd, 1996

Hoskyns, Barney, *Across The Great Divide: The Band And America*,
Penguin, 1993

Lee, CP, *Like The Night: Bob Dylan And The Road To The
Manchester Free Trade Hall*,
Helter Skelter, 1998

Monaco, James, *How To Read A Film*,
Oxford University Press, 1981

Prince, Stephen, *Savage Cinema: Sam Peckinpah And The Rise Of
The Ultra-Violent Movie*,
Athlone Press, 1998

Romney, Jonathan & Wooton, Adrian, (Eds), *Celluloid Jukebox,
Popular Music And The Movies Since The 50's*,
BFI Publishing, 1995

Roud, Richard, (Ed), *Cinema, A Critical Dictionary*,
Secker & Warburg, 1980

Shelton, Robert, *No Direction Home*,
William Morrow & Company, 1986

Shepard, Sam, *The Rolling Thunder Logbook*,
Penguin, 1997

Simmons, Garner, *Peckinpah: A Portrait In Montage*,
University of Texas Press, 1982

Sloman, Larry, *On The Road With Bob Dylan*,
Bantam Books, 1978

Warhol, Andy & Hackett, Pat, *Popism: The Warhol 60's*,
Hutchinson, 1981

Weddle, David, *Sam Peckinpah: 'If They Move… Kill 'Em'*,
Faber & Faber, 1996

Williams, Christian, *Bob Dylan, In His Own Words*,
Omnibus Press, 1993

Williams, Paul, *Performing Artist Volume One: 1960 – 1973*,
Omnibus Press, 1990

Williams, Paul, *Performing Artist Volume Two: 1974 – 1986*,
Omnibus Press, 1992

Magazines

The Bridge (UK)
PO Box 198
Gateshead
Tyne and Wear NE10 8WE
England

Dignity (UK)
Desolation Row Promotions Ltd
57 Tempsford
Welwyn Garden City
Herts. AL7 2PA
England

Isis (UK)
PO Box 1182
Bedworth
Warwickshire CV12 0ZA
England

On The Tracks (USA)
PO Box 1943
Grand Junction
Colorado 81502
USA

Internet Resources

Links to Bob Dylan film and TV sites can be found on the following Web pages:

Bringing It All Back Home (John Howells)
Includes tape reviews, general news and articles
http://www.punkhart.com/dylan/index.html

Expecting Rain (Karl Erick Anderson)
Includes general news, original art gallery, tour reviews and pictures.
http://www.expectingrain.com/

And more specifically:
http://www.skid-row.co.uk/bobdylan/

Acknowledgements

Thanks to Sean Body, my publisher at Helter Skelter, for steering me in the direction of this volume. Originally I thought of writing a book about one particular film featuring Dylan, but it soon became obvious that one about his entire output would be a far more exciting and challenging concept.

Early in 1999 I began amassing the material that I was going to look at for my researches. British cable TV had screened *Pat Garrett and Billy The Kid* on a fairly regular basis, as had BBC 2 with *Dont Look Back*. I'd had other items on video in my collection for over twenty years, but as I started doing background research into what was supposed to be available I realised that what I had was woefully inadequate. There was only one thing to do in those circumstances – contact EDLIS, the Internet Dylan resource group!

Through EDLIS and the usenet newsgroup 'rec.music.dylan' (RMD) a group of people offered their assistance in gathering videos and other information. From Japan, Itsuko Nishimura, sent me a painstakingly and meticulously compiled list, including every known feature film containing either a Bob Dylan song or reference!

From America, material was provided by the indefatigable and big-hearted Ron Chester, whose collection of Dylan and Dylan-related literature has to be seen to be believed. Ron was invaluable in finding text references that went way back to the 1960s.

Another American, without whose help this book would never have appeared is Jeff Klepper. Jeff, at his own expense, sent me package after package of items, every one of which was duly opened by Her Majesty's Customs & Excise officers. I only hope they had as much fun as I did watching all four hours of *Renaldo and Clara*! Thank you Jeff.

Encouragement and support came from Dylan webmeister, John Howells. His net site 'Bringing It All Back Home' at www.punkhart.com/dylan/index.html has a full filmography with links to all sorts of other interesting places and things Dylan. It was a pleasure to meet actor/musician, Mickey Jones and his wife Phyllis. Mickey provided me with not only a wealth of memories about his time with Dylan, but also allowed me to view his home-movie footage of the 66 tour – sincere thanks!

The final American I wish to thank this time round is musician and writer, Peter Stone Brown who took on the onerous task of fact checker and general factotum, often pointing me in the direction of areas that I'd overlooked in my original research. His contribution to this book has been enormous and is highly valued. The final product that you are holding in your hands is in no small way due to his efforts.

In the UK this book's genesis has been observed, helped and commented on by, what I have to call, the usual suspects. Namely, Alan Fraser who has once again proved a most useful friend, Craig Jamieson, the Cambridge scholar with a neat sideline in flying aircraft and knowing people who need people. Ben Taylor also offered his services once again and pointed me in the right direction. Derek Barker, editor of *Isis* magazine, has, as usual, been of great help in finding material.

A big thanks is due to Dylan's fellow actor – well, actually he was an extra in *Hearts of Fire* – Mark Makin, who sent me material from the production. As did Patrice Hamilton, long-time Dylan afficianado. She has provided several mementos that are included in the artwork of this book. A very big thanks Patrice!

In London, Richard Boon provided food, lodging and statistical support, and along with Richard Thomas gave me much help in the writing of this book. I'll never forget the day we missed Bobby Neuwirth by ten minutes, but there again, if you will go drinking in pubs!

Many thanks to my sister-in-law, Sue Malden, for tracking down several essential BBC documentaries.

Obviously in writing a book about film it's been a great help being a lecturer in film studies. Many thanks then to the School of Media, Music & Performance at Salford University, in particular my office mate and very good buddy, Andy Willis, has been invaluable in finding long lost articles and books that dealt with all aspects of film and Dylan film in particular. Thanks also to colleagues Dr Gareth

Palmer and Professor Ron Cook, who, as usual, have been very tolerant and understanding whilst this book has been written.

And finally, of course, all my love and thanks to Pam, my wife who cheerfully put up with mountains of videos and piles of reference material cluttering up the house while this book was in preparation. And once again she's patiently helped me grasp her IT wizardry and many other things – *Mi amore, mi corazon*!

FIREFLY PUBLISHING
An association of Helter Skelter and SAF Publishing

New Titles

Opening The Musical Box: A Genesis Chronicle : Alan Hewitt
Compiled by the editor of the definitive Genesis magazine *The Waiting Room*, *Opening The Musical Box* is a detailed and informative chronicle of the band's career: from early beginnings at Charterhouse school through to worldwide stardom. It is also the first book containing a detailed documentary of the solo recording careers and offshoot bands of Genesis members. Drawing on new interviews, packed with insights and anecdotes, and featuring the definitive discography, gigography and a guide to collectables, this is the ultimate compendium to one of the most successful and inventive bands of modern rock.
224 pages/8 photos/235 x 156mm ISBN 0-946719-30-6 UK £12.99

The Manic Street Preachers: Prole Art Threat: Bon Roberts
Drawing on new research and interviews with band insiders, Roberts charts the Manics' progress from Blackwood misfits to rock iconoclasts, through Ritchie Edwards' mysterious disappearance and its aftermath, on to the post-Ritchie mainstream pop stardom that culminated with hit singles such as 'A Design for Life,' and acclaimed albums *Everything Must Go* and *This is My Truth*…. Eschewing the more macabre and intrusive approach of most Manics' biographers, Roberts puts the emphasis back on the band's distinctive musical and cultural manifesto, documenting the rise and fall of The Manic Street Preachers' quest, in Ritchie's own words, 'to be the band that we never had when we were growing up'.
224 pages/8 photos/235 x 156mm ISBN 0-946719-25-X UK £12.99

Blowing Free: Thirty Years of Wishbone Ash: Mark Chatterton and Gary Carter
During the early 1970s golden era of progressive and heavy rock Wishbone Ash were one of Britain's most popular hard rock acts. Formed in 1969 around the twin-lead guitar attack of Andy Powell and Ted Turner, the group's music showcased blistering solos and a strong melodic sensibility. They became a staple favourite on the live circuit, and hit LPs quickly followed. In 1987, after a period in the wilderness, their original manager persuaded the band to reform and since then they have continued recording and touring to widespread international acclaim. The authors have produced a gripping account of the long and distinctive career of one of Britain's premier rock bands.
224 pages/8 photos/235 x 156mm ISBN 0-946719-33-0 UK £12.99

Soul Sacrifice: The Story of Santana: Simon Leng
This is the first ever biography of Carlos Santana – one of the most distinctive and influential guitarists of all time. His is a genuine 'rags to riches' story, and this book traces his life from a childhood spent playing Mariachi music on the streets of Tijuana through to worldwide superstardom. After receiving a Lifetime Achievement Award from *Billboard* magazine in 1996, Santana recently returned to the fray with his first studio album in seven years: *Supernatural* put Santana back at the *Billboard* number one spot, as did its first single, 'Smooth', and it won a multitude of awards at the first Grammy Award ceremony of the new millennium. Simon Leng has enjoyed unprecedented access to band members and associates, and most importantly Carlos Santana himself, .
224 pages 8 photos/235 x 156mm ISBN 0-946719-29-2 UK £12.99

Back Catalogue

Dancemusicsexromance: Prince: The First Decade: Per Nilsen
Documenting Prince's life from his humble Minneapolis beginnings to controversial, international stardom, before the artist's eventual rejection of his Prince persona and his adoption of a symbol instead of a name, *Dancemusicsexromance* is the first biography that gets to grips with one of the most contradictory geniuses of modern pop music. It is also the first in depth study of Prince's music during an extraordinarily creative ten-year period: from the funk-rock crossover platinum success of *Purple Rain* – which sold over 10 million copies in the US alone – to the intoxicating blend of soul, gospel, rock and dance that was *Sign O' the Times*. 'A serious and well-researched study.' *Publishers Weekly*
224 pages/24 photos/235 x 156mm ISBN 0-946719-22-5 UK £12.99

Jethro Tull: Minstrels in the Gallery: David Rees
The first ever biography of the band published on their 30th anniversary. This dates the band's career from the Rock 'n Roll Circus with the Rolling Stones in the 60s, through their megastardom in the 70s with platinum albums such as *Aqualung* and *Thick as a Brick*, and on to their place in the 80s and 90s as one of the great enduring rock acts. 'Brilliant, independently minded … A fine read for Tull fans and non-believers alike.' *Mojo*
224 pages/24 photos/235 x 156mm ISBN 0-946719-22-5 UK £12.99

Poison Heart: Surviving the Ramones: Dee Dee Ramone with Veronica Koffman
The autobiography of the seminal New York punk band's bassist and songwriter, that documents his fifteen years with the band. 'Former junkie, alleged street hustler and bass playing, helmet-haired founder member of The Ramones, Dee Dee's done a lot of living in his time.' *The Guardian*
'One of *the* great rock books.' *Q******
192 pages/20 b&w photos/235 x 156mm ISBN 0-946719-19-5 Paper UK £11.95

HELTER SKELTER

New Titles

No More Sad Refrains: The Life and Times of Sandy Denny: Clinton Heylin
Drawing on fresh interviews with Sandy's closest friends and musical collaborators, and with unprecedented access to her journals, diaries and unreleased recordings, Heylin has produced a portrait of a complex, driven and flawed genius who may well have been this land's greatest ever female singer-songwriter. Clinton Heylin is a highly respected historian of popular music, whose book *Dylan Behind Closed Doors* (1996, Penguin) was nominated for the Ralph J. Gleason award. 'No female singer of the last ten years could touch her.'
Greil Marcus, *Rolling Stone*, May 1978
256 pages/8 pages b&w photos/235 x 156mm ISBN 1-900924-11-2 Hardcover UK £18.99

Like a Bullet of Light: The Films of Bob Dylan: C.P. Lee
Using archive research and fresh interviews, C.P. Lee traces Dylan's celluloid obsession from his teenage adulation of James Dean through his involvement in documentaries like *Dont Look Back* and his enigmatic appearance in Peckinpah's *Pat Garratt and Billy The Kid*. It looks at the genesis of Dylan's dramatic directorial debut, *Renaldo and Clara*, and his starring role in mainstream *Hearts of Fire*. The author also presents an analysis of all Dylan's major appearances on TV and video. 'There is no doubt that C.P. has done it again ... thanks for getting it right.' Mickey Jones, drummer with Dylan during the *Dont Look Back* era.
192 pages/8 pages b&w photos/235 x 156mm ISBN 1-900924-06-4 UK £12.99

Rock's Wild Things: The Troggs Files: Alan Clayson and Jacqueline Ryan
The full sad, mad, funny story of the ultimate British garage band. While other bands of the *Sergeant Pepper* era were turning on and dropping out, the Troggs were knocking out raucously lascivious tunes like 'I Can't Control Myself'. Somehow, singer Reg Presley's mock-anthem 'Love is All Around' captured the spirit of the age. Respected rock writer Alan Clayson has had full access to the band and traces their history from 60s Andover rock roots to 90s covers, collaborations and corn circles. *The Troggs Files* also features the first-ever publication of the full transcript of the legendary 'Troggs Tapes', said to have inspired the movie *This is Spinal Tap*, together with an discography and many rare photographs.
224 pages/8 pages b&w photos/235 x 156mm ISBN 1-900924-19-6 UK £12.99

The Clash: The Return of the Last Gang in Town: Marcus Gray
Last Gang in Town is a fascinating study of the only band to fulfil punk's potential. It also paints an evocative picture of the mid-70s environment out of which punk flourished, as the author traces Strummer and co's origins from pub bands to US stadium rock status. This is a book to shelve next to Jon Savage's Pistols tome *England's Dreaming*. Previously published by Fourth Estate, this edition is fully revised and updated with a huge amount of new material. 'If you're a music fan ... it's important you read this book.' *Record Collector* 'A valuable document for anyone interested in the punk era.' *Billboard*
488 pages/8 pages b&w photographs/235 x 156mm ISBN 1-900924-16-1 UK £12.99

Calling Out Around the World: A Motown Reader: Kingsley Abbott
Calling Out features articles on the legendary hit factory songwriting partnerships such as Holland-Dozier-Holland, portraits of key musicians like James Jamerson and interviews with behind-the-scenes players, as well as profiles of all the major artists on the Motown roster and label supremo Gordy himself. Contributors include top music critics like Dave Marsh, Geri Hirshey, Richard Williams and John Rockwell. With a foreword by Martha Reeves and a full discography of UK Motown releases, this is an investigation into how a tiny, Mafia-funded indie label from middle America could dominate the pop charts of the era.
256 pages/8 pages b&w photos/235 x 156mm ISBN 1-900924-14-5 UK £12.99

Emerson Lake and Palmer: The Show That Never Ends: George Forrester, Martin Hanson and Frank Askew
Prog-rock supergroup Emerson Lake and Palmer were one the most successful acts of the 70s and, in terms of sound, artistic vision and concept, operated on a scale far in excess of any rivals. ELP enjoyed a huge profile from the off. Though punk rendered acts like ELP obsolete overnight, they hung on for a couple of years before splitting. Lake and Palmer went on to enjoy massive success in the US charts before being lured back to reform ELP in the early 90s. Drawing on interviews with band members and associates, the authors have produced a gripping and fascinating document of one of the great rock bands of the 70s.
256 pages/8 pages b&w photos/235 x 156mm ISBN 1-900924-17-X UK £12.99

Animal Tracks: The Story of The Animals: Sean Egan: Newcastle's finest emerged from the early-60s blues scene, when Alan Price and Chas Chandler recruited gravel-voiced Eric Burdon to front their new combo. They signed to Columbia Records and released their #1 reworking of 'House of the Rising Sun,'. The Animals built a huge international following – briefly on a par with the Beatles and the Stones – and forged a reputation for legendary live shows, before ego problems resurfaced and they split up. The Animals will be revered as one of the ultimate 1960s groups. Sean Egan has produced a compelling portrait of a distinctive band of survivors.
224 pages/8 pages b&w photos/235 x 156mm ISBN 1-900924-18-8 UK £12.99

Dead End Street: When Rock's Greatest Talents Lost Their Way: Peter Doggett: While other artists are usually revered for their later, more mature work, rock 'n' roll's prime movers have burned more briefly, with career trajectories traditionally following an arc pattern. Witty, compellingly argued and always outspoken, this book takes a no-holds barred look at many of rock's most sacred cows, from Elvis Presley to Oasis, via Bruce Springsteen, the Rolling Stones, Bob Marley, John Lennon, Joni Mitchell, Led Zeppelin, R.E.M. and dozens more. Often drawing on fresh interview material, it offers thought-provoking broadsides which overthrow the popular view of rock's greatest acts. Peter Doggett is Editor in Chief of *Record Collector* magazine.
256 pages/8 pages b&w photos /235 x 156mm ISBN 1-900924-20-X UK £12.99

Razor's Edge: Bob Dylan and the Never Ending Tour: Andrew Muir
Bob Dylan began a short tour in 1986, and has toured every year since. In 1988 he began 'The Never Ending Tour'. Dylan fanzine editor Andrew Muir documents the ups and downs of this trek, analyses and assesses Dylan's performances year in year out and tries to get to grips with exactly what it all means. Part rock criticism and part cultural analysis, this is a telling portrait of a rock star stuck on the live treadmill and a mature audience still spellbound by his every utterance. 'You can press your luck. The road has taken a lot of the great ones: Hank Williams; Buddy Holly; Otis Redding; Janis; Jimi Hendrix; Elvis... It's a goddamn impossible way of life.' Robbie Robertson
256 pages/8 pages b&w photos/235 x 156mm ISBN 1-900924-13-7 UK £12.99